The
Great
Fear
Race in the Mind
of America

Edited by

Gary B. Nash
University of California, Los Angeles

Richard Weiss
University of California, Los Angeles

HOLT, RINEHART AND WINSTON, INC.
New York   Chicago   San Francisco   Atlanta
Dallas   Montreal   Toronto   London   Sydney

Introduction

For the past decade and a half, the United States has been torn by almost continuous racial strife. Every segment of society is facing a major *crise de conscience* over the disparity between the promise and the reality of American life. The nation's formal commitment to human dignity and equality for all citizens is blatantly contradicted by persistent discrimination against large minority groups within American society. The causes and consequences of racism are being exposed and challenged as never before in our history. Yet while the scope of the open discussion of racism and its ramifications is new, the fact of it is very old. The confrontation of black, red, and white peoples on the American continent in the colonial period gave the factor of race unique significance in the evolution of our history. Racial attitudes have shaped the American experience since Europeans first set foot in the New World. This has been so true that, as occurs frequently with assumptions that are basic and pervasive, ascriptions of racial characteristics have escaped the rigorous analysis that other aspects of our thinking have received. We are only beginning to gain some insight into the ways that racist assumptions govern the perceptions and behavior of white Americans and are embedded in the institutions of our society.

Our heightened awareness of racism and its consequences derives from the present unprecedented ferment over racial injustice. Until recently, many Americans believed that formal emancipation in 1863 had ended institutional racism in the United States. Education, it was thought, was eroding vestigial racist feeling and would soon eliminate it altogether. Not until the advent of massive black protest movements was the attention of white America drawn to the persistence—and in some ways, the growth —of racism in America over the past century. In rebelling against second-class citizenship, blacks and other racial minorities have exposed facts about our society which most Americans were content to leave obscure. By challenging the symptoms and manifestations of prejudice, these minorities evoked the full range of racist feeling resident in white America.

In a proximate sense, this development began with the historic bus boycott of 1955 in Montgomery, Alabama. During that year, Montgomery Negroes boycotted city bus lines in protest over segregated seating. For twelve months, blacks organized car pools and refused to patronize segregated transportation facilities. At first, the bus company was contemptuous. Tradition had it that blacks were not unhappy with "the back of the bus" treatment and the community-wide organization necessary to make such a boycott effective was thought beyond the capacity of Negroes. But as the boycott's economic effects came to be felt, the company pressed for a settlement. The matter was finally settled in the courts. In June 1956, a federal court ruled that segregation on local public transportation was in violation of the Fourteenth Amendment. The blacks had won. In so doing, they shook many of the white community's myths about what Negroes were, how they felt, and what they were capable of achieving. This initial success inspired continued attacks on patterns of southern segregation, which traced back to the turn of the century.

The movement entered a new phase in 1960 when four students from a black college in Greensboro, North Carolina, entered a local variety store, made several purchases, and then sat down at a lunch counter and ordered coffee. They were refused service, but remained seated until the store closed. With this action, the era of the sit-in began. The same technique was used in restaurants, libraries, beaches, hotel lobbies, and other facilities public in nature. The federal government proved sympathetic and the offices of the Attorney General were used for negotiations with national chain stores to bring about desegregation of luncheon counters and other facilities.

Then in 1961, the Congress of Racial Equality inaugurated the historic freedom rides to test segregation and discrimination in interstate transportation facilities. During the spring and summer of that year, hundreds of "freedom riders" toured the South. Scores were arrested, but under continuing assault the edifice of segregation began to crumble. At the same time, the attack on racial injustice exposed the brutality which lurked so near the surface of American life. In struggling for their rights, blacks brought into plain view the violence that lay behind the formal and polite forms of discrimination. A shocked nation viewed scenes of electric cattle prods, fire hoses, and police dogs used against human beings. The bombing of black churches, the murder of civil rights workers, the threats, beatings, and intimidation employed against the struggle of an oppressed people for dignity and equality, was revealed as a running sore on the body politic. The myth of black contentment was shattered and the viability of the American social order brought seriously into question.

The Congress responded with a series of legislative enactments. The first Civil Rights Act passed since Reconstruction became law in 1957. While the measure was weak, it reversed Congressional policy established in the late nineteenth century of noninterference in matters of civil rights pertaining to blacks. Other legislation followed, strengthening the power of the federal government to act against discrimination in voting, education, employment, housing, and use of public accommodations. The Supreme Court, since the school desegregation decision of 1954, also has played a positive and crucial role in the civil rights struggle. It quickly became apparent, however, that these legislative and judicial triumphs only touched the surface of the problem. Their primary focus was the South and they attacked only the most obvious aspects of discrimination. Since antebellum days, the South had served as a scapegoat for the rest of the nation, diverting attention from the race problem elsewhere in the country. By concentrating on the pervasive racism below the Mason-Dixon Line, the remainder of the country, where most black Americans lived by 1960, managed to assume a rather righteous posture on racial issues, comfortably ignoring the more subtle but equally insidious forms of discrimination in its own backyard.

Events of the mid-1960s destroyed the notion that racism was a regional phenomenon. The urban upheavals of 1965–1967 forced recognition of the fact that the minority problem was national in scope. A series of major urban outbreaks began when Watts, a part of the black ghetto of Los Angeles, exploded in the summer of 1965. Before the rioting ended, thirty-five people, most of them blacks, had been killed and hundreds more injured. For two days after the National Guard arrived, Watts took on the aspect of a theater of war. More than 4000 people were arrested and property damage was estimated at over 35 million dollars. The Watts revolt was the most devastating racial upheaval since the Detroit outbreak of 1943. Whatever illusions existed about progress in race relations outside the South received a rude shock. Particularly distressing to white Americans was the fact that Watts was among the "nicer" ghettos in the nation. It lacked the crowding and congestion of ghettos in eastern and midwestern cities. The rate of home ownership was high relative to other ghettos. And it was thought to lack a history of racial tension. The nation was puzzled by the outbreak, and, rather belatedly, began to look for the causes of such a spontaneous outpouring of rage. The following year saw major riots in Chicago and Cleveland. Then in 1967, urban upheavals reached an unprecedented crescendo of violence and destruction. Beginning in June of that year in Tampa, Florida, uprisings flared in urban concentrations in every section of the nation. The most devastating occurred in Detroit at the end of July. For five days, violence ran unabated. Forty-three people were killed and scores more injured. By the third year of recurrent outbreaks urban racial upheaval appeared to be becoming a permanent part of the American way of life.

A few days after the Detroit uprising, President Lyndon B. Johnson established a commission, headed by Governor Otto Kerner of Illinois, to inquire into the causes of these civil disorders. The nine-member commission was composed entirely of moderates. Its two Negro members were Senator Edward W. Brooke of Massachusetts and Roy Wilkins, executive director of the NAACP. No radical or militant spokesman from the black community was included. Many voiced the fear that, given its composition, the commission's report would understate the grievances which lay behind the outbreaks and provide white America with a document to soothe its conscience. Quite the contrary happened. The commission's report, issued in the spring of 1968, charged white America with the primary responsibility for the racial disorders sweeping the nation. The commission concluded, "Our nation is moving toward two societies, one black, one white — separate and unequal." White society played a crucial role in determining the conditions in which blacks lived. "What white Americans have never fully understood — but what the Negro can never forget — is that white society is deeply implicated in the ghetto. White institutions created it, white institutions maintain it, and white society condones it." In its analysis of causes, the commission ascribed fundamental importance to "the racial attitudes and behavior of white Americans toward black Americans. . . . White racism is essentially responsible for the explosive mixture which has been accumulating in our cities since World War II." Viewing the events of the summer of 1967 as "in large part the culmination of 300 years of racial prejudice," the commission lamented the lack of awareness of this phenomenon on the part of the population at large. "Most Americans," the commission report stated, "know little of the origins of the racial schism separating our white and Negro citizens. Few appreciate how central the problem of the Negro has been to our social policy. Fewer still understand that today's problems can be solved only if white Americans comprehend the rigid social, economic, and educational barriers that have prevented Negroes from participating in the mainstream of American life."

The accusations of the Commission on Civil Disorders provoked outraged denials. Many shrank from the idea that our society, committed to ideals of human freedom and equal opportunity, could be labeled racist. The debate over the accuracy of the commission's findings, and the crucial importance of racial tension in America today clearly pointed to the need for serious and considered study of the role of racial attitudes in shaping the American experience. It is this need which motivated the authors of this volume. What are white racial attitudes? What are their origins? How have they been changed by historical forces? What functions have they served? To what extent have they permeated the institutions of American society? These are a few of the questions to which we have addressed ourselves. In nine analytical essays, we have explored white racial attitudes and their impact upon American society from the colonial period to the twentieth century. Along with blacks, other minorities—Indians, European and Asian immigrants, and Mexican-Americans—have come within our purview insofar as they have been objects of white racism. While we make no claim to definitiveness, it is our hope that this volume will shed light on this vital, but much neglected, aspect of the nation's history.

Los Angeles   Gary B. Nash
March 1970   Richard Weiss

Contents

1

Red, White, and Black

The Origins of Racism in Colonial America

GARY B. NASH

Racial attitudes in America have their origins in the culture of Elizabethan England, for it was in the closing decades of the sixteenth century that the English people, who were on the verge of creating an overseas empire in North America and the Caribbean, began to come into frequent contact with peoples whose culture, religion, and color was markedly different from their own. In the early responses of Englishmen to Indians and Africans lay the seeds of what would become, four centuries later, one of the most agonizing social problems in American history—the problem of racial prejudice.

I

Englishmen did not arrive at Jamestown, Virginia, in 1607, or at Plymouth, Massachusetts, in 1620, with minds barren of images and preconceptions of the native occupiers of the land. A mass of reports and stories concerning the Indians of the New World, many of them based upon the Spanish and Portuguese experience in Mexico, Peru, and Brazil, were available in printed form or by word of mouth for curious Englishmen crossing the Atlantic. From this literature ideas and fantasies concerning the Indians gradually entered the English consciousness.

These early accounts seem to have created a split image of the Indian in the English mind. On the one hand, the native was imagined to be a savage, hostile, beastlike creature who inhabited the animal kingdom rather than the kingdom of men. In 1585, prospective adventurers to the New World could read one description of the natives of North America which depicted them as naked, lascivious individuals who cohabited "like beasts without any reasonableness." Another account described them as men who "spake such speech that no men coulde understand them, and in their demeanour like to bruite beastes."[1] But Englishmen also entertained another more positive version of the New World native. Richard Hakluyt, the great propagandist for English colonization, described the Indians in 1585 as "simple and rude in manners, and destitute of the knowledge of God or any good lawes, yet of nature gentle and tractable, and most apt to receive the Christian Religion, and to subject themselves to some good government."[2] Many other reports spoke of the native in similarly optimistic terms.

This dual vision of the native matched the two-sided image of the New World refracted through the prism of the sixteenth-century European mind. In some ways prospective colonists fantasized the New World as a Garden of Eden, a land abounding with precious minerals, health foods, and exotic wildlife. The anti-image was of a barbarous land filled with a multitude of unknown dangers—a "howling wilderness" capable of dragging man down to the level of beasts.

In a rough way the two images of the Indian not only matched English visions of the New World, but coincided with the intentions of prospective settlers. In the early stages of colonization, when trade with the Indians was deemed important and the hope existed that the natives would lead the settlers to gold and silver—perhaps even to the fabled Northwest Passage to the Orient—the Indians were seen as primitive but winsome, as ignorant but receptive individuals. If treated kindly, they could be wooed and won to the advantages of trade and cooperation with the English. Only a friendly or malleable Indian *could* be a trading or assisting Indian. Thus, when thoughts of conducting trade and exploration from small trading stations on the coast were uppermost in the English mind, as they were between 1580 and 1610, the colonial leaders frequently portrayed the Indian in relatively gentle hues. Though the natives could be wary and "fearful by nature," wrote George Peckham in 1585, "courtesie and myldnes" along with a generous supply of "prittie merchaundizes and trifles" would win

[1] Edward Arber, ed., *The First Three English Books on America* (Birmingham, Eng., 1885), p. xxvii; Richard Hakluyt, *Divers Voyages touching the Discovery of America and the Islands Adjacent . . .,* Hakluyt Society Publications, First Series, VII (London, 1850), p. 23.

[2] E. G. R. Taylor, ed., *The Original Writings & Correspondence of the Two Richard Hakluyts,* Hakluyt Society Publications, Second Series, LXXVI (London, 1935), pp. 164–165.

them over and "induce theyr Barbarous natures to a likeing and mutuall society with us."[3] Also important in this optimistic view of the native was the need to quiet the fears of prospective colonists by assuring them that the Indians were not waiting to destroy them or drive them back into the sea.

When permanent settlement became the primary English concern, however, and land the object of desire, the image of the Indian as a hostile savage became ascendant in the English mind. Beginning with the James-town settlement of 1607 and intensifying with the great Puritan migration of the 1630's, Englishmen coming to the New World thought less about Indian trade, the Northwest Passage, and fabled gold mines and more about land. As the dreams of El Dorado evaporated, English attention centered on the less glamorous goal of permanent settlement. Now land became all-important, for without land how could there be permanent settlement? The Indian, who had been important when trade and exploration were the keys to overseas involvement, became an inconvenient obstacle. One En-glishman went to the heart of the difficulty in 1609: "by what right or war-rant can we enter into the land of these Savages, take away their rightfull inheritance from them, and plant ourselves in their places, being unwronged or unprovoked by them?"[4] It was a cogent question to ask, for Englishmen, like other Europeans, had organized their society around the concept of private ownership of land. They regarded it, in fact, as an important charac-teristic of their superior culture. Colonists were not blind to the fact that they were invading the land of another people, who by prior possession could lay sole claim to the whole of mainland America. The resolution of this moral and legal problem was accomplished by an appeal to logic and to higher powers. The English claimed that they came to share, not appro-priate, the trackless wilderness. The Indians would benefit because they would be elevated far above their present condition through contact with a richer culture, a more advanced civilization, and most importantly, the Christian religion. Samuel Purchas, a clerical promoter of English expan-sion, gave classic expression to this idea: "God in wisedome . . . enriched the Savage Countries, that those riches might be attractive for Christian suters, which there may sowe spirituals and reape temporals." Spirituals, to be sown, of course, meant Christianity; temporals to be reaped meant land. Purchas went on to argue that to leave undeveloped a sparsely settled land populated only by a few natives was to oppose the wishes of God who would not have showed Englishmen the way to the New World if he had not

[3] "A true reporte of the late discoveries . . ." in David B. Quinn, ed., *The Voyages and Colonizing Enterprises of Sir Humphrey Gilbert,* Hakluyt Society Publications, Second Series, LXXXIV (London, 1940), pp. 451–452.

[4] Robert Gray, *A Good Speed to Virginia* (London, 1609), in Wesley F. Craven, "Indian Policy in Early Virginia," *William and Mary Quarterly,* Third Series, I (1944), p. 65.

intended them to possess it.[5] Moreover, if the English did not occupy North America, Spain would; and the Indians would then fall victim to Catholicism.

Land was the key to English settlement after 1620. It was logical to assume in these circumstances that the Indian would not willingly give up the ground that sustained him, even if the English offered to purchase land, as they did in most cases. For anyone as property conscious as the English, the idea that people would resist the invasion of their land with all the force at their disposal came almost as a matter of course. Thus the image of the hostile, savage Indian began to triumph over that of the receptive, friendly Indian. Their own intentions had changed from establishing trade relations to building permanent settlements. A different conception of the Indian was required in these altered circumstances.

The image of a treacherous, uncooperative Indian caused great confusion in the English mind during the first years of the Virginia settlement when the Indians still entertained notions of profiting from the English presence. When Christopher Newport, the leader of the 1607 Jamestown expedition, made the first exploratory trip up the newly named James River, he was puzzled by what he encountered. The Indians, he wrote to his superiors in London, "are naturally given to trechery howbeit we could not finde it in our travell up the river, but rather a most kind and loving people."[6] Every new act of generosity—there is much evidence that the Indians provided the food that kept the struggling settlement alive over the first winter —was taken as another indication of Indian guile and treachery. Hospitality, eagerness to trade, curiosity at the newcomers, and the desire of some tribal leaders to use English support to defeat their enemies were all taken as evidence of the sly, treacherous qualities inherent in Indians.

What we see here is a subconscious attempt to manipulate the world in order to make it conform to the English definition of it. The evidence also suggests that the English stereotype of the hostile savage helped assuage a sense of guilt which inevitably arose when men whose culture was based on the concept of private property embarked on a program to dispossess another people of their land. To type-cast the Indian as a brutish savage was to solve a moral dilemma. If the Indian was truly cordial, generous, and eager to trade, what justification could there be for taking his land? But if he was a savage, without religion or culture, perhaps the colonists' actions were defensible. The English, we might speculate, anticipated hostility and then read it into the Indian's character because they recognized that they were embarking upon an invasion of land to which the only natural response

[5] Samuel Purchas, *Hakluytus Posthumus, or Purchas His Pilgrimes* (20 vols.; Glasgow, 1905–1907), XIX, p. 232.

[6] Gabriel Archer, "A relatyon . . . written . . . by a gent. of ye Colony," in Philip L. Barbour, ed., *The Jamestown Voyages under the First Charter, 1606–1609,* Hakluyt Society Publications, Second Series, CXXXVI (London, 1969), pp. 103–104.

could be violent resistance. Having created the conditions in which the Indian could only respond violently, the Englishman defined the native as brutal, beastly, savage, and barbarian and then used that as a justification for what he was doing.

This concept had a self-fulfilling quality to it. The more violence was anticipated, the more violence occurred. This is not to argue that hostility would have been avoided if the settlers had seen the native in a different light, since opportunities for mutual mistrust and hostility abounded. But certainly the chances of conflict were greatly enhanced by misperceiving the intentions of the Indian as he struggled within his own society to adapt to the presence of the Europeans.

There was hostility. In Virginia, after a period of uneasy relations punctuated with outbreaks of violence, the Indians mounted a concerted attack on the white settlements with the intention of driving the white man back into the sea. The Massacre of 1622 wiped out one third of the Chesapeake colony. The Indian victory was costly, however, for it left the English colonists with the excuse to set aside the old claim, frequently mentioned in the early years of settlement, of devoting themselves to civilizing and converting the natives. After 1622, most Virginians felt at liberty to attack the natives at will. A no-holds-barred approach was taken to what became known as the "Indian problem." Whereas before, the settlers had engaged in reprisals against the natives whenever they had been attacked, the English now put aside all restraint. As a leader in Virginia wrote revealingly after the Indian attack of 1622,

> Our hands, which before were tied with gentleness and faire usage, are now set at liberty by the treacherous violence of the Savages so that We may now by right of Warre and law of Nations invade the Country, and destroy them who sought to destroy us. . . . Now their cleared grounds in all their villages, (which are situate in the fruitfullest places of the land) shall be inhabited by us, whereas heretofore the grubbing of woods caused us the greatest labour.[7]

A note of grim satisfaction that the Indians had conducted an all-out attack can be detected. Hereafter one was entitled to devastate Indian villages and take, rather than buy, the best land of the area. It was a policy so profitable that the Virginia Council in 1629 reneged on a peace treaty that had been recently negotiated and proclaimed that on second thought a policy of "perpetual enmity" toward the natives was best for the colony.

After 1622 the stereotype of the Indian became less ambivalent. Little in his culture was found worthy of respect — in fact, he was deemed almost cultureless. More and more abusive words crept into English descriptions

---

[7] Edward Waterhouse, *A Declaration of the State of the Colonie and Affaires in Virginia* (London, 1622), in Susan M. Kingsbury, ed., *The Records of the Virginia Company of London* (4 vols.; Washington, D.C., 1906–1935), III, pp. 556–557.

of Indian society. Negative qualities were newly found and projected onto the natives. Whereas John Smith and other early leaders of the Virginia colony had written lengthy descriptions of the political organization, religion, and customs of the natives, Edward Waterhouse, writing after the Massacre of 1622, could only describe the Indians as "by nature sloathfull and idle, vitious, melancholy, slovenly, of bad conditions, lyers, of small memory, of no constancy or trust . . . by nature of all people the most lying and most inconstant in the world, sottish and sodaine, never looking what dangers may happen afterwards, lesse capable then children of sixe or seaven years old, and less apt and ingenious. . . ."[8] Samuel Purchas, writing in 1625 of the Virginia Indians, described them as "bad people, having little of Humanitie but shape, ignorant of Civilitie, of Arts, of Religion; more brutish then [sic] the beasts they hunt, more wild and unmanly then [sic] that unmanned wild Countrey which they range rather than inhabite; captivated also to Satans tyranny in foolish pieties, mad impieties, wicked idleness, busie and bloudy wickednesse. . . . ."[9] After the Indian attack of 1622 Englishmen in Virginia no longer needed to restrain their impulses or remind themselves of their obligation to convert the Indian.

In New England, despite the many differences in motives and means of colonization, attitudes evolved in much the same manner. In the first two attempts at settlement, on the coast of Maine in 1607 and at Plymouth in 1620, Anglo-Indian relations followed a pattern of initial wariness by the Indians, petty acts of violence and plunder by the white settlers, and then reciprocating and escalating hostility. When the great Puritan migration to New England began in 1630, the Indians were naturally apprehensive, though not hostile. John Winthrop, who led the Massachusetts Bay Colony throughout the 1630s, often mentioned the Puritans' obligation to convert the natives, giving the impression that he felt a real compulsion to "save their souls for Christ." But a careful reading of early New England literature suggests that with significant exceptions such as Roger Williams, the Puritans held the natives in contempt and would have preferred them all dead or removed from the region where they were building their "city on the hill." Winthrop remarked in his journal that the smallpox epidemic of 1617, communicated to the Indians by visiting fishermen, was God's way of "thinning out" the native population to make room for the Puritans. Another prominent Puritan referred to the epidemic, which ravaged the New England natives, as a "wonderful Plague." Later Winthrop wrote that the Indians "are neere all dead of the small Poxe, so the Lord hathe cleared our title to what we possess."[10] Rather than civilize or proselytize the natives, it was

---

[8] In Kingsbury, *The Records of the Virginia Company of London,* III, pp. 562–563.
[9] *Hakluytus Posthumus,* XIX, p. 231, in Roy Harvey Pearce, *Savagism and Civilization: A Study of the Indian and the American Mind* (Baltimore, 1953), pp. 7–8.
[10] In Pearce, *Savagism and Civilization,* p. 19.

easier to see them eliminated by European diseases and then to interpret this as God's wish.

In the Puritan mind there was always a tension between the inclusionist and exclusionist impulse, between the evangelical desire to convert the heathen and others who followed "false Gods," and the desire to keep the community pure by excluding deviant types. Despite many professions of concern for converting the natives, New England ministers made only a few perfunctory efforts in this direction. The same impulse which led to the expulsion of theologically deviant Puritans such as Anne Hutchinson and Roger Williams, or to the persecution of Quakers in Boston in the 1650s, was at the heart of the unwillingness to assimilate the New England Indians, even on the few occasions when they were converted to Christianity. Before the end of the first decade of Puritan settlement, the Indian had come to stand for Satanic opposition to the divine experiment being conducted in the Bay Colony. An Indian, when he attacked a white man, indirectly attacked God whose hand the Puritans saw in all that they did. In this sense, the Indians came to represent followers of Satan, savages pitting themselves against the Puritans' "errand into the wilderness." With the drama of colony building invested with divine guidance, with the hand of God seen in every act, to kill an Indian who had demonstrated his resistence or opposition to the Massachusetts Bay Colony, was only to destroy an opponent of God. When hostility with the Pequot Indians flared in 1637, and spread into a general war, the Puritans again saw evidence of divine intervention. The climax of the war came when the Puritans surrounded 500 Pequot men, women, and children in Mystic Fort and burned them to death. The Massachusetts leaders, suffused with a sense of mission, recorded that God "had laughed at his Enemies . . . making them as a fiery oven. . . . Thus did the Lord judge among the Heathen, filling the Place [the fort] with dead bodies."[11] To dehumanize the Indians was one means of justifying one's own inhumanity.

Two important concepts concerning the Indians were left in the English mind after the first period of painful confrontation. First, the image of the native as a hostile and inferior creature became indelibly printed upon the white mind. The Indian was noticeably different in color, though the colonists seemed to have made little of this. Far more important, he was uncivilized, and, it was generally concluded, incapable of civilization as Europeans defined it. As Roy H. Pearce has noted, the Indian was a constant reminder to the colonists of what they must not become. For men who were deeply concerned about the barbarizing effects of the wilderness, the Indian provided a means of measuring their own civility, culture, and

[11] John Mason, *A Brief History of the Pequot War* (Boston, 1736), in Alden T. Vaughan, *New England Frontier: Puritans and Indians, 1620–1675* (Boston, 1965), p. 145.

self-identity. "The Indian became important for the English mind, not for what he was in and of himself, but rather for what he showed civilized men they were not and must not be."[12] Not to control the Indian, therefore, was to lose control of one's new environment, and ultimately of oneself. This was the psychological importance of the Indian to the colonist.

At a more practical level was the problem of how to control the Indian. Defined as a savage, regarded in most cases as unassimilable, and inconveniently located in the path of English settlement, the Indian posed one of the colonists' most serious problems. At first colonial leaders had hoped that cultural interaction with the Indians would be possible. But it could only be on English terms. When the Indian threatened the white community, control and security became uppermost in the minds of the settlers. With the Indian now conforming to type, the colonists worked with grim determination to isolate this alien and dangerous subgroup and to control it strictly. A special status, inferior and subservient, was created for those Indians who wished to accept European culture and live within it on the white man's terms. The only other alternative for the native was to move out of the path of English settlement.

During the course of the seventeenth century thousands of Indians did choose to live within white society. Over the years they became dependent upon the iron-age implements of the European—the knife, gun, kettle, fishhook—and, most importantly, upon the white man's liquor. Gradually those Indians who chose to remain on the eastern seaboard lost their forest skills. Their culture slowly changed under the pressure of contact with a more technologically advanced society and their lot often was reduced to pathetic subservience as day laborers and sometimes as slaves. For these Indians—tamed, decultured, and utterly dependent—the colonist had only contempt. Unlike his brother on the frontier, the dreaded "savage," the domesticated Indian was looked upon as a despised menial.

The psychological calculus by which intentions governed attitudes can be illuminated further by studying the views of Anglo-Americans who genuinely desired amicable relations with the Indians. The Quakers of Pennsylvania and West New Jersey, who were the most important early practitioners of pacifism in the New World, threatened no violence to the Indians when they arrived in the Delaware River Valley in the last quarter of the seventeenth century. It was pacifism, not violence, that was on the Quaker mind. Though relations with the Indians would deteriorate in the eighteenth century, when Germans and Scotch-Irish streamed into Pennsylvania, it is significant to note that in the early years of settlement the pacifistic Quakers tended to view the Indian differently than their neighbors to the north and south. Though they regarded the native as backward and

[12] Pearce, *Savagism and Civilization*, p. 5.

"under a dark Night in things relating to Religion," they also saw him as physically attractive, generous, mild-tempered, and possessed of many admirable traits. William Penn, the Quaker proprietor of Pennsylvania, revived old speculations that the Indians were the "Jews of America," the descendants of the Lost Tribes of Israel, and found their language "lofty" and full of words "of more sweetness or greatness" than most European tongues.[13]

In other colonies, too, the image of the Indian began to change, at least within the reflective element of society, when the precariousness of the English position declined and when attacks on white communities subsided. In the first half of the eighteenth century a number of colonial observers began to develop a new image of the Indian. Unlike later writers from seaboard cities or European centers of culture, who sentimentalized the native into a "noble savage," these men knew of Indian life from firsthand experience as missionaries, provincial officials, and fur traders. Close to Indian culture, but not pitted against the native in a fight for land or survival, they developed clearer perspectives on aboriginal life. During the earlier period of hostility, the Indian had been regarded as virtually cultureless. Now all of the missing elements in the Indian's cultural make-up —government, social structure, religion, family organization, codes of justice and morality, arts and crafts—were discovered.

Thus, in 1705, thirty years after the last significant Indian attack in Virginia, Robert Beverley described the Indians in terms strikingly different from those employed by preceding generations, whose contacts, even in the best of times, had been highly abrasive. Beverley viewed the Indians not as savages, but as a cultural group whose institutions, modes of living, and values were worthy of examination on their own terms. He found aspects of Indian civilization reminiscent of classical Spartan life and much to be admired. In Beverley's view, the Indians' contact with European civilization, far from advancing their existence, was responsible for the loss of their "Felicity as well as their Innocence."[14]

John Lawson, who traveled extensively among the southeastern tribes in the early eighteenth century, also dwelled on the integrity of native culture and took note of many traits, such as cleanliness, equable temperament, bravery, tribal loyalty, hospitality, and concern for the welfare of the group rather than the individual, that often seemed absent from English society. Like Beverley, Lawson concluded that the Indians of the southern regions were the "freest people from Heats and Passions (which possess

---

[13] William Penn, *A Letter to the Free Society of Traders . . .* (London, 1683), in Albert C. Myers, ed., *Narratives of Early Pennsylvania, West New Jersey and Delaware* (New York, 1912), pp. 230, 234.

[14] Robert Beverley, *History of the Present State of Virginia* [London, 1705], ed. by Louis B. Wright (Chapel Hill, N.C., 1947), p. 233.

the Europeans)." He lamented that contact with the settlers had vitiated what was best in Indian culture.[15] Many other writers who did not covet the Indians' land or were not engaged in the exploitive Indian trade, agreed that the concept of community, which colonial leaders cherished as an ideal but rarely achieved, was best reflected in North America by the natives. As Pearce has noted, "the essential integrity of savage life, for good and bad, became increasingly the main concern of eighteenth-century Americans writing on the Indian."[16]

II

It was in an atmosphere emotionally charged by the tension between English settlers and Indians that the black man made his initial appearance in America. We know that the first Africans arrived in the colonies in 1619, though their status—whether slave or indentured servant—is uncertain. Not until the 1640s do we have any indications that Africans were being consigned to perpetual servitude and even then the evidence is scanty. But certainly by the 1660s, the indeterminate position of the African changed; hereditary slavery took root in the colonies. By the mid-eighteenth century, the black man in most colonies had been stripped of virtually all the rights accorded the white settler under the common law. In many colonies the black man was no longer defined as a legal person, but rather as chattel property—the object of rights, but never the subject of rights. A slave could neither appeal to nor testify in the courts; he had no rights to religion or marriage or parenthood; he could not own or carry arms; he could not buy or sell commodities or engage in any economic activity; he could not congregate in public places with more than two or three of his own race. Even education—the right to literacy—was forbidden slaves in many colonies, for it was thought that if the African was permitted to read, the germ of freedom might grow in him.

Much has been written concerning the evolution of this system of chattel slavery; and much has been learned by comparing it to slavery in the ancient world, where it was not based on race, and in the South American colonies of Spain and Portugal, where a less repressive and closed system of servitude developed than in British North America. But for our purposes the primary question concerns the effect of racial attitudes upon the evolution of slavery, and, conversely, the effects of slavery, once instituted, upon racial attitudes. Was racial prejudice against the African responsible for his consignment to slavery? Or were other factors, such as the great labor shortage in the New World, combined with the availability of Africans

[15] John Lawson, *A New Voyage to Carolina* [London, 1709], ed. by Hugh T. Lefler (Chapel Hill, N.C., 1967), pp. 209, 239.
[16] Pearce, *Savagism and Civilization,* p. 45.

and the example of slave trading set much earlier by Spain, Holland, and Portugal, responsible for a system of slave labor which cast the black man in such an inferior and degraded role that racial prejudice against him developed?

Certainly there was little about the first impressions of Africans that Englishmen formed in the late sixteenth century which augured well for the status of the African in English colonial society. Winthrop D. Jordan shows in his recent book *White Over Black: American Attitudes Toward the Negro, 1550–1812,* which is the most probing historical account we have of racial attitudes in early America, that Englishmen responded negatively to Africans even when their contacts were of a casual and exploratory nature. To begin with, the African's blackness was strange, troublesome, and vaguely repugnant. Englishmen were already familiar with people of darker skin than their own, for they had traded with people of the Mediterranean world and come into contact with Moors and occasional traders from the Middle East and North Africa. But they had not met truly black men, though they had probably heard of them. When these Englishmen, among the lightest-skinned people in the world, came face to face with one of the darkest-skinned people of the world, their reaction was strongly negative. Unhappily, blackness was already a means of conveying some of the most ingrained values of English society. Black—and its opposite, white—were emotion-laden words. Black meant foul, dirty, wicked, malignant, and disgraceful. And of course it signified night—a time of fear and uncertainty. Black was a symbol signifying baseness, evil, and danger. Thus expressions filtered into English usage associating black with the worst in human nature: the black sheep in the family, a black mark against one's name, a black day, a black look, to blackball or blackmail. White was all the opposites—chastity, virtue, beauty, and peace. Women were married in white to symbolize purity and virginity. Day was light just as night was black. The angels were white; the devil was black. Thus Englishmen were conditioned to see ugliness and evil in black. In this sense their encounter with the black people of West Africa was prejudiced by the very symbols of color which had been woven into English language and culture over the centuries.

Englishmen also were struck by the religious condition of the African, or what was considered to be his lack of religion. To the English, the Africans were heathens—an altogether Godless people. In an age when religion framed the life of society, this was taken as a grave defect. Though the universalist strain in their own religion emphasized the brotherhood of all men, and though the book of Genesis stressed the point that all men derived from the same act of creation, Englishmen took the Africans' heathenism as an indication of an almost irreparable inferiority.

Englishmen identified a third characteristic interacting with blackness and heathenism—what they called cultural depravity or "savagery."

Every new observation of African life added to their belief that the culture of Africans was vastly inferior to that of Europeans. The African's diet, for example, was revolting by European standards. He wore few clothes if any. His habitat was crude. He made war on his fellow men in what was deemed a hideously cruel way. All of this was imprinted on the English consciousness, as Jordan points out, and we find words like "brutish," "savage," and "beastly" creeping into English accounts of Africans. In almost all these respects the image of the African coincided with the image of the Indian after the first period of contact.

Strengthening and vivifying this impression of primitive men in a primitive setting was the extraordinary animal life of Africa. Englishmen were fascinated by the numerous subhuman species they encountered and none so fascinated them as the orangutan or chimpanzee. Though the English were familiar with monkeys and baboons, they had never encountered the tailless, anthropoid ape with his curiously human appearance and behavior, which still makes him a center of attention at zoos. When Englishmen came upon this strangely human creature they began to speculate about possible connections, as Jordan has indicated, between the "beastlike man" —the African—and the "manlike beast"—the orangutan. The logic was tortured, perhaps, but nonetheless Englishmen began discussing the possibility that the African was an intermediate specie between beast and man. To make matters worse, there were speculations about sexual unions between man and beast in Africa, a fantasy of overwrought English imaginations and an idea that probably suggested itself to Englishmen because promiscuity, bestiality, and sodomy were not uncommon in England at this time, and in fact were subjects of some concern.[17]

Thus a number of African characteristics—real and alleged—strongly and negatively impressed English venturers as the New World was opening up: the African's blackness, his heathenism, his cultural inferiority, his sexuality, and his bestiality. Because religion and cultural achievement were the primary reference points for Europeans of this age, it is probable that in this early period of contact the African's skin color was more a matter of curiosity than damning concern. Those who have read sixteenth-century accounts of the Irish, whose ancestral lands were being invaded by the English in this period, will know that the vocabulary of abuse used to describe Africans was applied also to Irishmen. They too were seen as culturally inferior, savage, brutish, and primitive. The blackness of Africans was an additional liability, given the connotations of color in the English mind, but perhaps not a crucially important one. Eventually, of course, blackness would be firmly linked with other negative qualities in the English anatomy of prejudice.

---

[17] Winthrop D. Jordan, *White Over Black: American Attitudes Toward the Negro, 1550–1812* (Chapel Hill, N.C., 1968), pp. 28–32.

It is important to remember that these early observations of Africans, like those of the Indians, reflect as much about the observer as the observed. We know now from careful research that Africa was not what Englishmen saw and recorded in that age of discovery. West Africa lagged behind western Europe technologically, though the differences were not so great as is usually imagined, but the area had nurtured a highly developed civilization. If art, social organization, and cultural traditions are criteria of advancement, Africa in the sixteenth and seventeenth centuries was far from primitive and backward. Englishmen saw in Africa not what existed there, but what they were psychologically prepared to see. They compared African culture with their own, which they took to be a universal model.

Further insight into the English reaction to Africans and Indians can be gained by comparing it to Spanish and Portuguese attitudes. Though England's colonial competitors regarded the natives of Africa and North America as primitive and inferior, the image they represented in their psychic landscape was far less negative and emotional. Geography explains much of this, for whereas the English of the sixteenth century were noted for their insularity, the Spanish and Portuguese, situated astride Europe and Africa, had been in near continuous contact with peoples of different races and cultures for centuries.

Because of this, Portugal, and to a lesser degree Spain, had an ethnic and cultural diversity not to be found in England. Over the centuries, the Iberian peninsula had been breached again and again: by Muslims between 711 and 1212, by Jews, Berbers, and North African Moors. As usually happens in history, the conquerors and the conquered fraternized, intermarried, and interbred. By the time England was first exposing herself to Africa, her European competitors, especially Portugal, had already amalgamated their bloodstreams with people of darker color and different cultures. This produced a tolerance for diversity in the Spanish and Portuguese cultures that was absent in the English, who had for centuries been relatively isolated from the rest of the world.

It would be unwise to conclude that the long warfare between the Portuguese and Moors and the centuries of contact with a variety of darker-skinned people eliminated racial prejudice among the Spanish and Portuguese in Europe or in their New World colonies. Racial consciousness *did* exist among these people, and with racial consciousness came feelings of racial superiority. There can be little doubt that the lighter one's skin, the greater one's social prestige in Spain and Portugal and in their colonies — a pattern which still exists. And yet because of their ancient exposure to and intermixture with people of darker skin, the Spanish and Portuguese, unlike the English, regarded racial intermixture as inevitable and attached no great moral significance to it. This difference in attitude would lead toward a gradual assimilation of races which in turn increased the tolerance for racial diversity.

A second factor which helps to explain the unusually virulent English reaction to Africans and Indians, not duplicated in Spain and Portugal, was the internal stresses England was undergoing at the time she first exposed herself to the outer world. This period of the late sixteenth and early seventeenth century, called the age of Puritanism, was a "time of troubles" for England—an era in which the traditional feudal society was giving way to a more modern social order. The beginnings of urbanization and industrialization, the breakup of the traditional church, the enclosure of land, and the decay of the guilds were all a part of this process. Englishmen of the late sixteenth century saw poverty and vagabondage on the rise, cities growing faster than they could absorb rural newcomers into the traditional close-knit scheme of life, alehouses and dens of prostitution multiplying, gangs of highwaymen and drifters roaming the country. England was experiencing not only rural dislocation but an associated "urban problem."

Puritanism, a religious reform movement bent on purifying the Church of England, must also be seen as a social response to this crumbling of the old order. Puritans were convinced that England was being threatened by dangerous currents of social change which encouraged the individual to free himself from the old institutionalized restraints. In religion, Puritans attempted to place the individual in a more direct relationship with his God by removing the traditional religious intermediaries—especially the Catholic Church. But individualism in other aspects of life was not greeted with similar enthusiasm, for it threatened to erode all the old symbols of authority, all the old instruments of corporate control in society—the church, the village community, the guild, even the father as patriarchal head of the family. Puritanism was the new religious and social doctrine which some men hoped would re-establish a morally secure and orderly world through new methods of social control, including a work-ethic which stressed industriousness as a way of serving God, and the formation of tight-knit Puritan congregations composed of people who would watch over and discipline themselves and each other. The keynotes of Puritanism were piety, discipline, order, self-restraint, and work.

The rise of Puritanism coincided with England's belated entry into the age of exploration. Puritans, and those around them, were simultaneously participants in an age of self-restraint and social discipline and an age of adventure, exploration, and discovery. As Winthrop Jordan has said, Elizabethan England reverberated with "the twin spirits of adventure and control."[18] Here was a society engaged in voyages of discovery and settlement overseas, as represented by Elizabethans such as John Hawkins, Francis Drake, Humphrey Gilbert, and Walter Raleigh, and simultaneously embarked upon attempts to reform themselves and society, as typified by such colonial leaders as William Bradford, John Winthrop, and Roger Williams.

---

[18] Jordan, *White Over Black,* p. 40.

In this vibrant atmosphere of discovery (a reaching outward) and self-scrutiny (a turning inward), Englishmen tended to use the newly found African black man, and later the Indian, as a foil. For men who were attempting to open up the New World while reorganizing the Old, the African and the Indian came to represent to the Englishman what he was fighting against in himself, what he must never allow himself to become. When we look at the English perceptions of Africans—their blackness, their nakedness, their sexuality—we begin to understand that Englishmen reacted emotionally and negatively because these strangers reminded them, at least at the subconscious level, of problems in themselves and their own society. A negative reaction to blackness stemmed both from the symbology of color in English culture and the awareness of "black deeds" at home; sexuality and bestiality were much on the English mind because of the Puritan emphasis on self-control and the guilt over licentiousness which were widespread in England. When Englishmen called the African bestial and savage, we may conjecture that they were unconsciously projecting onto black men qualities which they had identified and shrank from in themselves. Moreover, by contrasting themselves favorably to Africans or Indians, the English were better able to convince themselves of their own role as God's chosen people, destined to carry their culture and religion to all corners of the earth.

Of course not every settler who came to America in the early seventeenth century harbored deeply negative thoughts about Africans and Indians. Probably few of the Pilgrims and Puritans who colonized New England or few of the settlers in Virginia had met face to face with natives of Africa or North America or even thought very systematically about the culture and character traits of such people. But Africans and Indians *did* impress English adventurers of the late sixteenth and early seventeenth centuries in certain ways, and these impressions were recorded in books which literate men read or knew about. Thus, ideas and attitudes concerning red and black men were entering the collective English consciousness at just that time when England was making its first attempts to compete with Spain, Portugal, Holland, and France for possession of the New World. These first impressions would change under the pressure of circumstances in the New World. But the colonists first met these men from other continents with ideas and notions already in their heads, though the images were vague and half formed.

It is only with an understanding of these early attitudes and a knowledge of early Anglo-Indian relations that we can comprehend the connection between prejudice and slavery. No doubt the early English image of the African as a heathen, primitive creature made it easier for Englishmen to cast him into slavery. However, the Indian also was depicted in unfavorable terms as were the Irish and even the dregs of white English society. But among those seen in such a light, it was the Africans who were most vulnerable to economic exploitation because only they could be wrenched from their homeland in great numbers, often with the active participation of other Africans. Moreover, they were unusually helpless once transported to a distant and unfamiliar environment where they were forced into close association with a people whose power they could not contest. Certainly a latent and still forming prejudice against people with black skin was partially responsible for the subjugation of Africans. But the chronic labor shortage in the colonies and the almost total failure to mold the Indians into an agricultural labor force were probably more important factors. Winthrop Jordan has taken a middle position on this vexing question, writing that "rather than slavery causing 'prejudice,' or vice versa, they seem rather to have generated each other. . . . Slavery and 'prejudice' may have been equally cause and effect, continuously reacting upon each other, dynamically joining hands to hustle the Negro down the road to complete degradation."[19]

The effect of slavery on racial attitudes is less complicated. Once institutionalized in the American colonies, slavery cast the Negro in such a lowly role that the initial bias against him could only be confirmed and vastly strengthened. It was hardly possible for one people to enslave another without developing strong feelings against them. While initially unfavorable impressions of Africans and economic conditions which encouraged their exploitation led to the mass enslavement of men with black skins, it required slavery itself to harden negative racial feelings into a deep and almost unshakable prejudice which continued to grow for centuries to come. A labor system was devised which kept the African in America at the bottom of the social and economic pyramid. By mid-eighteenth century, when black codes had been legislated to ensure that slaves were totally and unalterably caught in the web of perpetual servitude, no further opportunity remained to prove the white stereotype wrong. Socially and legally defined as less than a man, kept in a degraded and debased position, virtually without power in his relationships with his white master, the African became a truly servile, ignoble, degraded creature in the perception of white men. In the long evolution of racial attitudes in America nothing was of greater importance than the enslavement of Africans in a land where freedom, equality, and opportunity were becoming the foundations of a new social order.

Whereas the white colonist almost always encountered the black man as a slave after about 1660, and thus came to think of him as a slavelike creature by nature, the English settler met the Indian, especially after 1675 when the last large-scale Indian wars until the nineteenth century occurred, far less frequently. When he did interact with the Indian, it was rarely in a master-slave context. The English settler learned how difficult it was to enslave the native in his own habitat. Thus, if the Indian had survived the

---

[19] Jordan, *White Over Black,* p. 80.

coming of white civilization, he usually maintained a certain freedom to come and go, and, more significantly, the capacity to attack and kill the white encroacher. Though he was hated for this, it earned him a grudging respect. The Anglo-Indian relationship in the eighteenth century was rarely that of master and slave, with all rights and power concentrated on one side.

In fact, the Indian and the white man were involved in a set of power relationships in which each side, with something to offer the other, maneuvered for the superior position. That the Indian was the ultimate loser in almost all these interchanges should not obscure the fact that for several hundred years the Anglo-American confronted the native as an adversary rather than a chattel.

The Anglo-Indian economic relationship illustrates the point. In almost every colony the Indian trade was of importance to the local economy in the early stages of development. Trade implied a kind of equality; each side bargained in its own interest; and in each exchange agreement had to be reached between buyer and seller. The long-term effect of the trade was attritional for the Indians because it fostered a dependence upon alcohol and the implements of European civilization, especially the gun. But even while their culture was transformed by this contact with a technologically advanced society, and even though they often were exploited by unscrupulous traders, the Indians maintained considerable power in the trade nexus. Just as the provincial government of South Carolina could bring a recalcitrant tribe to terms by threatening to cut off trade, the Iroquois tribes of New York could obtain advantages from the English by threatening to transfer their allegiance and their trade to the French. New York and Pennsylvania competed for decades for the Indian trade of the Susquehanna River Valley, a fact of which the Indians were well apprised and able to use to their own advantage.

In land transactions, though the Indian was again the ultimate loser, power was also divided between red and white. The Indian, unlike the African, possessed a commodity indispensable to the English settlers. Throughout the colonial period, provincial governments acknowledged an obligation to purchase rather than appropriate land. For several hundred years the two cultural groups negotiated land purchases, signed treaties, registered titles, and determined boundaries. These transactions had symbolic as well as legal meaning for they served as reminders that the Indian, though often despised and exploited, was not without power.

As in matters of land and trade, so it was in political relationships. Between 1652 and 1763, North America was a theater of war in four international conflicts involving the English, French, Spanish, and Dutch. In each of these wars the Indians played a significant role since the contending European powers vied for alliances with them and attempted to employ them against their enemies. Whether it was the English and French competing for the support of the Iroquois in New York or the English and Spanish wooing the Creeks of the Carolina region, the Indians were entitled to the respect which only an autonomous and powerful group could command.

Thus throughout the colonial period, the Indians alternately traded, negotiated, allied, and fought with the English. In each case power was divided between the two parties and shifted back and forth with time, location, and circumstances. Though he was exploited, excluded, and sometimes decimated in his contacts with European civilization, the Indian always maneuvered from a position of strength which the African, devoid of tribal unity, unaccustomed to the environment, and relatively defenseless, never enjoyed. The African in America was rarely a part of any political or economic equation. He had only his labor to offer the white man and even that was not subject to contractual agreement. He was never in a position to negotiate with the colonist and was only occasionally capable of either retaliating against his oppressors or escaping from them. This relative powerlessness, as compared with the Indian, could not help but effect attitudes. Unlike the native, the African was uniquely unable to win the respect of the white man because his situation was rarely one where respect was required or even possible. Tightly caught in a slave-master relationship, with virtually all the power on the other side, the African could only sink lower and lower in the white man's estimation. Meanwhile, the Indian, though hated, was often respected for his fighting ability, his dignity, solemnity, and even his oratorical ability. American colonists may have scoffed at the Enlightenment portrait of the "noble savage," but their image of the Indian came to have a positive side. The sociology of red-white and black-white relations differed; and from these variations evolved distinct white attitudes, in both cases adverse, but in significantly different ways.

The sociology of red-white and black-white contact differed in another important way—and in differing gave further shape to white attitudes. This was the area of sexual contact. White attitudes toward the black man cannot be dissociated from the fact that sexual relations, especially between white men and black women, were frequent and coercive throughout the eighteenth century, as graphically illustrated by the large mulatto population in America by 1800. The classic case of racial intermixture in the British colonies was in the West Indies where blacks made up as much as 80 percent of the population and white women were relatively unavailable. But in the mainland colonies, especially in the South, black women also became the object of extensive sexual exploitation by white slaveowners.

As Winthrop Jordan has explained in detail, the acceptance of interracial sex and the degree of guilt it engendered depended very heavily upon the availability of white women and the stability of family life in a particular area. In the West Indies, where sugar planters came to make a quick fortune and then return to "civilized" life in England, sexual relations with black women were extensive, but conducted without much guilt. No West Indian colony banned extramarital miscegenation and only the tiny island of

Montserrat prohibited racial intermarriage. A Jamaica planter summed up this unembarrassed view of interracial sex by writing in 1774: "He who should presume to shew any displeasure against such a thing as simple fornication [with a black woman], would for his pains be accounted a simple blockhead; since not one in twenty can be persuaded, that there is either sin; or shame in cohabiting with his slave."[20]

In English America, however, the situation was different. Colonists had come to plant white civilization as well as money crops, and interracial sex, given the strong prejudice that had developed against the Negro, was seen as a danger to individual morality, family life, and cultural integrity. In South Carolina and Georgia, where white women were greatly outnumbered by white men in the early years and where black women were plentiful, miscegenation was practiced frequently. But as the white female population grew, such sexual liaisons became socially unacceptable. Farther north, where slaves were proportionately fewer and white women more available, interracial sex was practiced less and condemned more. By the time of the American Revolution all the colonies had banned interracial marriage, although it is significant that South Carolina was the last to do so. That, of course, did not stop sexual contact outside of marriage between white men and black women (the reverse was rare for obvious reasons). To ban racial intermarriage was a way of stating with legal finality that the Negro, even when free, was not the equal of the white man. But by the same logic, to allow white men to exploit black women sexually outside of marriage was a way of permitting the white colonist to act out the concept of white social dominance. Racial intermingling outside of marriage, so long as it involved white men and black women, was no admission of equality but rather an intimate and often brutal proclamation of the superior rights of the white man.

The extensive sexual contact which white men had with black women, especially in the South, had no parallel in the case of Indian women. In the first place, they were not readily available except to an occasional fur trader or frontiersman in remote areas. Moreover, when accessible, it was not as a slave who was defenseless to resist the advances of a master with power of life and death over her. If an Indian woman chose to submit to a white man, it was usually on mutually agreeable terms. Thus the frequency and the nature of sexual relationships between white men and red women contrasted sharply with the liaison between the white man and black woman. In these differences we can find the source and meaning of a fear which has preoccupied white America for three hundred years—the fear of the black male lusting after the white woman. This vision of the "black rapist," so enduring in contemporary attitudes and literature, runs through the ac-

[20] [Edward Long], *The History of Jamaica* . . . (London, 1774), in Jordan, *White Over Black*, p. 140.

counts of the slave uprisings which occurred sporadically from 1712, when slaves revolted in New York, to the 1830s when Nat Turner led the bloodiest of all black insurrections. In large part this fear of the black man seems to have stemmed from feelings of guilt originating in the sexual exploitation of black women and an associated fear of the black avenger, presumably filled with anger and poised to retaliate against the white man. White attitudes toward the Indian only occasionally contain this element of sexual fear. Guilt seldom was aroused by the occasional and noncoercive contact with Indian women; thus the white man, when he encountered the hostile Indian male, rarely pictured his adversary as a sexual avenger. In eighteenth-century literature the Indian rarely is pictured as a frenzied rapist, lurking in the bush or stalking white women. Sometimes the Indian was viewed as a peculiarly asexual creature, which in turn created a confused image in the white mind of a hostile, and yet sexually passive, savage. It is further indicative of this fundamental difference in attitudes that in the colonial period miscegenation with Indians was prohibited only in North Carolina and briefly in Virginia, though sexual contact with Negroes was being banned everywhere in the colonies. A number of prominent colonial figures, including Robert Beverley, John Lawson, and William Byrd, publicly advised intermarriage of whites and Indians—a social policy unthinkable in the realm of black and white.

Arising from the fear of the black slave bent upon sexual revenge was the common perception of the Negro as a hypersexual creature, another view which has transited the centuries so enduringly as to suggest that it fills a need in the white psyche. In part, this myth originated in the vivid imprint which the African first made upon the English mind as a savage, naked, creature of the animal world where sexual urges went unrestrained. A century later in colonial America this image was intensified through the white settler's frequent sexual contact with black women. Little evidence can be found to show that the black woman *was* physiologically a more sexually responsive person. Instead, the white man *made* her into a symbol of sexuality because he could thus act out with her all of the repressed libidinal desires which were proscribed by his own moral code, and because by assigning to her a promiscuous nature he could assuage his own guilt that festered inevitably as a result of his illicit and exploitative activities.

Thus the degree and nature of contact between red and white and between black and white differed substantially in colonial America. In these differences lay the origins of distinct sets of attitudes toward the African and the Indian. The Englishman in America was constantly reminded by his contacts with the Indians of the advantages and the supposed superiority of his own civilization; likewise, he learned much about the control and coercion of a cultural subgroup within his midst. Through contact with the Indian, he worked out some of the problems of his own identity and destiny. Many of these lessons of control and many of these attitudes were transferred initially to the black African who began to trickle into the colonies in the 1620s. As the trickle broadened to a stream and new problems of control arose, the institution of chattel slavery hardened for Africans but not Indians, thus giving rise to new attitudes. The black man was consigned permanently to slavery; he was excluded from the rights upon which society in the New World was allegedly being built; he was incorporated into a system of close, intimate, servile, and inescapable contact. Because of this the black man became the object of a whole new set of attitudes that marked him off from the Indian with whom, initially, he had been loosely equated.

III

The American Revolution marked a turning point in the evolution of white racial attitudes. The radical patriot leaders were not greatly concerned about slavery in the colonies and did not initially plan to make its abolition a part of the revolutionary movement. Before the 1760s only a handful of colonial figures, mostly Quakers, had opposed the institution or lamented its effects on white society. Their voices resonated only weakly in a society where slavery had become accepted as natural, inevitable, and sanctioned by God. But in developing a revolutionary credo, in thinking out an intellectual justification for revolution, in mounting propaganda attacks on mother England, colonial leaders inevitably found themselves asking questions about institutions and values which they had not intended to challenge at the outset.

The arguments of the revolutionaries about liberty and the consent of the governed, about the natural rights of man, about equality, and against tyranny, contained intellectual dynamite. These stirring phrases led toward regions where even the most radical patriot leaders had not intended to go. The quarrel of radical leaders was not with the condition of colonial society but with the threatening actions of Parliament and the King's ministers. When James Otis or John Adams attempted to arouse the people with fiery pamphlets about inalienable rights, or the dignity of all men, or the abuse of power, they were pointing the finger at the English government and its attempts, as they said, to terrorize and tyrannize freedom-loving Englishmen in America. But the more they used words like "slavery" and "tyranny" in reference to English actions and the more they dilated upon equality, consent of the governed, liberty, and natural rights, the more difficult it became to ignore domestic slavery, which by the 1760s embraced 20 percent of the population in the colonies. Men who wrote about inalienable rights and human dignity, about the natural equality of men, could no longer overlook the anomalous plight of the Negro, even though it had nothing to do with the issues dividing the colonies and the mother country. The contradiction between arguing that all men were born free and equal and supporting a brutalizing system of perpetual servitude became obvious. For those who could not see the contradiction, American Tories and English writers gladly pointed it out. How could Americans treat Negroes "as a better kind of cattle . . . while they are bawling about the Rights of *human nature?*" asked one English official.[21]

Thus, as the Revolution approached, many revolutionary pamphlets undertook a discussion of slavery in the colonies. Calls for its abolition became more and more frequent. A Baptist pamphleteer wrote in 1774: "How can we reconcile the exercise of slavery with our professions of freedom." Another patriot writer chided his countrymen:

> Blush ye pretended votaries for freedom! ye trifling patriots! who are making a vain parade of being advocates for the liberties of mankind, who are thus making a mockery of your profession by trampling on the sacred natural rights and privileges of Africans; for while you are fasting, praying, nonimporting, nonexporting, remonstrating, resolving, and pleading for a restoration of your charter rights, you at the same time are continuing this lawless, cruel, inhuman, and abominable practice of enslaving your fellow creatures.[22]

The revolutionary emphasis on equality, liberty, and natural rights awakened Americans to the fact that slavery not only undergirded the economic structure of the colonies but was imbedded in their own minds. For the first time many Americans recognized that slavery was not only related to economic need but also to their assessment of the African—in other words, to their own prejudices. The more the revolutionaries thought of this, or were reminded of it by pamphleteers, the harder it became to square slavery with the unique virtue they were assigning themselves in the course of justifying their attempt to separate from what they condemned as a corrupt, exploitive, and tyrannical mother country. Slavery was an insult to the principles for which they were fighting. "Oh the shocking, the intolerable inconsistence! . . . This gross, barefaced practiced inconsistence," cried Samuel Hopkins of Rhode Island in 1776 in his call for emancipation of all slaves.[23] Slavery stood revealed in the era of the American revolution as a moral flaw, a violation of the ideology of equal rights, a contradiction of the American experience.

From this increasing awareness of white racial prejudice and the incompatibility of revolutionary principles with the position of the black slave

---

[21] Edward H. Tatum, Jr., ed., *The American Journal of Ambrose Serle* (San Marino, Calif., 1940), in Jordan, *White Over Black,* p. 291.

[22] [John Allen], *The Watchman's Alarm to Lord N____h* (Salem, Mass., 1774), in Bernard Bailyn, *The Ideological Origins of the American Revolution* (Cambridge, Mass., 1967), p. 240.

[23] *A Dialogue Concerning the Slavery of Africans . . .* (Norwich, 1776), in Bailyn, *The Ideological Origins of the American Revolution,* p. 244.

in America came a movement to end the slave system. A number of northern colonies abolished the slave trade or taxed it out of existence before the Declaration of Independence was signed. In 1775, the Continental Congress promised to abolish it throughout the colonies. Slavery was by no means dead, but the rhetoric of revolt against England had brought an ugly aspect of colonial life before the public view for discussion and reflection. It was one example of the radical and unplanned character of the Revolution. The defense of political rights had carried over into a social territory which was not directly related to the revolutionary struggle. Men who had started with a concern over their liberties had been sensitized by their own rhetoric to turn to the emancipation of slaves as an integral part of refabricating society along new and more enlightened lines.

The introspection of white Americans in the revolutionary era also brought men to ask what moral and social effects slavery was having on white society. Was it possible that the enslavement of Africans was perverting the white man as much as it was brutalizing the black? Had white masters placed themselves and their children in chains as well as their slaves? Jefferson, with characteristic insight, defined the nature of the problem:

> There must doubtless be an unhappy influence on the manners of our people produced by the existence of slavery among us. The whole commerce between master and slave is a perpetual exercise of the most boisterous passions, the most unremitting despotism on the one part, and degrading submissions on the other. Our children see this, and learn to imitate it; for man is an imitative animal. This quality is the germ of all education in him. From the cradle to the grave he is learning to do what he sees others do. . . . The parent storms, the child looks on, catches the lineaments of wrath, puts on the same airs in the circle of smaller slaves, gives a loose to the worst of passions, and thus nursed, educated, and daily exercised in tyranny, cannot but be stamped by it with odious peculiarities. The man must be a prodigy who can retain his manners and morals undepraved by such circumstances.[24]

Slavery was not abolished during the Revolution of course. The bright possibility that the new nation would begin by extending the principles of the Revolution to all its people ended in a discouraging story of backtracking, equivocating, and compromising. As the war against England wore on, the revolutionary idealism of the 1770s wore off. Men began to calculate their capital investment in slavery and to ask how a nation in a state of fiscal chaos could compensate slaveholders for their property if emancipation were decreed. Given the nearly universal belief in the inherent superiority of the white man, would it not be necessary to return

---

[24] Thomas Jefferson, *Notes on the State of Virginia*, Thomas P. Abernathy, ed. (New York, 1964), p. 155.

all Negroes to Africa? Even Jefferson, a voice of conscience in the South, believed that the Negro must not be allowed to "stain" the blood of the white race. "When freed," he wrote, the African slave "is to be removed from beyond the reach of mixture."[25] Other difficulties were found blocking the road to emancipation. The argument was put forward that while the war had been fought for inalienable human rights, it had also been fought for the protection of private property. Property rights and human rights collided, and human rights emerged second best.

By the 1780s it was apparent that while the social idealism of the revolutionary movement had produced considerable concern about trading in human flesh and enslaving one's fellow man, the basic assumption of the racial inferiority of the Negro never was seriously challenged. Among the many revolutionary figures who attacked the institution of slavery, only a handful were willing to confront the central concept of white superiority. Thus antislavery thought in the revolutionary era, like abolitionism in the nineteenth century, existed comfortably alongside racist assumptions concerning the inferiority of men with black — or red — skins.

Instead of abolishing slavery, the new American nation eradicated only the slave trade. Since the trans-Atlantic traffic in slaves was the ugliest facet of slavery, it was the logical target of reformist zeal. And because the demand for slaves was dropping by the 1770s, it was a policy which could be carried out without serious economic repercussions. Every state took some action against the slave trade between 1774 and 1794, although South Carolina and Georgia abolished it only for a few years before resanctioning it at the end of the century. In 1808, by act of Congress, the slave trade was legally ended.

The institution of slavery, meanwhile, generally went untouched, although in the northern states, where slavery was not of economic importance, abolition was legislated on a gradual basis. In fact, once the abolitionist crusade of the war years lost its impetus, the position of the free Negro, whose numbers had been swelled by thousands of private emancipations, became more and more circumscribed. By the end of the century, the institution of slavery, and racial attitudes supporting it, were hardening. After 1790 the free Negro, in both the North and the South, was subjected to increasing hostility, discrimination, and segregation. Once they had turned back the abolitionist crusade of the revolutionary period, white Americans became less concerned about the black slave than about black men who were not slaves. Southern states began passing laws prescribing heavier penalties for black felons than white, stripping away the legal rights of free Negroes, taxing free black men more heavily than whites, banning the free Negro from the polls and from political office, and forc-

---

[25] Jefferson, *Notes on the State of Virginia*, p. 139.

ing him out of white churches where he had been free to go and in some cases encouraged to go while a slave.

The final step in this reversal of abolitionist sentiment was to discourage or ban private emancipations. Virginia, earlier the most abolition-minded of the southern states, acted in 1806 to halt the wave of private emancipations that had begun in the revolutionary period. Every freed slave was required to leave the state within one year or be reenslaved. Within a year most of Virginia's neighbors—Kentucky, Maryland, Ohio, and Delaware—passed laws prohibiting free blacks from taking up residence within their boundaries. Thus we see a reversal of the drift of racial attitudes that had begun with the Revolution and a return to the admission that white men could not tolerate a mixed society unless the Negro was the object of their hostility and control.

It is one of the great ironies in the history of racial attitudes that the first steps to abolish slavery and the large number of private manumissions that occurred during the era of the American Revolution tended to increase the hostility of the white American toward his black countryman. The explanation for this is to be found first in the depths of racial prejudice that had developed in American society and, second, in the racial fear that had mushroomed in the eighteenth century. The black slave had been held in total subjection for so long that white men could hardly conceive of him as a free man. To free slaves was to concede to the Negro qualities which white society had said were absent in him—and whose absence justified racial slavery. White men had held almost unchallengeable control over black men for generations, justifying this on the basis that the African was inferior by nature. Now, with abolitionism facing them as a result of their own self-scrutiny, they found themselves at the brink of giving up a system of control and a sense of mastery which they had come to believe was natural and essential to the well-being of their society. It was almost as if the logic by which the African had been held in chains had been shattered. To compensate, a new system of control must be devised so that the free Negro, who remained a Negro after all, could still be dominated almost completely.

The second factor in the hardening of racial attitudes after 1790 was the fear which the free Negro inspired. He was feared because of the brutality of the slave system, which it was widely assumed would not be forgotten by the black man once he gained his freedom—and, with freedom, the opportunity to avenge past oppressions. The free Negro was feared because it was assumed that he would go to the aid of his black brothers and sisters who were still in chains. Often enough in the past slaves had revolted individually or in groups against their masters or white society at large. Who was to say that gradual emancipation might not end in a bloodbath? The free Negro also was feared because white men had exploited his women for decades, incurring a massive national debt which might be repaid by an assault in kind upon white womanhood. And he was feared because as a free black man he represented a loss of white dominion which had been exercised so unyieldingly in the past as to become almost a necessary support to the white American's sense of mastery over his world.

All of these apprehensions, a mixture of fantasies and realistic fears, combined and interacted, feeding upon each other in the white mind of the late eighteenth century. What would happen to the integrity of white culture, what would happen to the family, what would happen to the individual if the restraints which slavery had imposed on 20 percent of the population were suddenly thrown off? The Negro had been defined by white society as inferior, licentious, intellectually and morally inadequate. In view of this, most Americans who contemplated emancipation at the end of the eighteenth century reckoned that it would be necessary to recolonize the freed black man to his ancestral home in Africa, since genuine assimilation with white society was impossible.

Thus, after 1790, the free Negro as well as the slave, could look back on the revolutionary era with bitterness. What had been intended by many national leaders to be the dawn of a new era — and for many of them abolition was specifically included in their blueprints for "a virtuous republic" — emerged as the beginning of a new era of hostility and renewed determination by white men to restrain the black American, free or slave, in their midst. The course had been set for racial attitudes in America, and set so unswervingly that in the future only social and political convulsions would be able to alter patterns of thought imbedded in the mind and institutions of white society.

2

The Black Child-Savage in Ante-Bellum America

RONALD TAKAKI

During the tumultuous decade before the Civil War, a visitor from the North, traveling up the Mississippi River on a steamboat, sat down next to an Alabama nonslaveholding farmer. They probably talked about the river and the weather, the political emergence of the common man, and the wonders of the new technology and transportation in America. But, as many conversations today turn to a discussion of America's racial crisis, their conversation turned to the vexatious question of slavery. The visitor asked the farmer what he thought about emancipating the slaves. The farmer replied:

Well, I'll tell you what I think on it; I'd like it if we could get rid on 'em to youst. I wouldn't like to hev 'em freed, if they was gwine to hang 'round. They ought to get some country and put 'em war they could be by themselves. It wouldn't do no good to free 'em, and let 'em hang 'round, because they is so monstrous lazy; if they hadn't got nobody to take keer on 'em, you see they wouldn't do nothin' but juss nat'rally laze 'round, and steal, and pilfer, and no man couldn't live, you see, war they was—if they was free, no man couldn't live. And then, I've two objections; that's one on 'em—no man couldn't live—and this ere's the other: Now suppose they was free, you see they'd all think themselves just as good as we, of course they would, if they was free. Now,

27

just suppose you had a family of children, how would you like to hev a niggar feeling just as good as a white man? how'd you like to hev a niggar steppin' up to your darter?[1]

In his folksy way, the Alabama farmer had articulated his attitude toward the Negro. He believed the Negro was "so monstrous lazy." Since the Negro did not want to work, he must be kept in slavery. Otherwise, he would become a criminal; he would steal and pilfer rather than work. Thus the Negro would be lawless. Society, the Alabama farmer implied, must be based on law and order. Hence the white man could not live where the Negro was, if the Negro were uncontrolled. But, for the farmer, the Negro had a more disturbing quality—he was sexually threatening. The farmer was morbidly anxious about "a niggar steppin' up" to his "darter."

In his candid reply to the northern visitor, the Alabama farmer was expressing a racial prejudice shared by most white Americans, North and South. Indeed, one of the most salient realities of race relations in ante-bellum society was the ubiquity of prejudice against black people. During the 1850s an English traveler observed: "There seems, in short, to be a fixed notion throughout the whole of the States, whether slave or free, that the colored is by nature a subordinate race; and that, in no circumstances, can it be considered equal to the white."[2] Despite the different black-white population ratios in the North and South, and despite the Negro's different status in the free society of the North and the slave society of the South, whites everywhere in America held strongly negative feelings about Negroes —feelings that had evolved and intensified over a period of more than two centuries.

While the Alabama farmer was representing the anti-Negro feelings of the North as well as the South, he was also addressing himself to the essential and perplexing question of the Negro's place in America. White Americans had worried about this for generations. Since before the Revolution, whites had considered a variety of proposals: keep the blacks in slavery, transport them to Africa, emancipate and control them, or emancipate and offer them equality. During the first half of the nineteenth century, whites had to confront more seriously than ever before the crucial issues of race, nationality, and the status of blacks in American society. But why were they so concerned about this question during the Age of Jackson? How were their responses influenced by their images of the Negro as a black child-savage vis-à-vis their images of what whites as civilized men and America as a civilized society were or should be?

[1] Frederick Law Olmsted, *A Journey in the Seaboard Slave States in the Years 1853–1854 with Remarks on Their Economy,* (2 vols.; New York, 1904), II, pp. 218–219.
[2] William Chambers, *Things as They Are in America* (Philadelphia, 1854), p. 354.

I

The story of the antislavery crusade is familiar to most students of American history. We have been told how the northern states, under the liberal influence of the American Revolution, abolished slavery. We have been told about the northern moral struggle for the emancipation of black people in the South. We have been told about the northern men of good will—leaders like William Lloyd Garrison and Abraham Lincoln—who eloquently denounced the institution of slavery, and who in the end broke the chains of bondage. We have also been told about the hundreds of runaway slaves who followed the North Star to freedom. But often we do not recognize or we forget the reality of racism in the North, in the states above the Mason-Dixon Line.

During his visit to the United States in the early 1830s, Alexis de Tocqueville noticed that in the North the

> same schools do not receive the children of the black and of the European. In the theaters gold cannot procure a seat for the servile race beside their former masters; in the hospitals they lie apart; and although they are allowed to invoke the same God as the whites, it must be at a different altar and in their own churches, with their own clergy. The gates of heaven are not closed against them, but their inferiority is continued to the very confines of the other world. When the Negro dies, his bones are cast aside, and the distinction of condition prevails even in the equality of death.[3]

De Tocqueville saw that the Negro in the North was far from free. As Leon Litwack has demonstrated in *North of Slavery: The Negro in the Free States, 1790–1860,* the Negro was the unfortunate victim of oppressive *de jure* as well as *de facto* discrimination and segregation.

Everywhere in the North black children usually attended separate and inferior schools. Black people were barred from most hotels and restaurants, and they had separate sections in theaters and churches, invariably in the back. Transportation facilities often were segregated. The street car company in Philadelphia, for example, ruled that Negroes would be allowed to ride only on the front platform. New York City had separate bus cars—one for whites, one for blacks. Negroes who used the New York ferryboats were forced to stay on deck at all hours and in all weather conditions. Black people also were crowded into ghettos which developed in the North in the first half of the nineteenth century. When Negroes tried to escape from their slums, whites argued that their presence in white residential districts would depreciate property values.

[3] Alexis de Tocqueville, *Democracy in America,* (2 vols.; New York, 1945), I, pp. 373–374.

Most black people in the North, moreover, were stripped of the right to vote. Significantly the political proscription of blacks often was related to the constitutional extension of the suffrage for whites. The democratization of the suffrage in New York is a case in point. In 1821, the New York constitutional convention extended the vote to all free "white" male citizens of the state who possessed a freehold, paid taxes, had served in the state militia, or had worked on the highways. This amounted to universal manhood suffrage, but for whites only. The constitution, moreover, not only provided that the old property qualifications would still apply to Negroes but also increased the property requirement from $100 to $250. Twenty-five years later another New York constitutional convention met. This time a motion was made to strike out the word "white" and to remove the discriminatory prohibition. The motion was defeated, 37 to 63. The question was then submitted to a vote of the people, and the proposition to remove the property qualification for Negroes was defeated by an overwhelming vote of 85,306 to 223,834. Meanwhile, in Pennsylvania, the constitutional convention of 1838 provided for universal white manhood suffrage, and so disfranchised blacks completely. The new constitution then was ratified by popular vote. Thus, in New York and Pennsylvania, the political coming of age of the white common man signified the political degradation of the black man. The realization of universal manhood suffrage in the age of Jacksonian democracy often meant democracy for whites only.

While black people in the North were proscribed politically, they also were hindered economically. The first half of the nineteenth century was the age of the great market and transportation revolutions. It was an era of economic expansion, of steamboats, railroads, and factories; jobs were opening up for thousands of workers in the cities. Yet blacks benefited little from the growing need for labor because white workers often demanded the exclusion of blacks from the trades. The president of a mechanics association in Cincinnati was publicly condemned by his union because he had trained a black youth. After a young black cabinetmaker was hired in a shop in Cincinnati, the white workers forced their employer to fire him. A black seeking employment in New York was almost killed by the white dock workers who jealously considered the docks a white labor monopoly. Thus greater economic opportunity for white workers frequently meant greater economic proscription for black workers. Many blacks, including craftsmen, could not find skilled jobs and were forced into menial labor. In the 1850s, about 87 percent of New York's gainfully employed blacks had menial jobs, and nine out of ten blacks in New Haven were menial workers. Even black menials were increasingly displaced by Irish immigrants. In 1830, servants in New York City were mostly black; in 1850, they were mostly Irish.

While blacks struggled for economic survival, they also suffered the attacks of violent anti-Negro mobs, generally composed of white workers. Time and again in northern cities, white mobs invaded Negro ghettos, attacking and killing black people and destroying homes and churches. Philadelphia was the scene of several bloody anti-Negro riots. In 1834, a furious white mob, seeking to force blacks to leave Philadelphia and thereby remove black economic competition, assaulted the black community. Seven years later, in Cincinnati, angry white workers rushed into the Negro section of town. After they encountered fire from armed blacks, the white rioters dragged a cannon into the battle and forced the black defenders to retreat. Then the mayor tried to impose law and order. Authorities persuaded about 300 black men to go to jail for their own security, assuring them that their wives and children would be protected. The white mobs took advantage of the situation and again attacked the black community. Finally the governor of Ohio intervened and suppressed the disorder.

Painfully aware of the economic discrimination and mob violence confronting them, young black men became discouraged and bitter. A black youth complained,

> Why should I strive hard and acquire all the constituents of a man if the prevailing genius of the land admit me not as such, or but in an inferior degree! Pardon me if I feel insignificant and weak. . . . What are my prospects? To what shall I turn my hand? Shall I be a mechanic? No one will employ me; white boys won't work with me. . . . Drudgery and servitude, then, are my prospective portion.[4]

The black youth clearly recognized a frightening reality of northern society —this was a white man's country. No wonder, while Frederick Douglass struggled for the abolition of slavery and the realization of freedom within American society, an increasing number of black abolitionists adopted a separatist position during the 1850s. Profoundly alienated from white America, militant black leaders like Martin Delany advocated black emigration to South America and Africa. They declared that there was no hope for the black man in America, and that he must find his identity and freedom in a black country.

Black people in the North were the victims of segregation, discrimination, and violence. This oppressive structure of race relations was influenced by the images of the Negro long established in the minds of white Americans. While these images helped to shape the repression of black

[4] In Leon Litwack, *North of Slavery: The Negro in the Free States, 1790–1860* (Chicago, 1965), pp. 153–154.

people, the repressive system degraded and reduced them into conditions of poverty and illiteracy. Thus, the repression itself, reinforced the anti-Negro images whites held.

One of the striking characteristics of the Negro in the minds of white Northerners was his childlike quality. For many whites in the North, the Negro was the clownish and childish black minstrel; he was immature and needed the guidance of the superior white race. The Negro's childishness, moreover, often was associated with his alleged laziness. Whites frequently denounced the Negro as "indolent" and "good-for-nothing." The Connecticut Colonization Society, an organization designed to transport free Negroes to Africa, scolded the Negro for his lack of industry. Since whites viewed the Negro as lazy, they were sometimes amazed to see economically successful Negroes. While a black minister was visiting New England villages, white children noticed his neat clothes and scornfully screamed: "Hey nigger, where'd you get so much clothes?"[5] The connection between the Negro's immaturity and his improvidence was expressed succinctly by a white Pennsylvanian: "The Negro was simply unfit . . . he was naturally lazy, childlike. . . ."[6]

While northern whites viewed the Negro as a carefree child, they also feared him as a criminal. They often complained about what they thought was the Negro's tendency to steal. During the 1820s, the governor of Pennsylvania expressed apprehension about the rising crime rate among Negroes, and Pennsylvania newspapers repeatedly reported Negro burglaries, Negro robberies, and Negro assaults. Thus politicians and editors helped to stereotype the Negro as a criminal. An Irish song portrayed the Negro as a violent murderer. "When the negroes shall be free/ To cut the throats of all they see/ Then this dear land will come to be/ The den of foul rascality."[7]

The image of the Negro as a reprobate and criminal partially explains attempts by whites to restrict black migration into certain states during the early nineteenth century. Ohio and Indiana, for example, required entering Negroes to post a $500 bond as a guarantee against becoming a public charge and as a pledge of good behavior. Ohio politicians described the Negro as lazy and immoral, and warned that the Negro population of the state should not be allowed to increase by migration. The editor of an Indiana newspaper angrily declared in 1842: "We presume there is not a nigger in this town that has given his bond. . . ." He then demanded the enforcement of the law designed to discourage black migration into the state in order to "drive away a gang of pilferers."[8]

[5] In Robert Austin Warner, *New Haven Negroes: A Social History* (New Haven, Conn., 1940), p. 34.

[6] In Litwack, *North of Slavery*, pp. 155–156.

[7] In Litwack, *North of Slavery*, p. 164.

[8] Richmond *Jeffersonian*, in Emma Lou Thornbrough, *The Negro in Indiana: A Study of a Minority* (n.p., 1957), p. 62.

The images of the Negro as childlike, lazy, and criminal were reinforced by the conception of the Negro as inferior in intelligence. White parents told their children to improve themselves or they would be as "ignorant" as a "nigger." Since the Negro was mentally inferior, whites argued, he had no conception of civil liberty or capacity to take the first step toward civilization. A Philadelphia doctor, Samuel Morton, offered white Americans presumably scientific evidence of the Negro's inferior mind. He had measured the cranial capacities of English, American, German, Chinese, Indian, and Negro skulls, and had discovered that the skulls of the whites had a larger cranial capacity than the skulls of the others. His conclusion was inevitable: whites were more intelligent. But the skulls of the whites Morton had examined belonged to men who had been hanged as criminals. Thus, as Thomas F. Gossett has remarked, it "would have been just as logical to conclude that a large head indicated criminal tendencies."[9] Nevertheless, whites could seize the image of Negro mental inferiority in order to assert the supremacy of the white race and to justify the political, economic, and social oppression of black people. An Indiana senator, for example, declared in 1850: "The same power that has given him a black skin, with less weight or volume of brain has given us a white skin, with greater volume of brain and intellect; and that we can never live together upon an equality is as certain as that no two antagonistic principles can exist together at the same time."[10]

What probably worried northern whites most was their image of the Negro as a sexual threat to white women and white racial purity. During an anti-Republican parade in New York in 1860, floats showed a thick-lipped Negro embracing a white girl, and a Negro leading a white woman into the White House. In 1821, white citizens of Pennsylvania petitioned the legislature to declare mixed marriages void and make it a penal act for a Negro to marry a white man's daughter. Northern states such as Indiana and Illinois prohibited interracial marriages, and white social sentiment vigorously discouraged black and white relationships. "It is true," observed de Tocqueville, "that in the North . . . marriages may be contracted between Negroes and whites; but public opinion would stigmatize as infamous a man who should connect himself with a Negress, and it would be difficult to cite a single instance of such a union."[11]

The demand for the exclusion of Negroes from certain territories and states often involved a sexual fear of the black man and the horror of miscegenation. In a petition to the legislature of the Indiana Territory, whites sought to prevent the settlement of Negroes because white "wives and daughters . . . will be insulted and abused by those Africans." At the Illinois

[9] Thomas F. Gossett, *Race: The History of an Idea in America* (Dallas, 1963), p. 74.
[10] In Litwack, *North of Slavery*, p. 66.
[11] De Tocqueville, *Democracy in America*, I, p. 373.

constitutional convention of 1847, a delegate explained that the lack of a restriction on Negro migration was tantamount to allowing Negroes "to make proposals to marry our daughters."[12] Some northern whites demanded the disfranchisement of the Negro because they feared that black suffrage could lead to amalgamation. A delegate to the New York constitutional convention of 1821 favored such disfranchisement because he wished to avoid the time "when the colours shall intermarry." In their effort to deny the suffrage to Negroes, Wisconsin Democrats argued that the extension of political rights to Negroes would encourage them to "marry our sisters and daughters."[13]

School segregation was also influenced by fears of interracial unions. In 1842, whites petitioned the Indiana senate to establish the separation of the races in the public schools. The question was referred to the committee on education. In its report supporting the exclusion of Negro children from white schools, the committee argued that the Negro race was inferior and that the admission of Negro children "into our public schools would ultimately tend to bring about that feeling which favour their amalgamation with our own people." When Massachusetts prohibited racial discrimination for admission to public schools in 1855, a northern newspaper cried: "Now the blood of the Winthrops, the Otises, the Lymans, the Endicotts, and the Eliots, is in a fair way to be amalgamated with the Sambos, the Catos, and the Pompeys. The North is to be Africanized. Amalgamation has commenced."[14] Thus, in the view of many whites, segregated education was a bulwark of white racial purity.

Even white abolitionism in the North was based partly on an abhorrence of racial mixing and miscegenation. Many white abolitionists condemned slavery because it promoted interracial sexual unions. Some Indiana abolitionists, for example, declared that they were "opposed to the amalgamation of the white and black inhabitants of our country, and . . . that the only means by which it can be prevented, is to abolish slavery, so that colored females, may be instructed in their moral and religious duties, and be placed under the protection of righteous laws." They also warned that the loose morals of slaves would "cause a compound of the human species."[15] For these abolitionists, antislavery meant, among other things, a crusade against miscegenation.

This northern concern for white racial purity was a basis for the oppo-

[12] In Eugene H. Berwanger, *The Frontier Against Slavery: Western Anti-Negro Prejudice and the Slavery Extension Controversy* (Urbana, Ill., 1967), pp. 20, 36.

[13] Respectively in Litwack, *North of Slavery*, p. 77, and Berwanger, *The Frontier Against Slavery*, p. 36.

[14] Respectively in Thornbrough, *The Negro in Indiana*, p. 163, and Litwack, *North of Slavery*, pp. 149–150.

[15] Respectively in Thornbrough, *The Negro in Indiana*, p. 127, and Berwanger, *The Frontier Against Slavery*, p. 24.

sition to the expansion of slavery into the western territories. Northern resistance to the expansion of slavery often involved racial prejudice. The Wilmot Proviso of 1846, prohibiting slavery in the territories acquired from Mexico, was antislavery; yet the intention of the proviso was anti-Negro. The sponsor of the proviso, David Wilmot of Pennsylvania, wanted to exclude Negroes from those lands. On the floor of Congress, Wilmot declared: "I plead the cause and the rights of white freemen. I would preserve to free white labor a fair country, a rich inheritance, where the sons of toil, or my own race and own color, can live without the disgrace which association with negro slavery brings upon free labor." For Wilmot, "men born and nursed of white women are not going to be ruled by men who were brought up on the milk of some damn Negro wench!"[16] A few years later, another antislavery leader, Abraham Lincoln, candidly stated that "the separation of the races is the only perfect preventive of amalgamation," that "a very large proportion" of the Republic Party supported racial separation, and that the "chief plank in their platform—opposition to the spread of slavery—is most favorable to that separation."[17] Thus, David Wilmot and many other Republicans of the 1850s believed that the territories should be reserved for whites only.

A range of images of the Negro can be found in the white mind of the North. The Negro was a child: he was lazy, irresponsible, and mentally inferior. But, these characteristics of laziness and ignorance along with immoral and criminal tendencies also implied a savage quality. The Negro was untrained and unsocialized; he was dominated by his passions, especially sex. He lived in the section of town called "New Liberia" or "New Guinea" or "Little Africa"; these places were associated with vice, promiscuity, and immoral entertainment. As many whites imagined him, the Negro was identified with Africa—a dark and wild continent. Thus the savage Negro, they concluded, was unfit for and should not be a part of civilization in America.

II

If the image of the Negro minstrel was popular among whites in the North, the image of Sambo was equally widespread below the Mason-Dixon Line. The minstrel and Sambo had many qualities in common. As southern whites imagined him, Sambo—the typical plantation slave—was child-like, docile, irresponsible, happy, and lazy. Indeed, whites frequently described the Negro as "a grown up child," and usually referred to adult slaves as "boys and girls." A traveler in the South commented that slaves

[16] In Berwanger, *The Frontier Against Slavery,* pp. 125–126.

[17] Speech at Springfield, Illinois, June 26, 1857, in Roy P. Basler, ed., *The Collected Works of Abraham Lincoln,* (9 vols.; New Brunswick, N.J., 1953), II, pp. 408–409.

"never become men or women." In the judgment of slavemasters, who saw themselves as guardians, the slave must be "governed as a child."[18] Furthermore, slavemasters cherished the bonds of affection that they said existed between themselves and their dependent childlike slaves. In his *Black Diamonds Gathered in the Darkey Homes of the South,* published on the eve of the Civil War, proslavery writer Edward Pollard of Virginia exclaimed:

> I love to look upon his [the slave's] countenance shining with content and grease; I love to study his affectionate heart; I love to mark that peculiarity in him, which beneath all his buffoonery exhibits him as a creature of the tenderest sensibilities, mingling his joys and his sorrows with those of his master's home.[19]

Yet, while white southerners fondly remembered the boyishness of their slaves, they also complained about their laziness. Slavemasters constantly commented on the need to supervise their black laborers; otherwise they would not work. Like the Alabama farmer, whites in the South argued that the Negro was improvident; he would not "lay up in summer for the wants of winter," and would not "accumulate in youth for the exigencies of age." Thus if he were free, he would "become an insufferable burden to society. Society has the right to prevent this, and can only do so by subjecting him to domestic slavery."[20] William Gilmore Simms gave this argument literary expression. In his novel *The Yemassee: A Romance of Carolina* (1835), the slave Hector responded to a proposal that he be freed: "I d___n to h___ll, massa, if I gwine to be free! . . . De ting aint right; and enty I know wha' kind of ting freedom is wid black man? Ha! You make Hector free, he turn wuss more nor poor buckra—he tief out of de shop—he git drunk and lie in de ditch. . . ."[21] Obviously, white southerners explained, the Negro must be kept in slavery; otherwise he would surely become a perpetual burden to American society.

White southerners often noted the contentment of their slaves. In 1859, a southern planter scribbled into his diary: "The hands as usual came in to greet the New Year with their good wishes—the scene is well calculated to excite sympathies; notwithstanding bondage, affections find roots in the heart of the slave for the master."[22] White southerners loudly pro-

---

[18] George Fitzhugh, *Sociology for the South,* in Harvey Wish, ed., *Ante-Bellum: Writings of George Fitzhugh and Hinton Rowan Helper on Slavery* (New York, 1960), p. 88; C. G. Parsons, *An Inside View of Slavery,* in D. W. Doyle, *Etiquette of Race Relations in the South* (Chicago, 1931), p. 54.

[19] Edward Pollard, *Black Diamonds* (New York, 1968), pp. 57–58.

[20] Fitzhugh, *Sociology for the South,* p. 89.

[21] William Gilmore Simms, *The Yemassee* (New York, 1962), p. 392.

[22] Gustave A. Breaux, Diary, January 1, 1859, Breaux Papers, Tulane University Library.

claimed to the North and to Europe that the slaves of the South were the happiest people in the world. In his description of the life of a Virginia slave, a novelist remarked that the Negro worked little and spent the rest of his time "singing, dancing, laughing, chattering, and bringing up pigs and chickens. . . . In point of general happiness, it would not be amiss to alter an old adage and say: 'As merry as a negro slave.'"[23]

While this evidence about slave behavior shows that southern whites thought slaves were Sambos, it does not prove that slaves were indeed Sambos. To be sure, the South was a Sambo-making machine. Slavemasters sought to create a Sambo, to break the slave's spirit, and to mold the perfect slave. As Kenneth Stampp has shown in *The Peculiar Institution,* slavemasters developed elaborate techniques of slave control. Hopeful that contented slaves would be obedient, slavemasters sometimes used kindness to control their slaves. A Georgia planter, for example, explained:

> Now, I contend that the surest and best method of managing negroes, is to love them. We know . . . that if we love our horse, we will treat him well, and if we treat him well he will become gentle, docile and obedient . . . and if this treatment has this effect upon all the animal creation . . . why will it not have the same effect upon slaves?[24]

But if slavemasters offered their slaves presents and holidays as incentives for good conduct, they also knew that strict slave discipline was essential and that their power must be based on the principle of fear. Senator James Hammond of South Carolina, who owned more than 300 slaves, fully understood the need for the absolute submission of the slave to his master. "We have to rely more and more on the power of fear," he declared. "We are determined to continue masters, and to do so we have to draw the rein tighter and tighter day by day to be assured that we hold them in complete check."[25] Slavemasters also tried to brainwash the slave into believing he was racially inferior and racially designed to be a slave. They tried to give the slave a sense of helplessness and a feeling of dependence upon his master. They kept him ignorant and illiterate and told him that he was unfit to look out for himself. Thus they compelled the slave to become a dependent child.

Slavemasters had designed an awesome system of slave control. But the need for a Sambo-making machine could mean that slaves were not Sambos, but were engaged in resistance against slavery and the master class. Hence slavemasters were obsessed with the problem of slave control. This is not to say that no docile and happy slaves existed in the ante-

---

[23] Quoted in Natchez *Free Trader,* September 20, 1858.

[24] Kenneth Stampp, *The Peculiar Institution: Slavery in the Ante-Bellum South* (New York, 1956), p. 163.

[25] In Stampp, *The Peculiar Institution,* p. 146.

bellum South. Many slaves, especially household servants, behaved like Sambos. But slaves who behaved or acted in this way were sometimes, perhaps often, playing the role of the loyal and congenial slave in order to survive. As ex-slave Frederick Douglass reported, slaves were fearful of punishment, and consequently when they were asked about "their condition and the character of their masters, [they] would almost invariably say that they were contented and their masters kind." Thus many slaves wore smiling masks. "It is a blessed thing," Douglass explained, "that the tyrant may not always know the thoughts and purposes of his victim."[26]

The image of the slave as a Sambo had special significance for the ante-bellum white southerner. The whole western world of the nineteenth century was ideologically opposed to southern slavery, and thus the South sought to defend and justify its peculiar institution as a positive good. If southern whites could show their moral critics that slaves were happy and dependent children, then perhaps they could convince them that slavery was justifiable. Southerners repeatedly emphasized their claims about the ties of affection binding the master-slave relationship, and the "pleasant intercourse between master and slave." They proudly announced that "ours is a patriarchal institution now, founded in pity and protection on the one side, and dependence and gratitude on the other."[27] Concerned about the need for an ideological defense of slavery, southerners believed that one of the strongest arguments against emancipation was the assertion that slavery was a paternalistic rather than a profit-oriented system of labor.

White southerners needed a Sambo not only to demonstrate to the world the integrity of slavery but also to convince themselves that slavery was moral. Since the era of the Revolution, whites in the South had been bothered by the contradiction between their peculiar institution and the principles upon which the nation was founded. Even after the invention of the cotton gin in 1793 and the subsequent expansion of cotton cultivation had made slavery a more profitable system of labor in the early nineteenth century, white southerners continued to apologize. "Slavery," admitted the governor of Mississippi in 1825, "is an evil at best."[28] And even after the Nat Turner insurrection of 1831 frightened the South into a rigid defense of the peculiar institution, many southerners still were troubled about the question of the morality of slavery. "This, sir, is a Christian community," a Virginian anxiously explained in 1832. "Southerners read in their Bibles, 'Do unto all men as you would have them do

[26] Frederick Douglass, *Life and Times of Frederick Douglass* (New York, 1962), pp. 64, 192.

[27] J. J. Pettigrew, in *De Bow's Review,* 25 (1858), p. 293; Roger Pryor, in *De Bow's Review,* 24 (1858), p. 582.

[28] In Percy Lee Rainwater, *Mississippi, Storm Center of Secession, 1856–1861* (Baton Rouge, La., 1938), p. 12.

unto you'; and this golden rule and slavery are hard to reconcile." A slave-holder wrote in his diary in 1858: "Oh what trouble,—running sore, constant pressing weight, perpetual wearing, dripping, is this patriarchal institution! What miserable folly for men to cling to it as something heaven-descended. And here we and our children after us must groan under the burden—our hands tied from freeing ourselves."[29]

Thus, southern proslavery polemicists had to convince their fellow southerners that slavery was indeed right. "We must satisfy the consciences," they declared, "we must allay the fears of our own people. We must satisfy them that slavery is of itself right—that it is not a sin against God. . . ."[30] Time and again southern defenders of slavery compared the condition of the Negro in Africa with the condition of their slaves in the South. Here the slave had an "enlightened," "humane," and "Christian" master. Here the slave was "submissive," "docile," "happy," "conscious of his own inferiority and proud of being owned & governed by a superior."[31] Hence the image of the slave as a Sambo, as a happy child, helped to comfort the anguished consciences of many white southerners.

The need of white southerners for a Sambo was more profound than a need for a proslavery argument and the mitigation of guilt: the image of Sambo helped to assure them that the slave was controlled and contented. Surely a happy slave would not protest violently against his bondage; surely he would not slit his master's throat at night. Yet, while they were fond of the image of the happy Sambo, white southerners were also terrified by the specter of the rebellious savage. Anxiously aware of the successful and bloody slave revolts in St. Domingo in the 1790s, they undoubtedly believed an American official in Haiti when he claimed that "Negroes only cease to be *children* when they degenerate into *savages*."[32] White southerners understood that the black savage was crucially different from the black child—he could kill. After the violent and brutal suppression of the Denmark Vesey slave conspiracy in 1822, a worried South Carolina gentleman exclaimed: Our Negroes are "barbarians who would *if they could,* become the destroyers of our race."[33] This southerner's fear was not wholly without grounds. A few years later in Southampton, Virginia, Nat Turner and his fellow slave rebels took up the knife against their oppressors and killed nearly sixty whites. White southerners were appalled

[29] Respectively in Charles G. Sellers, Jr., *The Southerner as American* (Chapel Hill, N.C., 1960), p. 48; and Ernest T. Thompson, *Presbyterians in the South, 1607–1861* (Richmond, Va., 1963), p. 533.

[30] In Sellers, *The Southerner as American,* p. 51.

[31] Galveston *News,* Dec. 6, 1856; Charleston *Mercury,* Oct. 20, 1858; J. G. M. Ramsey to L. W. Spratt, April 23, 1858, Ramsey Papers, University of North Carolina Library.

[32] In *De Bow's Review,* 14 (1853), p. 276, italics added.

[33] In William W. Freehling, *Prelude to Civil War: The Nullification Controversy in South Carolina, 1816–1836* (New York, 1966), p. 59.

by the violence of Nat Turner; they denounced the rebels as a "band of savages." "It will long be remembered in the annals of our country," wrote a Virginian, "and many a mother as she presses her infant darling to her bosom, will shudder at the recollection of Nat Turner. . . ."[34] White southerners did not think the Nat Turner revolt was a boyish prank.

Indeed, they almost constantly worried about servile insurrections. A former Louisiana planter said he knew "times here, when there was not a single planter who had a calm night's rest; they then never lay down to sleep without a brace of pistols at their side." The wife of a Georgia planter observed that the slaves were "a threatening source of constant insecurity, and every southern *woman* to whom I have spoken on the subject, has admitted to me that they live in terror of their slaves." During the 1850s, southern newspapers frequently reported news about slave unrest and "evidences of a very unsettled state of mind among the servile population."[35] Here was a society constantly on edge with fear of black rebellion.

The white southerners' fear of slave rebellions often was associated with their apprehensions about the "benighted" continent of Africa and the Negro's original savagery. During the late eighteenth century, this fear was a factor compelling southerners to limit and prohibit the importation of slaves from Africa. After the suppression of the Vesey slave conspiracy in 1822 white Charlestonians could not forget the awesome Gullah Jack, a witch doctor from Angola who gave the Vesey slave rebels a strange feeling of confidence and invincibility. In their opposition to the African slave trade during the 1850s, southerners argued that the introduction of Africans among "our present civilized and happy negro population" would "render them unhappy, discontented and insubordinate, the spirit of insurrection and revenge would take the place of respect and affection they have for their owners now."[36] Thus, many white southerners wanted to keep the African savage away from their domesticated slave—their happy child.

In the minds of white southerners, Africa was a jungleland of savages and cannibals. They read reports about the terrible barbarism and brutality of Africa in books such as J. Leighton Wilson's *Western Africa: Its History, Condition and Prospects.* In a review of Wilson's book, the Charleston *Mercury* commented in 1856: "The prospects [of good] for Africa, can only begin when her people shall be made, by a power and will superior to their own, to obey the first lay of God—the foundation of all the laws of God—

[34] T. R. Gray, *The Confessions of Nat Turner,* in appendix of Herbert Aptheker, *Nat Turner's Slave Rebellion* (New York, 1968), pp. 130–131.

[35] From Frederika Bremer, *The Homes of the New World; Impressions of America,* (3 vols.; London, 1853), II, p. 451; Frances A. Kemble, *Journal of a Residence on a Georgia Plantation in 1838–1839* (New York, 1961), p. 342; New Orleans *Picayune,* Dec. 24, 1856.

[36] In Joe G. Taylor, *Negro Slavery in Louisiana* (Baton Rouge, La., 1963), p. 58.

and be coerced to earn their bread in the sweat of the brow."[37] Thus the African's laziness was associated with his savagery. Southerners also read in their newspapers vivid descriptions of untamed Africans eating snails and grasshoppers. The New Orleans *Delta,* for example, offered its readers the following illustration of life in Africa.

> Pity the sorrows of a European traveling through the bush and partaking of the hospitality . . . of a native, there is fished up out of the big pot of soup a black head, with the lips drawn back and the white teeth grinning, and such a painful resemblance to the faces around him that for a moment he wonders which of the younger members of the family has been sacrificed to the exigencies of the occasion. But he is reassured, and discovers that he is not eating man, but monkey.[38]

No doubt white southerners tried to remind themselves that the Negro in the American South had been transformed into a "cotton-picking Christian." But many whites fearfully believed that the Negro, if returned to Africa, would become an idolatrous cannibal, and they continued to associate the Negro in America with their images of his African homeland and savage ancestry.

To white southerners, the Negro's savagery was also related to his sexuality. In his description of the Negro's "pleasurable emotions," Dr. Samuel Cartwright of New Orleans reported in the 1850s that "in the dance called *putting juber,* the odor emitted from the men, intoxicated with pleasure, is often so powerful as to throw the negro women into paroxysms of unconsciousness, vulgo hysterics." White southerners were gravely concerned about the black man as a sexual threat to the white woman. Thomas Jefferson thought black men preferred white to black women "as uniformly as is the preference of the Oran-utan for the black women over those of his own species."[39]

III

In the minds of white Americans, North and South, the Negro was a peculiar, often contradictory, mixture of child and savage. Of course, there were important regional differences in the functions of the images for northern and southern whites. Unlike segregation in the North, slavery in the South was the target of widespread moral criticism during the first

---

[37] Charleston *Mercury,* July 17, 1856.

[38] New Orleans *Delta,* Nov. 21, 1858.

[39] Samuel Cartwright, "Natural History of the Prognathous Species of Mankind," reprinted in Eric McKitrick, *Slavery Defended: The Views of the Old South* (Englewood Cliffs, N. J., 1963), p. 145; Jefferson, *Notes on the State of Virginia,* Thomas P. Abernathy, ed. (New York, 1964), p. 133.

half of the nineteenth century. Western civilization condemned it, and many southerners themselves had troubled consciences about their peculiar institution. Thus, for southerners, the image of the Negro served not only to defend slavery but also to reduce the level of their anxiety based on their moral qualms about its perpetuation. Furthermore, while Negroes constituted only about 2 percent of the northern population in 1850, they composed about 33 percent of southern society. Though the black-white population ratio was higher in the South than in the North, Negroes below the Mason-Dixon Line had an unmistakeable status: they were slaves. Hence, northern whites had to rely more extensively than southern whites on anti-Negro images to underscore the inferior status of the free Negro in the North.

But more important, the image of the Negro served a need shared by whites, North and South; it performed an identity function for white Americans during a period when they were groping for self-definition. It is significant to note the way that whites imagined the Negro in relation to themselves: the Negro was mentally inferior, naturally lazy, childlike, unwholesome, and given to vice. He was the antithesis of themselves and of what they valued: industriousness, intelligence, and moral restraint. These, of course, were values which whites associated with civilized society.

These values had no sectional boundaries. In reality southerners were chivalrous men with feet of money. Though they proclaimed a devotion to the Cavalier ideal, though they articulated an allegiance to honor and the life style of a gentleman, and though they sometimes expressed an indifference to money making, they actually shared many values with the acquisitive Yankee. White southerners were enthusiastically involved in business enterprise and expansion, land and cotton speculation, and profit making based on the production of cotton and the exploitation of black labor. They, too, believed in the principle of accumulation.

In the age of the transportation revolution and Jacksonian democracy, these values had a special significance. As social analysts like Alexis de Tocqueville, George R. Taylor, and Marvin Meyers have observed, white Americans were engaged in frantic efforts to open up new economic opportunities, to cultivate new farms, to build factories, to construct canals and railroads, to ship more steamboats up and down the Mississippi River, to create more markets, and to accumulate money and material goods. Thus the image of the Negro as lazy and the denunciation of the Negro's alleged idleness helped whites to establish more clearly in their own minds the values of a materialistic and success-oriented society.

Furthermore, the opening up of society and the acceleration of social mobility during the age of Jackson intensified white racial anxieties, which in turn triggered greater repression of black people. Society was becoming more democratic. But the democratization of society, whites thought, required the reinforcement of caste lines. As the class structure loosened, whites felt the need to tighten the caste structure. Of course, the *de facto* caste lines were already rigid. But white Americans believed that the openness of American society during the Jacksonian era made necessary the establishment of a *de jure* caste system. As whites abolished property qualifications for the suffrage, they felt compelled to disfranchise blacks in order to keep them out of the political power structure and to define the political nation as white.

For half a century or more, whites in America had been concerned about their national identity. During the American Revolution, they had come to view themselves as one people. But for many, race was intricately tied to nationality. This relationship was violently asserted in the age of Jackson. During the 1830s, for example, white boys in Philadelphia drove blacks from Independence Square with stones and clubs, screaming "niggers had nothing to do with the fourth of July."[40] In the judgment of white Americans, not only was America a white nation; America also had a special destiny. If Negroes were not controlled, if they were not set apart, if they amalgamated with whites, then America's nationality surely would be stained. America's destiny as a white and civilized nation would be destroyed. No wonder Thomas Jefferson, expressing not only his political conviction but perhaps also guilt over sexual relations with a black woman, declared in 1814 that Negro "amalgamation with the other color produces a degradation to which no lover of his country, no lover of excellence in the human character can innocently consent."[41] For white Americans like Jefferson, the two—nation and human character—were interwoven.

In the minds of ante-bellum white Americans, then, the black child-savage represented what whites thought they and the American nation were not, and more important, should not become. Their images of the Negro helped them to identify themselves not only as white but also as civilized, and to define civilization in America during the age of Jackson. As sociologists and psychologists have shown, a group defines deviancy and punishes deviants in order to reinforce its identity and norms. As this study of racial attitudes before the Civil War suggests, the images of the Negro as a deviant helped to define the identity and norms for white Americans at a time when their society was experiencing rapid change.

Here was a crucially important reason why white Americans, North and South, worried about the horror of miscegenation, and the Alabama farmer bristled at the thought of a "niggar steppin' up" to his "darter." The anxiety went deeper. It was related to the disturbing awareness that white men themselves, especially white men in the South, were engaging

[40] In Edward R. Turner, *The Negro in Pennsylvania, Slavery—Servitude—Freedom, 1639–1861* (Baltimore, 1911), p. 146.
[41] In Winthrop D. Jordan, *White Over Black: American Attitudes Toward the Negro, 1550–1812* (Chapel Hill, N.C., 1968), p. 547.

in sexual relations with black women. "Under slavery, we live surrounded by prostitutes," a southern white woman complained.

> Like the patriarchs of old, our men live all in one house with their wives and their concubines; and the mulattoes one sees in every family partly resemble the white children. Any lady is ready to tell you who is the father of all the mulatto children in everybody's household but her own. Those, she seems to think, drop from the clouds. My disgust is sometimes boiling over.[42]

Her bitter claim was not unfounded: there were half a million mulattoes in the South in 1860. White southern men, however, could not admit that racial amalgamation did occur in the ante-bellum South, for they viewed themselves as the custodians of civilization.

---

[42] Mary Boykin Chesnut, *A Diary from Dixie* (Cambridge, Mass., 1961), pp. 21-22.

3

Two Steps Forward, One Step Back

Racial Attitudes during the Civil War and Reconstruction

LARRY KINCAID

Angry, jeering protestors filled the room on July 13, 1863, when New York City draft commissioners met to draw the names of New York's first conscripts. More protestors—perhaps 500—waited menacingly outside the building clutching bricks, clubs, and iron bars. As a draft official reached into a large selection machine, a shot sounded and a brick crashed through a window. A shower of bricks followed, and the mob charged into the room. Selection machines toppled, official papers and records flew through broken windows and doors, chairs and desks crashed, draft officials and policemen slumped to the floor, bruised and bloody. Within minutes, the draft headquarters was ransacked and set ablaze. When a policeman attempted to organize fire fighters, protestors clubbed him senseless and left him dying in the street.

Surging through the streets, the mob grew in size and fury. Perhaps 4000 men, women, and children—mostly working-class Irish immigrants—gathered outside the Twenty-first Street Armory, which they showered with bricks and paving stones. A hundred men rushed the front door. Soldiers inside greeted them with a blast of bullets that felled half a dozen leaders. Heedless, the mob shoved ahead through the doors and into the building, which they looted and burned. The guards escaped—barely—through a back door. Fire wagons called to extinguish the blaze were overturned, firemen were beaten, horses were maimed and killed. Soldiers hurriedly sent to disperse the crowd with blank cartridges were attacked and sent scurrying for safety, leaving canteens, rifles, and bayonets scattered behind.

Victorious, the rioters focused their hatred on a new object—the black population of New York. Breaking into small squads and raiding parties, rioters raced through black residential areas, cursing, clubbing, stoning, stabbing, and shooting as they ran. Before them, black men, women, and children fled in panic. Dozens fell or were caught and beaten; some were clubbed to death; a few were hanged and burned. Early in the evening hundreds of rioters gathered outside New York's Orphan Asylum for Colored Children where about 600 black children lived on charity. While rioters cheered, women and children flowed through the building, stripping it of furniture, clothing, food—anything that could be carried away. A small force of police managed to extinguish torches tossed into the building as the orphans escaped. Then the defenders fled and flames consumed the building. Again, firemen sent to the scene were beaten and their equipment was wrecked.

The next day, the crowds of working-class rioters grew still larger and more destructive. Shouting angry insults and threats, they brought a reign of terror to black residential sections. Wild chases ending in barbaric cruelty were common. Rioters even stormed a police station where black women and children had taken refuge. They were turned back only after long, fierce fighting.

Looting, beating, murder, and arson continued for two more days before the army and the police restored order. When the dust and smoke finally began to clear, hundreds of New York's black citizens huddled together in improvised shelters, reflecting on the hatred New York's white working class felt for them. Rioters had murdered at least a dozen black men, women, and children, beaten scores more, and left thousands homeless and destitute—all for the crime of being black.

Less than two years after the New York riot, Representative George W. Julian, a radical Republican from Indiana, recorded in his diary a wondrous spectacle—"the greatest event of this century"—he had witnessed in the House of Representatives.

> The result for a good while remained in doubt and the suspense produced perfect stillness. When it was certainly known that the measure had carried, the cheering in the hall and densely packed galleries exceeded anything I ever before saw and beggered description. Members joined in the shouting, and kept it up for some minutes. Some embraced one another, others wept like children. I never before felt as I then did, and thanked God for the blessed opportunity of recording my name where it will be honored as those of the signers of the Declaration of Independence. What a grand jubilee for the old

battle-scarred Abolitionists. Glorious fruit of the war. I have felt, ever since the vote, as if I were in a new country. I seem to breathe better, and feel comforted and refreshed.[1]

Julian had witnessed the House's approval of the Thirteenth Amendment, which abolished slavery in the United States. In February 1865, the House and Senate by two-thirds majorities recommended its adoption. By December, three-fourths of the free states had ratified it. A year later, in 1866, Congress enacted a civil rights law to preserve the freedom the amendment guaranteed.

I

These two events—the New York riot and the adoption of the Thirteenth Amendment—symbolize the polarization of racial attitudes that occurred during the Civil War.

Of the two, the action of the New York rioters is the more easily explained. In schools, in churches, in books, and in the streets most white people in the North learned that black-skinned people were inherently dirty, immoral, ignorant, childlike, occasionally vicious, and fit only for menial occupations—a race of savage children.

Northerners did not reflect antiblack attitudes with equal intensity. New Englanders generally showed less prejudice than other northerners; residents of southern Ohio, Indiana, and Illinois, most of whom had migrated from slave states, generally showed more. Northerners who lived in cities, where the black population was concentrated, usually showed more prejudice than farmers, most of whom lived in relative isolation and saw black people rarely, if at all. Educated professionals, especially ministers, showed less prejudice than members of other occupational groups, especially manual laborers and factory workers, who lived closest to the black ghettos and viewed black men as both sexual and economic rivals. Democrats were much more actively racist than Whigs, and, later, Republicans. Irish immigrants, who were not only poor urbanites, manual laborers, and Democrats, but themselves the victims of intense prejudices on the part of native Americans, harbored perhaps the most intense antiblack prejudices in the United States outside the South.

But wherever white northerners lived, whatever they did for a living, whatever their religious, educational, or social background, generally they believed that black people belonged to an inferior race. Even many aboli-

---

[1] "George W. Julian's Journal—The Assassination of Abraham Lincoln," *Indiana Magazine of History,* 11 (1915), p. 327.

tionists shared these assumptions, though they often were more inclined than most to include admirable traits in the black stereotype.

In the South, racist attitudes justified slavery. In the North, they justified an elaborate system of segregation. Though both black northerners and white abolitionists fought these segregation laws in the decades before the Civil War, and occasionally won significant victories, progress was slow and insubstantial.

In the late 1850s, moreover, as the nation stumbled toward civil war, antiblack feeling in the North increased significantly. This development, often overlooked by historians, at first glance may seem paradoxical. Between 1854 and 1860, northerners became more openly opposed to slavery and tolerant of abolitionists than ever before. Several northern states enacted "personal liberty laws" designed to obstruct implementation of national fugitive slave laws. The Republican party emerged to resist the expansion of slavery into United States territories and almost overnight became the dominant party in the North. Proslavery Democrats, meanwhile, lost support throughout the North.

But these developments did not reflect a growing sympathy in the North for black people, free or enslaved. Rather they indicated a rapidly growing dissatisfaction with southern political leadership, methods, and purposes. Persistent southern opposition to free homesteads, to appropriations for internal improvements in frontier states, and to tariff protection for northern industries; southern insistence that the Missouri Compromise be nullified and the upper Louisiana territory be opened to slavery; southern intimidation and arrogance in the House and Senate; southern efforts to establish slavery in Kansas against the will of the majority of settlers; southern defenses of slavery and criticisms of industrial capitalism; southern efforts to deprive Congress of the power to keep slavery out of United States territories—all combined to convince a majority of northerners that southern leaders, the "Slave Power," exerted a baneful influence on national development that should be reduced. To achieve this purpose indirectly, northerners organized the Republican party to oppose the spread of slavery beyond the states in which it already existed. This step, Republican partisans hoped, would chasten southern leaders, limit their power, and set slavery on the path to ultimate extinction. Thus the "enemy" to which Republicans pointed was not racial prejudice and segregation; it was not even slavery. It was the "Slave Power" and the alleged determination of southern leaders to impose both their leadership and slavery on the nation.

Northern Democrats were eager to obscure what Republicans actually favored. They hardly could hope to discredit Republicans in the North by accusing them of opposing the influence of the "Slave Power" and the spread of slavery. So Democrats accused Republicans of favoring two ideas northern voters overwhelmingly opposed: emancipation and racial equality. The

North's leading Democrat, Senator Stephen A. Douglas of Illinois, for example, charged that "the Abolition Party [that is, the Republican party] really think that under the Declaration of Independence the negro is equal to the white man, and that negro equality is an inalienable right conferred by the Almighty, and hence that all human law in violation of it are null and void."

Douglas, of course, repudiated this view. "The signers of the Declaration of Independence had no references to the negro whatever, when they declared all men to be equal." They were speaking only of white Europeans and their posterity. They did not include "the negro, the savage Indian, the Fejee, the Malay, or any other inferior and degraded race, when they spoke of the equality of men." This fact did not necessarily mean that black people should be enslaved. The white citizens of each state could decide what rights they wished black people to enjoy. If the people of Maine, for example, wished to confess that they "were no better than negroes," Douglas would not quarrel with them. But his Illinois constituents certainly were better than Negroes and should retain a monopoly of political power.

> A negro is not and never ought to be a citizen of the United States. . . . The Almighty [had not] made the negro capable of self-government. . . . Do you desire to strike out of our State Constitution that clause which keeps slaves and free negroes out of the States, and allow the free negroes to flow in, and cover your prairies with black settlements? Do you desire to turn this beautiful State into a free negro colony, in order that when Missouri abolishes slavery she can send one hundred thousand emancipated slaves into Illinois, to become citizens and voters, on an equality with yourselves? If you desire negro citizenship, if you desire to allow them to come into the State and settle with the white man, if you desire them to vote on an equality with yourselves, and to make them eligible for office, to serve on juries, and to adjudge your rights, then support Mr. Lincoln and the Black Republican Party.[2]

Charges like these put Republicans in an awkward and dangerous position. If Republicanism became identified in the popular mind with abolitionism or racial equality, the party would quickly die. At the same time, most Republicans did oppose slavery and did rely heavily on growing antislavery feeling in the North. Moreover, they included in their ranks nearly all politically active abolitionists, humanitarians, social reformers, and racial egalitarians in the North. They could not simply declare that they had no desire to interfere with slavery or that they opposed racial equality as strongly as Douglas himself. Nor could they easily dissociate themselves from the document that party organizers had made the cornerstone of Republicanism, the Declaration of Independence.

[2] Robert W. Johannsen, ed., *The Lincoln-Douglas Debates* (New York, 1965), pp. 45, 127–129, 299.

Republicans tried to walk a middle path. To counter Democratic accusations, they emphasized that the party was the defender of the interests of white men, not black. Though insisting that slavery was morally wrong, they stressed that they did not propose to interfere with it in the states where it already existed; they merely wished to prevent its expansion. Though insisting that black men were "created equal" in their right to life, liberty, and the pursuit of happiness, they stressed that this conviction did not commit Republicans to racial equality. Responding to Douglas, Lincoln expressed the view of most Republicans.

> I am not, nor ever have been in favor of bringing about in any way the social and political equality of white and black races.—that I am not nor ever have been in favor of making voters or jurors of negroes, nor of qualifying them to hold office, nor to intermarry with white people; and I will say in addition to this that there is a physical difference between the white and black races which I believe will forever forbid the two races living together on terms of social and political equality. And inasmuch as they cannot so live, while they do remain together there must be the position of superior and inferior, and I as much as any other man am in favor of having the superior position assigned to the white race. . . . I have never seen, to my knowledge, a man, woman or child who was in favor of producing a perfect equality, social or political, between negroes and white men.[3]

A few Republicans, mostly New Englanders and abolitionists, disagreed with Lincoln. Many of them did support political and civil equality, if not social equality, and did not hesitate to defend their views publicly. But most Republicans shared Lincoln's attitudes, and were eager to reassure northern voters that they, as much as Douglas, thought black men proper objects for white discrimination.

It was this partisan struggle that caused northern whites to become more antiblack as they became more antislavery. In order to make their indictment of Republicans utterly damning, Democrats stressed the "Negro question" and reminded northern voters again and again of the most negative and frightening characteristics of the black stereotype. Scrambling to escape damning association with black people, most Republicans repeatedly emphasized that black men belonged to an inferior race and that Republicans did not like them either. Thus, both political parties in the late 1850s not only spoke of black people to northern voters more than ever before, but they spoke of them in ways virtually guaranteed to increase the contempt and fear white northerners felt for black-skinned people. Called upon to suggest a way to improve race relations in the United States, most Republicans could only urge that black people be encouraged to leave the country for homes in Africa or South America. The Chicago convention that

---

[3] Johannsen, *The Lincoln-Douglas Debates,* pp. 162–163.

nominated Lincoln for the Presidency in 1860 was reluctant even to endorse the Declaration of Independence, fearing that their action might imply they believed in racial equality.

II

Threats and accusations turned to bullets and blood in the summer of 1861. Shortly after Lincoln's narrow election (he received less than 40 percent of the popular vote), seven states of the Deep South announced their withdrawal from the United States. Late in February, representatives from these states gathered in Montgomery, Alabama, and formed the Confederate States of America. On April 12, Confederate guns in the harbor of Charleston, South Carolina shelled Fort Sumter until the federal garrison surrendered. Lincoln immediately called for 75,000 volunteers to compel obedience to federal authority in the South. By May, Union and Confederate troops had clashed in border areas, and four more states had joined the Confederacy. On July 21, northern and southern forces collided at Manassas Junction in Virginia. After several hours of indecisive fighting, raw federal soldiers began a retreat that soon became a frenzied flight for safety. For a few days it seemed that southern troops would follow the Yankees into Washington and seize the capital. Throughout the North, lingering hopes for reconciliation or a short war flickered out. Realists now looked ahead to a long period of hard fighting.

The outbreak of war triggered a sharp increase in racial hatred among white northerners. Spurred by a natural desire to find a scapegoat for the disaster that had befallen white men, made anxious by the political chaos and economic slump that followed secession, filled with fear that war would enable "two or three million semi-savages" to escape slavery and flood into northern states, white northerners launched antiblack tirades and demonstrations on an unprecedented scale.

Democratic politicians and publicists were especially active purveyors of racial hatred. Badly divided and disorganized, their party suffered massive political defeats in the North in 1860. Abandoned by their southern allies, their power was at an all-time low. Northern racism seemed to be their salvation. Properly aroused and manipulated, it might be the lever that would pry Republicans out of power. As in the past, the sincere racism and political needs of their party pushed them to the forefront of racial propagandists. More frantically than ever before Democrats set out to associate Republicanism with abolition and racial equality, and added the warning that Republican policies would lead soon to a black inundation of the North.

Initially, most Republicans responded to Democratic charges as they had before the war: they tried to assure northern voters that they bowed to nobody in their dislike of black people. Convinced that disaster awaited their party if a majority of northerners began to think that party leaders favored either abolition or racial equality, Republicans across the nation repudiated both policies. In Congress, on the day after the disaster at Manassas Junction, Republican legislators hurriedly resolved that the war would not be fought to destroy slavery, but to preserve the Union. It would end as soon as the states were reunited. Republicans also tried to allay fears of a black inundation by arguing that it probably would not occur, that the warning was simply a Democratic political trick. If escaping blacks did reach the North, however, Republicans promised that they would be returned to the South, or "voluntarily colonized" outside the United States.

But great wars work great changes. Between 1861 and 1865, the attitudes of Republican leaders toward the place of black people evolved with bewildering speed, and a majority of voters in the North followed where the Republican party led. When war began, most Republican politicians supported racial discrimination in the North and announced their willingness to guarantee slavery a perpetual existence in the South. By July 1862, Republican congressmen had offered financial assistance to any slave state that would adopt a policy of gradual emancipation, had freed enslaved black people of the District of Columbia and the territories, and had declared that anyone held in slavery by a supporter of the rebellion was forever free. In January 1863, President Lincoln announced the emancipation of all enslaved people living in rebellious areas. The Republican party platform of 1864 called for the abolition of slavery throughout the nation. After the party's sweeping victory, Republicans returned to Washington to act out the drama described by Representative George W. Julian—the passage of the Thirteenth Amendment. In April 1866, when Republicans enacted the nation's first Civil Rights Act, President Andrew Johnson observed that they were granting the black race legal protection "infinitely beyond any that the General Government has ever provided for the white race."[4] Yet when Republicans embodied this protection in the Fourteenth Amendment, and carried the issue to the people, they again received the support of a decisive majority of voters throughout the North.

This extraordinarily rapid and extensive alteration of northern attitudes is usually attributed primarily to the influence that Lincoln himself stressed—the logic of military needs. Certainly, this played its part. With hundreds of thousands of white southerners in the army, enslaved black laborers (male and female) probably comprised half of the Confederate labor force. Moreover, the black labor force represented an investment of over $2,000,000,000 by the South's most powerful economic interest group. If the Confederate cause could be deprived of that labor, or if large numbers

[4] J. D. Richardson, ed., *A Compilation of the Messages and Papers of the Presidents, 1789-1897* (10 vols.; Washington, D.C., 1896–1899), VI, p. 413.

of planters could be persuaded to reject the Confederacy to protect their investment, Union prospects would brighten considerably. Many northerners also believed that foreign powers, especially Great Britain, would be less likely to intervene in behalf of the South if the North adopted abolition as a war goal.

But other considerations were perhaps just as important. The growing conviction that slavery was the root of the war undoubtedly widened the appeal of abolition. For years antislavery leaders had traced the aristocratic, secessionist tendencies of southern society to the egotistical arrogance bred by the slave-master relationship. Before the war, William Seward spoke of the "irrepressible conflict" between slavery and freedom, and Lincoln had warned that "a house divided against itself" could not stand. Though both insisted that conflict need not end in war, when war came most people in the North were inclined to agree with the abolition propagandists who declared that slavery caused the war and that if slavery did not die with the Confederacy, North and South some day would be drawn into war again. Even conservatives like the noted Catholic publicist, Orestes Brownson, reluctantly decided that a Union "reconstructed on the basis of slavery" would not long survive. "There would soon be disaffection at the South; there would be disaffection at the North; and there would always be disaffection in the consciences of all good men, of all true Christians in all sections, created and sustained by the moral and social plague of slavery."[5] The death of slavery was, in short, the price of permanent peace. Nothing less would serve.

War-born hatred also affected northern thinking. The culmination of years of sectional animosity, secession itself became a significant irritant. Most northerners thought their constitution the most perfect system of government devised by man. The action of secessionists threatened the survival of that government and thus angered northerners of every political persuasion. The shame and humiliation occasioned by the ease with which secession was accomplished and the rout at Manassas Junction also inspired hatred. Once war began in earnest, the horrible toll of battle became the most important generator of northern hatred. Confederates killed or wounded 10,000 Union soldiers at Shilo and 10,000 more during the seven days' battle in the wilderness of Virginia. They killed 5000 men in a single day at Antietam and killed or wounded 12,000 more in a few hours at Fredericksburg. By the summer of 1863, southern soldiers had killed over 50,000 Union troops, and wounded and crippled another 100,000. Not since the Napoleonic wars had battle losses reached such staggering dimensions. Death and sorrow invaded nearly every northern household, and hatred grew. Some of it focused on the Republicans who controlled the

---

[5] *Brownson's Quarterly Review* (1861) in Frank Freidel, ed., *Union Pamphlets of the Civil War* (2 vols.; Cambridge, Mass., 1967), I, p. 151.

government; some of it focused on the black population whose presence in the country seemed somehow to be the ultimate cause of the war; most of it focused on the men doing the killing—white southerners. To strike at slavery was to strike at them.

Neither military necessity, nor the conviction that sectional peace required the abolition of slavery, nor the war hatred account for the rapidity, extent, or direction of the revolution in northern thinking, however. For one thing, the short-range disadvantages of emancipation easily could outweigh any long-range advantages, as Democrats in the North insisted. If the North made abolition a war aim, southerners would be more determined than ever to fight until utterly exhausted. The policy also might cause the defection of critically important border slave states that had remained in the Union. Certainly, it seemed likely to erode severely support for the Union cause in both the border states and the midwest. Besides, even if the present and future interests of the Union seemed to require the abolition of slavery, they hardly required national citizenship and federal guarantees of civil equality for black people. Most leading Republicans, including the President, had already endorsed the idea of colonizing the black race outside the United States. The government was placing Indians on reservations. Aliens often had to wait years for citizenship and full civil equality. Any of these policies or a combination of them would have been much more in keeping with traditional attitudes than the policy Republicans actually adopted. They might even have permitted white southerners to define the postemancipation status of black people in the South, as President Johnson urged.

Why did Republicans go beyond mere abolition and attempt to raise emancipated black people to civil equality? No simple answer will suffice. Paternalism and humane sympathy played a role. The plight of thousands of displaced, hungry, homeless freedmen doubtless moved men in the North. So did the fate of the blameless black victims of the New York draft rioters. But the situation of blacks, North and South, had been miserable for years and had prompted little fellow-feeling or sympathy on the part of white northerners.

Part of the answer lies in the elusive realm of northern idealism. As the war dragged on, white northerners had to make sacrifices that hatred alone would not justify. To send themselves off to die by the hundreds of thousands, northerners needed some positive ideal, a sense of sacred purpose. In the beginning, preservation of the Union had been that purpose. Most northerners agreed with Lincoln when he declared that the struggle embraced "more than the fate of these United States. It presents to the whole family of man, the question, whether a constitutional republic, or a democracy—a government of the people, by the same people—can or cannot maintain its territorial integrity, against its domestic foes." Americans had proved that ordinary men could create and administer a democratic republic. They now had to prove that such a government could survive internal dissension. Success would vindicate the right of men to rule themselves. Failure would "put an end to free government upon the earth."[6]

Lincoln perhaps needed no larger vision of the war than this, but other northerners did. As the war dragged on from one battlefield to another, as the lists of dead and wounded swelled to hundreds of thousands, the preservation of a political arrangement seemed to be a cold, prosaic, and narrow objective. It hardly could justify such carnage. Besides, it was an ideal clouded with ambiguity. Southerners insisted that the Declaration of Independence justified secession. They also insisted that they, not northerners, were defending the Constitution and the sacred right of self-government. They labeled the Union a tyrannical oppressor—an accusation that gained force as the Lincoln administration encroached upon the traditional constitutional rights of citizens, states, and the other branches of government.

An emotional, religious, naive, and democratic people, northerners needed an unclouded vision of the war that could engage their feelings and profoundest ideals. Increasingly they found that vision in the idea that they were God's agents in a "new birth of liberty." Northern abolitionists long had hoped that the North would play this role and began to urge it upon people as soon as the war began. Orestes Brownson promptly agreed. "The Union is and must be sacred to liberty. Here man must be man, nothing more and nothing less. Slaves must not breathe our atmosphere."[7] All across the North, preachers, teachers, publicists, and pamphleteers reiterated this theme to an increasingly receptive audience. Then, in 1863, Julia Ward Howe set the idea to music, and it became the North's marching song:

> Mine eyes have seen the glory of the coming of the Lord.
> He is trampling out the vintage where the grapes of wrath are stored.
> He has loosed the fateful lightning of his terrible swift sword.
> His truth is marching on.
>
> . . .
>
> In the beauty of the lilies Christ was born across the sea.
> With a glory in his bosom that transfigures you and me.
> As he died to make men holy, let us die to make men free,
> While God is marching on.

The ideological and emotional needs of war filled many northerners with a new idealism. The old and cherished conviction that the United States was uniquely God's nation gained a new dimension. As Lincoln re-

---

[6] Richard N. Current, ed., *The Political Thought of Abraham Lincoln* (Indianapolis, Ind., 1967), 180–181.

[7] Freidel, *Union Pamphlets of the Civil War,* I, p. 140.

marked at Gettysburg: the North had resolved that "these dead shall not have died in vain; that this nation under God shall have a new birth of freedom; and that government of the people, by the people, for the people, shall not perish from the earth."

Gratitude also played a part in the North's decision to abolish slavery and extend civil equality to black people. By 1863, army enlistments had fallen sharply and showed no promise of rising. The casualty lists were appalling; enlistment bonuses attracted few new recruits; the draft was greeted with widespread resentment and resistance. By the middle of the year, the Union army was clearly in serious trouble that not even victories at Gettysburg and Vicksburg could wholly remedy. The stage was set for one of the most important events in the history of the war—the appearance of black men in Union blue.

This development, too, was startling. During the American Revolution, black and white soldiers fought side by side. But at the beginning of the war, when leading black and white abolitionists urged the nation to recruit black troops, most white northerners rejected the idea. To many, racial pride was at stake: if white men could not save the Union, certainly black men could not. Some feared that black recruitment would further antagonize Confederates and alienate border state Unionists. Others believed that black troops were too ignorant, too cowardly, too unreliable ever to fight well. They predicted that white men would desert by the thousands rather than fight side by side with black men. Bowing to popular opinion, Lincoln refused to recruit black soldiers even after Congress authorized this action.

The hard necessities of war, however, soon undercut preconceptions, abstract arguments, and deep prejudices. As the lists of dead and wounded grew longer, opposition to the recruitment of black men began to evaporate. Though restricted to segregated units, by early 1863 several thousand black soldiers composed regiments all along the battle lines. By late 1863, black troops had fought courageously in half a dozen battles, and by the war's end, nearly 180,000 black men had entered the Union army, and 68,000 had died.

Closely followed in the press and widely publicized, the performance of black troops dramatically affected many white northerners. In 1862, Charles Francis Adams, Jr., opposed arming black men. In July 1863, he remarked that black troops were "so much a success that they will soon be in fashion." Charles Dana, a reporter, declared that "the bravery of the blacks in the battle of Milliken's Bend completely revolutionized the sentiment of the army with regard to the employment of Negro troops." From Michigan, a Republican partisan happily observed that "it is daily being proved that the negro can take care of himself; that he ardently desires freedom; that he knows how to conduct himself as a free man; that he will fight, too . . . . The negro loves freedom, and will fight to obtain it." An

Irish Democrat from Wisconsin put the matter more simply: "I never believed in niggers before, but by Jasus [sic], they are hell for fighting."[8]

Many white northerners never became reconciled to the recruitment of black soldiers, but most—especially those in the army—appreciated their help. As a result they more readily accepted the idea that black people should enjoy not only freedom, but civil equality. It seemed only simple justice to acknowledge that men who fought to preserve the nation deserved its protection.

Northern racism also played a part in the decision to link civil equality with emancipation. Because they seemed expensive and impractical, the colonization plans of Lincoln and other leading Republicans never gained much support among either white or black Americans. Thus the postwar racial adjustment would have to be made in light of the knowledge that the vast majority of black people would remain in the United States. This fact revived the prospect that the northern states might be flooded with emancipated black people fleeing oppression in the South. A way did exist, however, to alleviate northern anxieties. If the nation guaranteed black people that they would be as free (or freer) in the South as in the North, they would have no reason to leave the South. They could stay where climate, customs, and companions presumably were more congenial—incidentally sparing the North the agonies of racial adjustment. Some northerners even predicted that black northerners soon would move to the South.

Many northerners were little affected by any of these considerations or developments. Most northern Democrats and many conservatives ardently condemned the Emancipation Proclamation, the decision to arm black men, the Thirteenth Amendment, the Freedmen's Bureau, the first Civil Rights Act, and the Fourteenth Amendment. Indeed, each step the government took in the direction of guaranteeing racial equality drew from them angry protests and hysterical predictions of doom and degradation.

Nor did Republicans participate in the new mood of sympathy and friendliness with equal enthusiasm. Radicals not only supported civil equality but hoped that the nation would give blacks political power. Conservative Republicans, on the other hand, only with reluctance agreed that citizenship and civil equality for blacks were in the national interest. Moderates, who comprised the bulk of the party and its supporters, moved between these two extremes, their attitudes usually more dependent upon external conditions than on any firmly held convictions or beliefs.

But the emotions generated by war—hatred, idealism, gratitude—combined with military needs, traditional racism, and the widespread belief

[8] Dudley T. Cornish, *The Sable Arm; Negro Troops in the Union Army, 1861–1865* (New York, 1966), pp. 132, 147; V. Jacque Voegeli, *Free but Not Equal; The Midwest and the Negro During the Civil War* (Chicago, 1967), pp. 123–124.

that slavery was an obstacle to progress and destructive of republican institutions to produce what Lincoln called a "fundamental and astounding"
change in the status northern white voters were willing to accord black
people in America. Though most white northerners continued to believe
that black people belonged to an inferior race, a majority also were persuaded that regardless of racial disabilities, blacks deserved freedom and
equality before the law.

Lincoln's death on Good Friday, April 15, 1865, sanctified this new
attitude. The president never publicly supported civil equality for black
people. Indeed, he seems to have hoped until the day he died that they would
choose to emigrate to some new land. But in the minds of most northerners,
Lincoln and freedom for the black race were synonymous. He had made
emancipation a war purpose; he had called upon black men to fight for the
Union and their freedom; he had praised the contribution of black soldiers;
he had informed Congress shortly after his re-election in 1864, that "if the
people should, by whatever mode or means, make it an Executive duty to
re-enslave" those freed by the war, "another, and not I, must be their instrument to perform it."[9] Little wonder that millions of northerners emerged
from their shock and sorrow with their dedication to freedom renewed and
intensified.

III

Albion Tourgee was one of the thousands of northerners who went
South to make a new life in the decade after the Civil War. He also was an
active and ardent Republican who believed that black people deserved
political and legal equality. Settling in North Carolina, he soon was engaged
in fierce political battles that lasted until 1879, when he gave up and returned to the North to write of his experiences. In one of his novels, *A Fool's
Errand* (1879), Tourgee drew on his wide knowledge of political and racial
attitudes in the North and South to summarize the ideas that dominated
the two regions when the war ended:

The Southern Idea of the Situation

We have lost our slaves, our bank stock, everything, by the war. We have
been beaten, and have honestly surrendered; slavery is gone, of course. The
slave is now free, but he is not white. We have no ill will towards the colored
man as such and in his place; but he is not our equal, can not be made our equal,
and we will not be ruled by him, or admit him as a co-ordinate with the white
race in power.

[9] Current, *The Political Thought of Abraham Lincoln,* p. 313.

The Northern Idea of the Situation

The negroes are free now, and must have a fair chance to make themselves something. What is claimed about their inferiority may be true . . . but true or false, they have a right to equality before the law. That is what the war meant, and this must be secured to them. The rest they must get as they can, or do without, as they choose. [10]

Obviously, these are two very different ideas. How were they to be reconciled? How could Republicans preserve the freedom and establish the civil equality of black people in a restored Union when most white southerners were determined to relegate blacks to the bottom of southern society and a large minority in the North were more actively antiblack than ever before? Finding an answer to this question was one of the major challenges facing Republicans during the postwar decade that historians call the era of Reconstruction.

To the task, they brought great strengths. Most Republican politicians and voters were wedded firmly to their party. They were convinced that it was the repository of most of the nation's political virtue, that it alone could devise a settlement that would preserve the gains of the war and seal the defeat of the Confederacy, that it alone could steer the nation into a new era of industrial growth and national prosperity. Moreover, Republican leaders enjoyed unprecedented political power. A sudden turn in the tide of war and a successful effort to link the northern Democratic party with treason had brought Republicans substantial gains in the elections of 1864. When the war ended in April 1865, the party controlled the presidency, both houses of Congress by two-thirds majorities, and the governorships and legislatures of all but two or three small northern states. Most of the United States Supreme Court Justices were Republicans; the Chief Justice, Salmon P. Chase, was a well-known radical.

But Republican politicians also faced large obstacles. Though united on most long-range goals, they often disagreed sharply among themselves about methods, especially when they confronted the questions of how to punish southern whites, aid southern blacks, and remake southern society. Republican "radicals" believed that national development required the eradication of every vestige of the "Slave Power." Consequently they wished to strip most white southerners of political power, enfranchise black men, and let them work with whatever white allies they could find in the restructuring of southern society. The army would be used to protect and maintain the radical regimes. Republican conservatives, on the other hand, believed that national development required prompt, thorough reconciliation between white northerners and southerners; they wished to be generous in their

---

[10] Albion Tourgee, *A Fool's Errand* (New York, 1880), pp. 121–122.

dealings with defeated Confederates, even if some of the nation's promises to emancipated black people had to be compromised. Moderate Republicans, who comprised the bulk of the party in Congress and in the nation, ranged between these two extremes. They wished to protect black people and insure that ex-Confederates could never again threaten the Union; they also wished to hasten reconciliation. The anger generated by this clash of ideas was aggravated by personal rivalries and personality conflicts, which seemed to crop up incessantly.

Republicans faced other difficulties. Lincoln's death deprived the party of a skillful and sensitive leader. It also placed a former slaveowner and southern Democrat in the White House. Widely admired for his devotion to the Union, Andrew Johnson had been selected to run with Lincoln while serving as military governor of Tennessee. Wishing merely to strengthen the claim that they represented all pro-Union factions, Republicans had assumed that Johnson would sink into obscurity, like most previous vice-presidents. Instead John Wilkes Booth thrust him into the nation's highest office. What he would do there, how he would get along with Republican Congressional leaders, what he would do to southern whites and for southern blacks, no one knew, and Johnson, notoriously reserved, was not inclined to say.

Northern Democrats also could prove troublesome. Northern Democratic leaders opposed both emancipation and civil equality for black people, wished to halt the erosion of state powers that war had permitted, and hoped to control the political strength of returning southern whites. Consequently, they became the ardent advocates of complete forgiveness for ex-Confederates, prompt restoration to full political power, and state control of postwar race relations. Though demoralized and depleted by the defeats of 1864, the Democratic party continued to command the support of about 45 percent of the North's voters, a number that Republican missteps quickly could swell.

Finally, white southerners themselves were a potential source of difficulty. Dispirited by defeat, ravaged by war, unrepresented in Congress, they stood helpless for the moment. But in every ex-Confederate state except Mississippi, South Carolina, and Louisiana, whites comprised a substantial majority of the population. In every southern state, they possessed nearly all of the money, land, education, social prestige, and political experience—in short, all of the things that constitute social power. They also controlled most of the region's newspapers. Whatever short-range settlement Republicans might devise, eventually white southerners would control the destiny of the South and the balance of power in the nation—that is, unless Republicans launched a social and economic revolution. Republican leaders could not ignore this fundamental fact if they wished to effect a lasting settlement in the South.

Convinced that white southerners would never permit black people to enjoy genuine freedom or civil equality, radical Republicans did wish to revolutionize the South. Most Republicans rejected this solution, however. Temperamentally moderate, fearful of precipitating a reaction among northern voters, hopeful that many southern whites were at last ready to be reasonable, most Republican leaders preferred to cooperate with southern whites rather than to coerce them. They hoped to devise a settlement that would not only protect the Union and preserve the new freedom of black people, but treat defeated southerners generously.

The settlement they developed became the Fourteenth Amendment to the Constitution. The first of the amendment's five sections established the status of black people not only in the South, but throughout the nation. It declared that all persons born in the United States were citizens of the United States and of the state in which they lived. It also prohibited states from making or enforcing laws that limited the privileges and immunities of United States citizens; from depriving any person of "life, liberty, or property, without due process of law"; and from denying any person "equal protection of the laws."

The remaining sections of the amendment were designed to limit the power of white southerners to injure the Union. Section Two reduced the voice of the southern whites in the House of Representatives and the electoral college by subtracting all disfranchised adult males from the population upon which national representation was apportioned. Section Three barred from state and national offices all men who had violated explicit oaths to support the Constitution when they aided the Confederacy. Section Four demanded full payment of the national war debt and prohibited payment of the Confederate war debt or compensation for emancipated black people. In Section Five, Congress reserved the power to pass laws to enforce the several provisions.

Republican moderates regarded this as a fair and generous settlement, and they hoped that many white southerners would agree. The amendment seemed to protect black people and the nation with a minimum of offense to conciliatory white southerners. Though it prohibited discriminatory legal codes and barred some prominent southerners from high public office, it left intact the regimes that Andrew Johnson had permitted white southerners to construct immediately after the war. Though it reduced southern power in the national government, it did not challenge white supremacy in the South. Most ex-Confederates were permitted to guide and direct the regeneration of the war-mangled region and to speak for the states at the national level. To those barred from high office for violating their oath to the Constitution, the amendment held out the promise of eventual pardon. No white man was denied the right to vote; no black man was given that right. White southerners merely were refused the right to count the disfranchised black population when determining how many representatives they deserved. The amendment did not give black people land, nor did it guarantee them an education. Economically and intellectually, they would remain subordinated to the white population.

But hopes that the amendment would lead to cooperation between Republican leaders and white southerners soon were blasted. Andrew Johnson thought that the amendment was harsh and punitive and that it encroached too much on the traditional rights of states. He urged southern leaders to reject it. So did leading Democrats, who assured white southerners that the North would never support such revolutionary proposals. Encouraged by these words and reluctant to participate in what they regarded as the Republicans' efforts to humiliate them, southern legislators overwhelmingly refused to ratify the Fourteenth Amendment. Between October 1866, when Texas rejected the amendment, and February 1867, when it was defeated in Louisiana, more than 1500 state legislators voted "no." Fewer than 100 voted "yes." Of the eleven ex-Confederate states, only Tennessee adopted the amendment.

Cooperation gave way to coercion in the wake of the decision of the ten ex-Confederate states. In March 1867, Republican congressmen enacted with near unanimity the first Military Reconstruction Act. This decision was the result of a confusing crosscurrent of pressures and a complicated legislative struggle, but we can isolate the major concerns and considerations that lay behind it. First, the overwhelming rejection of the Fourteenth Amendment made it apparent that the existing regimes in the South were not eager to cooperate with Republicans and could not easily be made to reconsider their action. Second, a spectacular, bloody riot in New Orleans and continuous reports from northern officials stationed in the South made it clear that those regimes could not or would not protect the lives and property of southern Unionists, upon whom northern Republicans depended for support and to whom they felt obligated. Third, both the rejection of the amendment and the failure of white southerners to protect Unionists outraged Republicans, who generally regarded southern leaders as both arrogant and evil. Finally, Republicans feared that if they did not settle the southern question promptly, Andrew Johnson and his allies might soon win back enough support in the North to regain control of Reconstruction. Prodded by their feelings of obligation, self-interest, anger, and fear, and by their particular view of the national interest, Congressional Republicans agreed to give politics in the South a new framework and a new complexion.

The Military Reconstruction Act and the supplements that followed dictated sweeping changes in southern political institutions. Congress declared the governments of every ex-Confederate state but Tennessee invalid. Southerners would have to write new state constitutions and establish new governments. While this reconstruction occurred, the states remained subject to military supervision. White southerners barred from office by the Fourteenth Amendment could not vote for delegates to the constitutional convention nor serve in them. At the same time, all adult black men in these states gained the right to vote, and new state constitutions had to guarantee suffrage impartially before Congress would consider approving them. Even after all of this was done, Congress would not consider readmitting representatives from southern states until those states had ratified the Fourteenth Amendment.

This policy has been denounced often during the last century. In 1867, the opponents of Military Reconstruction labeled it vindictive, irresponsible, cruel, and tyrannical. Attributing it to the Republicans' radical faction, they predicted the policy would generate a race war, "Africanize" the South, and make a joke of government and justice. Soon, they warned, decent white folk would not be able to live in the South. Until recently, historians have been impressed by these partisan accusations and various elaborations by southerners in the late 1860s and the 1870s. They also have been ashamed of the North for permitting black men to vote and hold office while denying that right to some white men. Consequently, many historians have echoed the political rhetoric of the time.

In fact, the radicalism of Military Reconstruction has been exaggerated greatly. Many of the features of the policy did originate with radical Republicans, but its evolution was shaped by moderates in both the House and Senate. They made certain that nothing too radical found its way into the final program. The disfranchisement of white voters affected very few southerners, and these lost only the right to vote for delegates to the state constitutional conventions. Black men, on the other hand, though given the right to vote, did not gain either the economic independence or the guarantee of education without which they could hardly hope to protect that right. The army was available to protect southern Republicans, but its supervision was brief, mild, and limited.

Military Reconstruction was a compromise solution to the southern question, and as radical leaders feared and predicted, it further alienated white southerners without adequately disarming them. Since they remained a majority, their overthrow of the Republican regimes was only a matter of time—and not a very long time at that. Between 1868 and 1869, black and white southern Republicans did manage to draft and ratify new constitutions in most ex-Confederate states and gain control of the state governments. They helped to ratify the Fourteenth Amendment and elect Grant president in 1868. They also helped to ratify the Fifteenth Amendment, which prohibited states from denying anyone the right to vote simply because they were black or had once been enslaved.

In the face of massive white resistance, however, southern Republicans could not retain power. Despite sporadic federal intervention intended to protect them from the terrorism of the Ku Klux Klan and other militant conservative white groups, southern Republicans lost ground steadily. In 1869, Democrats (or Conservatives, as they often called themselves) regained control of Tennessee. By 1870, they controlled Virginia and North

Carolina. The next year, they returned to power in Georgia. In 1874, Alabama, Arkansas, and Texas ousted Republican regimes. Mississippi did the same in 1875. By 1876, when Republicans nominated Rutherford B. Hayes for president, southern Republicans controlled only South Carolina, Louisiana, and Florida, which they ruled as besieged garrisons in enemy territory with the aid of the United States Army. One of President Hayes's first acts in 1877 was to abandon fully the policy of coercion. Recalling federal troops from the remaining bastions of Republican power, he tacitly informed southern Democrats that Republicans no longer would assume responsibility for protecting the rights, lives, and property of black people in the South.

Many rationalizations bolstered this decision but the basic reason for Hayes's action was simple. By the mid-1870s, most Republicans no longer felt moved to compel white men—not even southern white men—to respect the rights of black men. Caught up in the politics of industrialization, removed from the idealism that the war had inspired, less able to sustain the hatred of white southerners that war had encouraged, burdened by the scandals of the Grant administration and the economic collapse of 1873, Republican leaders and voters were swept along by the resurgence of racism that afflicted the nation in the late nineteenth century. C. Vann Woodward has compared the result to a bank transaction. During and immediately after the Civil War, Republicans

> ran up a staggering war debt, a moral debt that was soon found to be beyond the country's capacity to pay, given the underdeveloped state of its moral resources at the time. After making a few token payments during Reconstruction, the United States defaulted on the debt and unilaterally declared a moratorium that lasted more than eight decades.[11]

IV

Republicans launched Reconstruction in part because they wished to guarantee the freedom and civil equality of black people in the South. It is thus tragically ironic that instead of achieving this purpose, instead of making the South a better place for freedmen, Reconstruction actually intensified racial hatred and virtually insured the ruthless resubjugation of blacks.

The sources of increased racial hatred were numerous. One of the most important had little to do with black people themselves, but with what they represented in the South. Early identified with northern Republicans and soon their active political allies, black men inevitably became the principal objects of the hatred and frustration that defeated white southerners felt toward the victorious Union. Doubtless ex-Confederates would have

[11] C. Vann Woodward, *The Burden of Southern History* (New York, 1961), p. 84.

preferred to strike directly at northern Republicans. But since they could not, black men quickly became a convenient and inviting substitute.

The sudden collapse of the traditional restraints on black people provided another important source of more virulent racism. For two centuries white southerners had regarded black men as savage children and had relied upon slavery to maintain social and personal control of the "savages" in their midst. As Winthrop Jordan points out, they had early grown accustomed to thinking that the end of slavery would mean "a cataclysmic, entire, and irrevocable disintegration of indispensable restraints."[12] One can easily imagine, then, the feelings that emancipation occasioned. Suddenly the status of black people in the South was a matter of complete uncertainty. In the eyes of a majority of northerners and in the United States Constitution, they were free citizens, equal to white citizens before the law, and entitled to vote, hold office, and sit on juries. In the eyes of most white southerners, they remained savages—threats to the lives of white people and the values of southern civilization; though freed from the control of planters, black people somehow had to be subordinated to white authority. In this situation, the fears built up by more than 200 years of slavery— fears of sexual assault, of bloody revenge, of rampant immorality, of economic collapse, of the triumph of barbarism—swept furiously through white southern communities.

Social disorganization and economic desolation further augmented old fears and prejudices. Living in a region in which traditional class lines and personal relationships were suddenly blurred or obliterated, white southerners of every social position found themselves exposed and alone. Forced to make their way in a land stripped of its wealth, most found themselves driven downward economically. At the same time, they saw black men gain the right to own land, to work for themselves, to vote, and to obtain the education that white men often lacked. As the social and economic distance between poorer white men and black men lessened, the need of white men for some firm status differential became increasingly acute. More than ever before, the sense of innate white racial superiority became the one secure peg upon which white men could hang their sagging sense of self-esteem.

Finally, politics contributed significantly to worsening race relations in the South during Reconstruction. For the first time, white men had to compete with black men for political power and influence. Racist appeals and warnings became ·potent—and therefore irresistible—weapons in almost any political contest. Inevitably, white politicians engaged in the effort to overthrow Republicans bombarded southerners with lurid, frightening accounts of black corruption, incompetence, and brutality.

A generation-long reign of terror, legal oppression, and persecution

[12] Winthrop D. Jordan, *White Over Black; American Attitudes Toward the Negro, 1550–1812* (Chapel Hill, N.C., 1968), p. 578.

of the Negroes in the South resulted from these pressures. If racial fears were to be quieted, if racial control was to be re-established, if racial superiority was to be psychologically reassuring and economically effective, racial supremacy could not exist merely in the realm of words and ideas. It had to be brought into the world of affairs. It had to be expressed in actions and embedded in laws and institutions. Ku Klux Klansmen, lynch mobs, self-appointed "nigger hazers," and race-baiting politicians organized and spearheaded the drive to resubjugate black people. White southerners recognized that they could not restore chattel slavery. Most may not even have wished to. But they could make certain that black men were put "in their place" and did not move again.

Ironically, the tragic fate of blacks in the South probably only increased the hatred and contempt white Southerners felt for them. Somehow men of Christian conscience had to justify to themselves and the outside world the cruelty and ruthlessness of the white South's assault on black men. In order to justify the barbarity of the assault, the barbarity of the victims had to be painted in more and more lurid hues. The more inhumanely white Southerners behaved, the more they had to believe in the inhumanity of black Southerners. It is little wonder that shootings and hangings gave way to grisly tortures and death by burning, or that southern defenses of their actions and indictments of black "bestiality" became more strident with the passage of time, or that humiliating Jim Crow laws multiplied as they became less necessary objectively.

In the North, the failure of Reconstruction permitted indifference to become the dominant attitude on the race question. Among Democratic partisans, racial hatred had reached its peak during the three or four years immediately after the war. Having appealed to racial fears and hatreds throughout the war, Democratic politicians saw no reason to stop in 1865. Indeed, as Republicans became increasingly committed to preserving the civil equality of black people in the South, the issue seemed more clearly drawn than ever before. Had not white southerners thrown themselves upon the nation's mercy? And were Republicans not trying to heap degradation on top of defeat by placing black and white on the same plane? Were they not trying to create a black dictatorship in order to ensure the triumph of racial amalgamation and "African barbarism" in the South?

But in 1870, Democratic hatemongering began to fall off sharply. Unable to defeat Republicans on the racial issue alone, Democratic leaders accepted the Reconstruction amendments and Military Reconstruction as accomplished facts and subordinated antiblack tirades to issues they hoped would be more effective—Republican corruption and extravagance, the multiplying scandals of the Grant administration, and the economic policies they insisted lay behind the severe depression that began in 1873. As success rewarded the Democrats' "new departure," and as Republican regimes in the South collapsed, northern Democrats rapidly lost interest in the race issue, leaving Republicans to carry on the debate alone.

But Republicans were losing interest, too. The intensity of the debate depended almost wholly on the intensity of the racial fears, humanitarian ideals, gratitude, and practical political needs of white northerners. And by the mid-1870s, all had diminished considerably. Racial fears eased with the return of postwar normalcy and the growing awareness that the widely anticipated black inundation of the North had not occurred. Humanitarian sympathies lessened sharply when the Reconstruction amendments became a part of the Constitution and war-born idealism (and idealists) began to die. The ratification of the amendments and the consolidation of Republican power in the North also diminished the political importance of Southern black voters, especially when those voters proved unable to maintain their political independence in the South. Gratitude for black soldiers' contributions to victory faded as the war itself faded from memory. All the while, a new generation of white Americans was trying to cope with the emerging problems generated by rapid urban and industrial expansion. It is hardly surprising that by the time President Hayes decided to withdraw federal troops from the South, most supporters of Reconstruction felt black people had gotten as much as they deserved from the nation and would now have to make their own way in the world. Contemplating the fate of black people in the South, they felt neither outrage nor indignation. Like their political opponents in the North, they felt indifference.

Some northerners fought the drift to apathy. In the early 1870s, as Reconstruction regimes toppled, leading Republicans often tried to rouse the conscience of the North and check the violence directed against their black allies. Even after the final withdrawal of federal troops in 1877 Republicans and northern reformers, black and white, remained strongly committed to civil and political equality for black people. Reminding the government of its moral and legal responsibility to protect the rights of black southerners, they angrily criticized the Republican party for its dereliction.

But the tide could not be reversed. After a generation of arguing and fighting about the proper status of black people in America, most Republicans had grown tired of the subject. By the mid-1870s, talk about the nation's responsibility usually came only at election time, when Republicans wished to make political capital out of lingering war hatreds and humanitarian sympathies and hoped to revive their claim to the allegiance of black voters in the North. Rarely after 1875 did Republican leaders attempt to launch a sustained debate about the situation in the South, and they said virtually nothing about discrimination in the North.

The failure of Reconstruction did not merely make most northerners indifferent to the fate of black people in America. It deepened the prevailing conviction that black people were morally and intellectually inferior. In part, racist assumptions had been reconfirmed and intensified by the flood of antiblack propaganda that the political feuds of Reconstruction had called forth. Between the end of the war and 1870, when racist hate-mongering began to taper off, northern white racists deluged the North with vivid descriptions of the ignorance, sexual licentiousness, political childishness, and essential barbarism of black people, North and South.

The impact of this political propaganda should not be exaggerated, however. To a large extent, its influence was countered by the egalitarian preachments of Republican partisans. During the struggle to launch Reconstruction, Thaddeus Stevens declared that to "honest Republicans" "negro equality" meant

> just this much and no more: every man, no matter what his race or color; every earthly being who has an immortal soul, has an equal right to justice, honesty, and fair play with every other man; and the law should secure him those rights. The same law which condemns or acquits an African should condemn or acquit a white man. The same law which gives a verdict in a white man's favor should give a verdict in a black man's favor on the same state of facts. Such is the law of God and such ought to be the law of man. This doctrine does not mean that a negro shall sit on the same seat or eat at the same table with a white man. That is a matter of taste which every man must decide for himself. The law has nothing to do with it.[13]

Though few white men in the North would have announced themselves in favor of black equality so emphatically, the idea articulated by Stevens was persuasive and ennobling—especially when Democrats attacked it viciously. It cannot be overemphasized that insofar as the struggle to control Reconstruction was a propaganda war, it was won by the advocates of racial civil equality. The Reconstruction amendments are their monument. For the most part, racial propaganda only confirmed the faith of the already converted.

Guilt feelings occasioned by the failure of Reconstruction were a much more prolific source of antiblack attitudes. As Reconstruction regimes became notorious for corruption and their inability to establish harmonious race relations, white supporters of Reconstruction had to confess that they had been wrong. They had acted hastily and unwisely and had caused southern whites and blacks needless suffering. This admission, of course, generated guilt feelings. A few Republicans tried to exorcise them by joining the Liberal Republican movement in 1872 and condemning Grant and the regular party. Other shuffled the blame back to white southern conservatives, whom they insisted never gave Reconstruction regimes or black

---

[13] Harold M. Hyman, ed., *The Radical Republicans and Reconstruction, 1861–1870* (Indianapolis, Ind., 1967), p. 375.

voters an opportunity to prove themselves. As leading Republicans moved toward a reconciliation with moderate white southerners in the mid-1870s, however, Republicans increasingly were inclined to throw the burden of failure—and guilt—onto black voters themselves. Blacks, they declared, had been given a splendid opportunity to prove themselves and earn the respect of white people, North and South. Instead, they had proved they did not deserve either civil or political equality.

Black southerners served Republicans as scapegoats in another important way. When Republicans stopped actively intervening in southern affairs to protect the constitutional rights of black citizens, those who sympathized with the black people had to find some way to justify their inaction. Some blamed the party; some blamed the nation as a whole. But Republicans who could do neither became increasingly attracted to the arguments of white southerners who insisted that black people were so inferior that the survival of white civilization demanded their ruthless suppression. In other words, men of conscience in the North, like those in the South, became more deeply racist in order to live with themselves and the nation's indifference to the fate of black people. Thus the way was prepared in the North for the rampant racism of the late nineteenth century.

V

A cynic, looking at racial attitudes and race relations in the United States in 1880, might have said that much had happened in thirty years, but not much had changed. Most whites, North and South, believed more firmly than ever that black people belonged to an inferior race. In the South, this conviction sustained and justified a highly successful effort to keep black people economically and socially subordinated to white people. In the North, it justified widespread discrimination and permitted northerners to relegate blacks to the worst jobs and the poorest parts of town.

Looked at from another point of view, however, the era of Civil War and Reconstruction was one of unparalleled importance in the evolution of racial attitudes and race relations. Emancipation and Reconstruction did not bring genuine freedom to black people in the South, nor did they bring them equality before the law; but these were the essential preconditions for the winning of both. For all its limitations, freedom was better than slavery. Though persecuted and economically exploited during Reconstruction, black people in the South gained the right to move, to own land and money, and to gain an education; black women gained a measure of freedom from the sexual exploitation of southern white men. After emancipation, black people could begin to develop stable families, churches, and businesses. At last they could draw back, lick the wounds inflicted by slavery, gather their strength, and prepare for the day when the battle for equality could be joined again.

In the North, too, the Civil War and Reconstruction significantly affected the development of race relations and, ultimately, racial attitudes. For one thing, the war brought black men a much needed measure of pride and confidence. At a critical moment in the nation's life, they had given money and blood to preserve the Union and extend the range of liberty. White men might forget this fact, but black leaders would not, and the memory enhanced both their self-esteem and their claim to fair treatment in the United States. At the same time, the adoption of the Reconstruction amendments moved the struggle for racial equality to a new level. Before the war, black reformers had been forced to expend most of their energies in a vain attempt to persuade the North to abolish slavery and provide minimal civil rights for black people. Suddenly, with the ratification of the Fourteenth and Fifteenth Amendments, the Constitution became the ally of black people. After 1869, no one could say, as Chief Justice Roger Taney had in 1857, that black Americans were not United States citizens or that they were not entitled to civil and political equality. Even when southern violence and northern prejudice prevented the enforcement of laws designed to implement the amendments and the Supreme Court began to interpret them narrowly, the guarantees of citizenship were plainly incorporated in the basic law of the land. Consequently, black leaders could turn their attention to tactical questions and begin to devise methods for gaining in practice rights already granted in principle.

The era also significantly affected the long-range development of white attitudes. Though Reconstruction ultimately failed to establish a new civil and political order in the South, it did enable Republicans to include in the Constitution an indelible repudiation of racism—a fact of no small weight in a nation of Constitution worshipers. White men would long continue to discriminate against black men in clear violation of the Constitution, but the amendments were reminders that at a moment in the past white men had behaved toward black men in a way consonant with the democratic principles of the nation. The Reconstruction amendments rebuked succeeding generations and established a standard against which men of conscience would continue to measure themselves and their society. If the steps toward creating racial equality during the Civil War and Reconstruction turned out to be small ones, they were critically important, as first steps always are.

4

Found Cumbering the Soil

Manifest Destiny and the Indian in the Nineteenth Century[1]

PHILIP BORDEN

The Indian has never occupied a very positive niche in the American mind. From the beginning of settlement until the late nineteenth century, large numbers of white Americans thought of the Indian as little better than a benighted barbarian. Later, when the Indian had been removed as a threat and no longer competed with white men for land, Americans began to pity his state, but their characterization of him always remained negative.

In early colonial times only a few challenged the belief in the total depravity of the Indian. But for an increasing number, the image began to take on positive aspects as early as the beginning of the eighteenth century. This trend was strengthened by currents of European opinion. Enlightenment philosophers had begun to conceive of the Indian as noble in his bearing, as a natural, simple, and passionate being. The Indian was part of the environment, yet undeniably of the family of man. Although the characterization was favorable, it continued to picture the Indian as an alien. Europeans saw the Indian as a natural curiosity and often lamented that the conquest of nature would make his demise inevitable. To be sure,

[1] "Aborigines, n. Persons of little worth found cumbering the soil of a newly discovered country. They soon cease to cumber; they fertilize." Ambrose Bierce, "Devil's Dictionary," *Collected Works of Ambrose Bierce* (12 vols.; New York, 1909–1912), VII, p. 13.

American observers, particularly near the frontier, saw reason to give more attention to Indian barbarity and violence and to view English conquest with less regret. But the confidence of Americans in the unity of creation and a leaning toward a conception of nature as beneficent tended to neutralize objections to the European idea of the "noble savage."

Events of the nineteenth century altered the beliefs that shaped American actions toward the Indian. As always in American life, the mental picture of the Anglo-American was shaped less by Indian actions than by the needs of white culture. The need to expand, to assert their nationality, and to deal with other problems of race soon cast a shadow across the earlier more favorable image of the Indian. The nobility which some intellectuals had granted the Indian's character faded before 1840, as the Indian became a barrier to the extension of white life and culture. White Americans reasoned that for the welfare of the Indian, to say nothing of the safety of white frontiersmen, it was necessary to keep the Indian removed from civilized men. New waves of westward migration in the 1840s and 1850s broke up the so-called permanent Indian frontier, that area beyond the Mississippi River which had been promised to the Indian forever in the removal treaties of the 1830s. Removal came to mean the piecemeal penning of Indians. The basic picture of the savage Indian established in the seventeenth century was reinvoked until his culture was crushed. Not until the 1870s did the government officially recognize the Indian for what he had progressively become: not a member of a sovereign nation, but rather part of a dependent minority. At this point, it became safe for white Americans to consider the possibility of absorbing the Indian into their culture on a large scale. The Dawes Act of 1887 officially acknowledged that the Indian could assimilate only as the early immigrants had—by acquiring property and using it to build personal wealth and self-reliance. This attitude became the official government stance until the New Deal period.

During the nineteenth century, even the most concerned and "liberal" Americans had difficulty perceiving Indians as individuals with viable and widely varying cultures. Indians refused to participate in American values and aims, which were regarded by whites as indisputably superior. White Americans did not question their right to expand and to take their civilization with them. In their relationships with the Indians, they continued to stress the basic virtues of individualism, hard work, rationality, and assimilation. Confident of their own moral superiority, they rarely considered that the Indians had a culture worth preserving. Dedicated either to possessing the continent or to getting on with business, white Americans viewed Indians first as part of the wilderness to be cleared for civilization, then as wayward but dangerous children to be prepared for adulthood in the higher white culture through appropriate discipline.

Government Indian policy was a product of pressures from both sympathetic and hostile groups. Thus the federal government, with almost cyclical regularity, first punished Indians and then took steps to meliorate their suffering. Even at its best, government policy lacked sympathetic administration in Indian territories. And the best intended actions taken by the government were frequently based upon the needs of some mythical savages, rather than those of the real Indians. Whether motivated by pity or greed, white Americans established a record of almost uniform failure in dealing with Indians in the nineteenth century. The story of red-white relations became one of the growing dependence of the Indian upon white culture and his inability to sustain his own culture even when left alone. The destruction of so much of the unique Indian culture was not the necessary result of red and white confrontations, as many nineteenth-century Americans thought. It was rather a ramification of white ethnocentrism and technical superiority.

I

The imaginative literature of the nineteenth century provides clues to the problem of how the image of the Indian was formed and transformed. The picture of the Indian that emerged contained elements of nobility and savagery, combined with sexual overtones. It usually varied according to the distance of the observer from the scenes of white and red interaction.

The Indian bulked large in the quest of American intellectuals for an indigenous literature to testify to their nationhood. The attempt to develop cultural independence had characterized American literary output since the late eighteenth century. Many believed that an American literature would have to voice American themes and utilize American settings. These themes and settings included the Indian and the frontier as the most distinctive characteristics of American life. At the beginning of the nineteenth century, therefore, the Indian began to assume a prime place in American poetry, plays, and fiction. As a literary figure, he continued to increase in importance throughout the pre-Civil War period.

The dominant images in popular literary works and histories were negative or equivocal, although they often contained heroic overtones. Most Indian characters represented projections both of unfavorable aspects of white culture and favorable aspects of the American past. In both cases, they were wholly out of keeping with what little was known about the Indian himself. The images in historical literature, even when certified as "objective," were similarly distorted. Historian Francis Parkman, for example, found the Indian to be "man, wolf, and devil, all in one."[2] Parkman allowed the Indian a place in the prehistory of America; but after Euro-

[2] In William Brandon, "American Indians and American History," *American West,* 2 (1965), p. 16.

pean settlement, he saw the native only as an impediment to the higher destinies of Anglo-Saxon culture. Although he accused the novelists of the day like James Fenimore Cooper of creating unduly romantic images, Parkman's accounts were regarded as unduly harsh by more sympathetic literary figures, such as Herman Melville.

For the romantic intellectuals of the 1830s and 1840s, the pervasive view of Indian savagery often was tempered by their own passion for primitivism. Frequently, they retained a sense of the nobility of the savage because they did not always consider the progress of civilization and primitivism to be antithetical. Henry David Thoreau, in particular, attributed to the Indian precisely those qualities of harmony with nature, freedom from constraint, and simplicity in life which he feared civilization had squeezed out of men. Thoreau approached the Indian as an ethnologist and humanitarian. While he collected specimens of Indian culture, he foresaw the triumph of technological civilization and called upon the Indian to accommodate himself to it. Thoreau likened the civilization overtaking the Indian to the railroad overtaking his Walden. His trip into the woods was an attempt to capture for himself the peace, harmony, and self-sufficiency of the Indian spirit, just as his need to leave the woods anticipated their future. But even sympathetic thinkers like Thoreau did not deny Indian savagery; they only saw redeeming virtues in it.

To primitivism and savagery in the Indian's character were added sexual characteristics. Until about the 1830s, the Indian's image had no special sexual implications. Then novels and tales began to depict an Indian who symbolized forbidden sexuality. Perhaps this was because of the increased and prolonged red and white contacts. More likely, it related to changing beliefs among Americans linking sex with sin. The attitudes of many educated white men in the nineteenth century toward feminine purity and sexual aloofness created women who could not be sexually attractive to "decent" men and who could be "objects of lust" only for Negroes, outlaws, and Indians. Southern whites had for some time projected onto blacks sexual feelings they forbade themselves. Now white men of all sections projected their unfulfillable sexual desires onto Indians, seeing in them sexual aggressiveness and lust. There were other implicitly sexual themes in the literature of this era. Relationships among men in ambivalent sexual situations characterized the popular sea tale of the nineteenth century, and also the tale of the woods. In these isolated settings men existed without women and were unrestrained by traditional mores. In the tales of the woods, homosexual relationships were often symbolized as liaisons between shady characters. Constrained by the rules of polite society in the centers of culture, some white men sought male companionship in the woods or at sea—and often with Indians.

Cooper's portrayal of Natty Bumppo and Chingachgook illustrates several of these themes. Again and again Natty rejected feminine companionship in favor of "the woods" and his Indian companion. Much of Natty's strength was derived from his Indian characteristics. He was able to live in the woods like a natural man, though, fortunately, without losing his white, civilized nature. And Natty's dislike of effete eastern urban culture was related to his immersion in the Indian love for nature. Chingachgook was not only a good and honest friend, but a keen observer and a thinker whose cunning and loyalty aided his white companion on numerous occasions. However, even Cooper could not forgo a critical thrust at his most heroic Indian. For Chingachgook's savagery doomed him to a love of scalping and eventually to drink and degradation.

Because the savagery with which the Anglo-American invested the Indian extended to his sexuality, stories of Indian captivity had great popularity, as did novels warning against the evils of miscegenation. Narratives detailing the horror of being taken alive by Indians often were replete with infanticide and molestation. Interracial sex was more dreaded than capture in many instances. Perhaps this was because it often substituted a voluntary rejection of white values for the forced accommodation of unpredictable capture. Concern over miscegenation between whites and reds was far more intense in the nineteenth century than in earlier periods and paralleled the general increase of fear among white Americans about the nature of their sexuality and about the growing number of free Negroes in their midst.

Negative attitudes about miscegenation between reds and whites, absent in earlier times, were manifested now in forms reminiscent of the long-standing fears about white-black intercourse. Even William Gilmore Simms, like Thoreau one of the more judicious interpreters of Indian life, forced his most important Indian hero, Lenatewa, to become the victim of a mortal revenge as he knelt to propose to a white girl. Predictably, half-breeds, the products of interracial sex, had no place in either red of white culture. Their lot among "Savages, who know neither love nor delicacy," however, was easier than among whites who presumably knew both.[3] The fact that they were of mixed blood should have placed their status in white society between reds and whites. That they were held in lower esteem than Indians themselves reveals much about white guilt concerning miscegenation.

The fear of the white man, made Indian by mixed marriage or voluntary association, and the general evocation of the Indian as a bloodthirsty brute were perhaps most typically expressed in Robert Montgomery Bird's popular novel of the mid-century, *Nick of the Wood; or the Jibbenainosay.* Bird painted the Indian in stark colors of animality. He allowed no human hues or shadings in his portraits. Not only did the Indian initiate horrifying attacks, tortures, and captures, but his lack of character also led him to

[3] Pierre-Antoine Tabeau, in Wilcomb E. Washburn, ed., *The Indian and the White Man* (New York, 1964), p. 91.

participate as a willing tool in the schemes of lustful whites. The interest of the book does not center upon the portrait of the Indian, which was negative, unrealistic, and wooden, so much as it does upon the images of the whites.

Bird's whites were photographic negatives of the reds. Their brutality and hatred of the Indians was excused by the atmosphere of Indian savagery which they breathed. All of the characters perceived, if dimly, the vague sexual threat hanging over women and children in frontier communities. The center of interest, however, was not a sexual symbol, but a symbol of Christian peace and love. He was Nick of the Woods, or Bloody Nathan Slaughter, a wandering Quaker peddler known to Indians and frontiersmen as a biblical fool. Bloody Nathan had earned his facetious nickname because of his refusal to resort to violence under any conditions, even Indian attack.

As Quaker Nathan led a party of whites through the woods, into and out of Indian clutches, they continually discovered evidence of the Jibbenainosay, a "spirit that walks" named by the Indians. The Jibbenainosay always appeared when Indians threatened a community. He always left as evidence of his visit a dead Indian with a tomahawk buried in his head and a cross carved in his chest. The Jibbenainosay's acts were not simply murders. They epitomized the wrath of a Christian and civilized nation; for the Jibbenainosay killed the Indian with the savage's own weapon and then engraved the corpse with the dominant symbol of white civilization.

Of course the Jibbenainosay turned out to be none other than Nathan Slaughter. Bloody Nathan had assumed a dual role in order to avenge the earlier massacre of his family by Indians. In the climax of the story, Nathan not only wrought vengeance upon the perpetrator of the original bloody deed with an uncontrolled frenzy that clove "skin, cartilage, and even bone," but then reverted to a savage himself, leading a posse of whites in the complete devastation of an Indian village.[4] Psychologically maimed by the slaughter of his loved ones before his eyes, Nathan had responded in a just way. Christian by day, avenger by night, he dealt the savages a civilizing blow they could understand. The Christian avenger was not a criminal but a hero for Bird and his readers.

Although Bird lived on the Kentucky frontier, he wrote for easterners. The image which his work and that of other novelists evoked was modified by the observations of missionaries and traders. Missionary efforts were as old as the Massachusetts Bay Colony and in the nineteenth century involved large expenditures by private groups and the federal government. The reform impulse of the first third of the nineteenth century threw wave after wave of missionaries into the wilderness to preach Christianity to the Indian, to effect lightning conversions, and to found schools. After

---

[4] Robert Montgomery Bird, *Nick of the Woods; or the Jibbenainosay* (New York, 1853), p. 359.

the missionary effort declined, the government continued to attempt to reconcile the Indian to his fate by religion.

Missionary efforts, despite small successes, were disappointing. Before 1840, this was due to the exalted expectations and confused purposes of the missionaries, their focus on immediate results, and their failure to realize that in order to achieve success they had not merely to inform and awaken their Indian listeners, but also to recognize their widely divergent cultural tendencies. Even if the Indians could overcome their breeding, however, they rarely could overcome their image among whites, so conversion availed them little. A second period of intense missionary activity followed the Civil War. It too collapsed primarily because of the hostility of the United States Army and the Catholic Church. Throughout, missionaries were handicapped in trying to come to grips with the problems of Indian conversion by the fear and pity that characterized the white attitude toward the Indian. Even had the missionaries been better prepared, however, the hunger for land that characterized frontier life would have ensured the failure of Indian assimilation.

Though their success in proselytizing Indians was small, missionaries did influence the eastern image of the Indian. Many missionaries furnished sympathetic and sensitive accounts of Indian society. One example was the Moravian, John Heckewelder, a figure of the transition period from the eighteenth to the nineteenth centuries, who wrote an admiring and detailed analysis of the life of the Delawares. He related their hunting culture to the primitive communism of their lives and, while regretting their refusal to adopt Christianity, he frequently praised their character. Heckewelder believed that the Delawares lived their lives as decently as heathens might, and that in many ways they were more virtuous than most Christians. Heckewelder's accounts, along with those of the ethnologist-geologist, Henry Rowe Schoolcraft, furnished inspiration and concrete evidence for literary artists like Henry Wadsworth Longfellow and James Fenimore Cooper, who used them to construct poems, novels, and fantasies albeit without Heckewelder's or Schoolcraft's sense of responsibility to the Indians themselves.

Traders comprised another group with considerable Indian contact. By and large, since the eighteenth century they had carried into the forest every traditional myth relating to the noble savage. But the myths were quickly shattered. The more "generous" the image was at the outset, the greater the modification life on the frontier usually brought. Lewis O. Saum, in *The Fur Trader and the Indian,* notes that a number of observers did not reserve all of their criticism for the Indians, but lavished it on whites as well. They found the intermingling of civilizations mutually destructive. They measured this devolution in terms of the rising number of half-breeds, increased drinking and promiscuity, and sharp trading.

Intensely practical men, the fur traders came to see the Indian as a man motivated by self-interest, but one who failed rationally to follow self-interest through to a prudential and work-oriented style of life. The Indian ate when hungry, did not save, followed his impulses, worked no more than necessary, remained passive and incurious, and cared little for personal hygiene. The fur trader found these characteristics offensive, threatening, and difficult to understand. Not acculturated to them from an early age like the Indian captives, he was far less willing to reject the advantages of civilization in favor of Indian life. Like most Americans, he tended to judge the Indian in terms of white values and to find him wanting. The fur trader preferred to separate civility from civilization and, like many missionaries, to find in Indian "culture" only a veil for wilder traits.

Traders, however, almost universally acknowledged one positive Indian characteristic: the dignity and nobility with which the Indian carried himself. By and large, this was seen as a result of his comfort in nature and his reserved character. Not only fur traders, but often easterners identified a dignified demeanor as an Indian characteristic. Drunkenness among Indians particularly disgusted observers because the dignity of the Indian's bearing was the focus of so much of the white respect he achieved. Alcohol led the Indian to a complete personal disregard, uncharacteristic debauchery, and, ultimately, loss of the elevated carriage that was his most positive characteristic in the white mind.

The relative unity of the white American image of the native obscured the fact that Indian personality and culture were far from monolithic. Personality variations among Indians were considerable. Indian cultures varied substantially from area to area, and even from tribe to tribe. Complex patterns of tribal interaction and hostility sometimes had nothing to do with the white man. That such a uniform interpretation of "the Indian" emerged, signifies more about the qualities of the observers than the observed.

The general image of the Indian as a nomad, for instance, fitted well the attributes of savagery whites gave him. However, as accurate description it applied loosely only to a minority of Indians, and absolutely only to some of the Plains Indians with whom Americans experienced large-scale contact only after the image had been formed. Similarly, beliefs about Indian religion, the role of women, tribal democracy, and competition did not correspond with the realities of hundreds of tribes spread over thousands of miles of extremely varied terrain.

The tribe itself often was an artificial unit which was culturally and socially, rather than politically, significant. Among many groups tribal meetings were infrequent. Rarely was it legitimate for a chief or any other tribal officer or unit to give away land. Chiefs were often temporary officers, elected not for purposes of political policy but out of respect or for religious or other attributes. Even the social hierarchy in Indian groups, thought to relate to the abilities of warriors, often was related to other qualities, such as religion, hunting ability, or, in some cases, wealth. The clan and other family groupings, the secret society, and other hunting and warring groups most frequently formed the core of Indian social and political life. Moreover, a dominant belief among most Indian tribes was that nature and land were a common wealth and belonged to God alone. Land was not the possession of tribes, clans, or individuals, and could not be transferred by human actions such as treaties. Ultimately, government officials dealt with fictional Indian leaders and bargained for objects which the leaders often did not consider they owned. This was especially the case with the nomadic tribes, who believed that they had the right to follow their livelihood wherever it led them, and whose "need" for territory was far greater than that of "civilized" farmers. But the idea of firm tribes and chiefs was convenient for a rapacious land policy, and so it was taken as the norm. Thus, even if land treaties had not been unfairly negotiated, they would have failed to stay Indian wrath because until after the Civil War they were inconsistent with the values of the Indians themselves.

The list of myths that confused the nineteenth-century picture of the Indian was as long as Indian life was rich and varied. Indian personality and society were as complex, varied, and self-sustained as white. But American society, preoccupied with economic growth and westward expansion, and certain of its superiority, could only stereotype the Indian who stood in the way.

II

The early years of the nineteenth century, which saw the image of the Indian in the white mind take on characteristics of unmitigated savagery, were also years of tremendous confidence, optimism, individualism, and expansion in American life. The negative image of the Indian was dramatized against the background of a stridently nationalistic and expansive white culture. Until the issue of Negro slavery increasingly forced its way into the American mind, the national mood reflected the belief that the obstacles to reform were minor, that there was little Americans could not accomplish if they set their minds to it. The revivalist sects and renewed missionary vigor, as well as the numerous political action, utopian and religious community experiments testified to the restless optimism of American life and the belief that the perfect society could be built by virtuous individuals. Moreover, beginning with the era of large-scale expansion to the West following the War of 1812 and aided by developments in travel and communications, Americans began to feel that it was their ordained fate to inhabit the continent from east to west. By the mid-1840s the idea had a label—Manifest Destiny—and became an important part of American life and politics. Americans also possessed a sense of the inevitable progress of their civilization and its role in the world at large. There was little feeling for reds or blacks except as they presented obstacles to the idea of progress.

The negative image of the Indian and growing white self-confidence implied to many that the Indian, like the frontier itself, must be cleared in order to extend American values. Similarly, many believed that the progress of American civilization itself cured social ills. Unable to expand without confronting Indians, Americans rationalized their removal to remote places. Unable to cope with the complexities of reconciliation between the white and red races or to understand the physical needs and cultural qualities of the civilizations they opposed, Americans preferred to trust to the progress of time to solve the problem, or to hope that the problem would simply disappear.

The arguments justifying Indian removal were not based upon avarice alone. A few eastern congressmen and intellectuals wished to remove Indians from the presence of whites in order to preserve the integrity of the more primitive Indian culture. The paradoxical combination of self-interest and humanitarian support for the policy of removal reflected a tension in the American mind between the virtues of the frontier wilderness and those of civilization—a tension which was being resolved in favor of civilization. Despite the veneration of Indian culture and dislike of frontier opportunism by sympathetic easterners, so long as they regarded purging savagery as a precondition for the triumph of civilization, their ideology made the Indian expendable and aided speculators, homesteaders, and expansionists. The image of uncivilized, aggressive Indians obscured the thin line between interest and ideology.

Americans saw themselves as the inevitable inheritors of the continent. At best, the removal of Indians from their path was a way of buying time until Americans could afford to meet frontier racial problems. It was analogous to the desire of slave breeders and white liberals to solve southern racial problems by returning freed blacks to Africa. At worst, and despite its motives, removal had the effect of a genocidal attack upon Indians. Expansion and removal were factors in the same equation. Insofar as the former remained an unchallenged assumption, the Indian was foredoomed.

The unofficial policy of Indian removal antedated the official Indian Removal Act of 1830. It developed with the rapid expansion of the national domain. The earliest federal policy was cognizant of the Indian's plight. Henry Knox, Secretary of War under the Continental Congress and later in Washington's Cabinet, foresaw the need to deal fairly with the Indian as an alternative to destroying him. From time to time before the Louisiana Purchase, other national politicians attempted to interpret the commerce clause of the Constitution so as to regulate Indian trade and relations, especially where liquor was concerned. However, much of the official good will was negated because the power of enforcement often was left in the hands of local authorities. Through the early nineteenth century, the federal government continued to empower territorial governors to superintend Indian affairs. Because governors were often appointed in return for political services, were sometimes land speculators themselves, and determined their policies according to the needs of their white constituents, the most enlightened national policies would have been imperiled. Furthermore, national policy was benevolent only infrequently, and under the guise of securing the borders of the United States, treaties often were imposed on frontier Indian by force.

The idea of removal began with Thomas Jefferson. The Louisiana Purchase tested Jefferson's Indian principles as it tested his Constitutional ones. The Purchase brought large numbers of Indian tribes under United States authority, and Jefferson early began to think in terms of transporting them across the Mississippi River for the good of all involved. Along with his Constitutional amendment enabling purchase, Jefferson submitted to Congress another amendment authorizing the purchase of several parcels of land then in Indian hands. Both failed. Jefferson instructed Indian agents to persuade tribes to move. When a Cherokee delegation "marched on Washington" in 1808 with the request that they be allowed to stay and purchase their lands from the government, Jefferson strongly voiced his preference for removal. Nevertheless, Jefferson, and Madison after him, took only tentative steps in the direction of removal. Neither was willing to commit force to the project of Indian relocation, although they sometimes tacitly sanctioned it among the territorial governors. This created an unpredictable policy and a series of potentially volatile border situations. Some governors, especially in the South, were moderate in Indian affairs. But others, like William Henry Harrison of the Indiana Territory, were unscrupulous in their land dealings and overbearing in their use of armed pressure. Thus, before the War of 1812, removal was an ideology but not an official policy. With local exceptions, it was not pushed vigorously. Red-white relations were not therefore calm. The increasing number of migrants, unchecked by federal restraints, frequently applied extralegal pressures on the Indians, who replied with violence of their own.

The War of 1812 was a turning point. American rhetoric of conquest and expansion, coupled with rising levels of tension in frontier areas made the Indian especially receptive to British promises of protection. Many tribes, though not all of them, joined the British. In return the British promised to protect Indians from American depredations and to establish an official and independent Indian state as a buffer between its more westerly holdings and the United States. But before the war concluded it became obvious that the British were both unwilling and unable to make good their pledges. In disillusionment, some Indians began slipping back to the American side or fading into political neutrality. In 1815, the Treaty of Ghent ending the war delivered the Indians into the hands of the Americans.

With the postwar tide of migration to the West rising sharply, with American confidence growing, and with the need to detach the Indian from the British now ended, the national pressure for Indian removal intensified. Moreover, white Americans could now use Indian support for the British in the war as a justification for any kind of postwar policy.

Equally important, the folklore of the war created new heroes whose fortunes were bound up with Indian fighting. One of the most significant of these was Andrew Jackson, who participated in several bloody Indian battles and emerged from the war with a wide reputation as a brutal and implacable Indian foe. With Jackson, and later William Henry Harrison, elected partly as a result of their frontier and anti-Indian images, and with governors frequently campaigning on anti-Indian platforms, little in the way of evenhanded justice might be anticipated by the tribal chief.

Although the violent situation of border hostility did not change after the war, Presidents Monroe and Adams and the Congress all became more receptive to a policy of large-scale removal. While they still did not employ it as the sole solution to the "Indian problem," increasing numbers of tribes found themselves pressed to sell their land and move beyond the reaches of "civilization." The pressure came from Indian agents and superintendents charged by the federal government to make treaties. Adams had used the federal treaty power judiciously but widely and insisted on equity in treaty negotiations.

Despite Adams' reluctance, enough Indian removal treaties had been negotiated by the time of Jackson's inauguration to leave the area east of the Mississippi River largely free of Indians and to make removal the dominant fact of American Indian life. Without a strong federal law to restrain states and localities, many treaties were negotiated locally. Adams intervened on behalf of the Creeks in Georgia, for example, but was ignored by both the governor and his own federal marshals.

By the end of Monroe's presidency removal had become official government policy. In 1823, Secretary of War John C. Calhoun officially recommended the purchase of Indian land in the East, the clearing of lands west of the Mississippi, and the removal of Indians there at government expense. In Calhoun's view, Indian interests must be guarded, but "our opinion, and not theirs, ought to prevail, in measures intended for their civilization and happiness." He knew that ultimately a policy "less vigorous may protract, but cannot arrest their fate."[5]

Calhoun hoped and believed that after a suitable period of separation and education for civilization, the Indian's savagery would be sufficiently diminished to permit him to live among white men in peace. At the same time as he began to put his ideas on removal into practice, Calhoun secured

[5] In Laurence F. Schmeckbier, *The Office of Indian Affairs; Its History, Activities, and Organization* (Baltimore, 1927), p. 59.

the establishment of a Bureau of Indian Affairs within the War Department to replace and broaden the duties of its outmoded and understaffed Superintendent of Indian Trade. Although the bureau was still drastically undermanned, L. M. McKenney, who continued in office, was a talented administrator and was able to bring some rationality to the chaotic land purchases of the preceding years.

This hesitant beginning to official Indian relocation became rigorous policy under President Andrew Jackson. The crux of the issue as it passed to Jackson was not simply Indian removal but the use of coercion in Indian removal. The process of removal had been approved in principle by all of his predecessors in the nineteenth century. It was now an accomplished fact with the exception of one area in the old Northwest and several areas in the South.

Jackson voiced his views on the Indian question in his first annual message. Despite a conciliatory tone, he urged that the few "savages" inhabiting American lands must give way to the 12 million Americans already blessed with civilization. He reshuffled the Bureau of Indian Affairs, and rid himself of bureaucrats and politicians who would oppose his plan of removal by any means. Heretofore the treaty process had called for agreement in principle between the government and Indians, followed by government purchase of Indian lands, provision of a new territory in which to settle, and assistance in moving. The Jackson administration regularized this process, but also unofficially sanctioned chicanery, intimidation, and bribery in land purchases, and inadequately funded removal procedures and provisions. The administration often left the process in the hands of military rather than civilian authorities. The result was sometimes outright destruction, as in the case of the Winnebagos; sometimes futile resistance, as in the case of the Sac and Fox; and sometimes decimation in moving, as in the case of the Creeks.

In formulating a policy, Jackson reacted to political pressure from the South, an area of strong support for his candidacy. In the South, the issue of Indian removal often was tied to land speculation, especially when the territories upon which the Indians were living were known to contain valuable minerals. Of the tribes that offered special problems in removal during Jackson's administration, only the Sac and Fox were in the North. The Creek, Choctaw, Chickasaw, and Cherokee nations all lived in the midst of southern civilization. The Seminoles also lived in the South, but in less habitable and cultivated regions.

Removal of the Cherokee was not the most brutal and bloody example of relocation but it represented best the marriage of frontier convenience and Indian myth. Jackson had based the rationale for his policy on the assumptions that Indians were savages, that cultivation defined land ownership, and that Indians were independent nations requiring treaty negotiation. According to each of these assumptions, the Cherokee should not have been removed. If by savages was meant a hunting society, or one practicing "pre-Christian" or bloody rites, the Cherokee were the least savage of American Indians. They had been the focus of intense missionary work and comprised a more largely—though unevenly—Christianized body than almost any other tribe. They were settled and pursued a farming existence. Furthermore, they had gathered many of the trappings of success in terms of the white work ethic: they held numerous black slaves, they possessed a school system of note, they were economically prosperous, they were peaceful.

The Cherokee were not unaware of their precarious position in the South. Foreseeing a fate similar to other southern tribes moved off their land by fraud and coercion, Cherokee leaders met on July 4, 1827, to draft a constitution as a separate nation. But the inauguration of Jackson, together with the discovery of gold on Cherokee land, doomed the tribe to the usual fate. The state of Georgia promptly passed laws nullifying all treaty obligations with the Indians and creating for the Cherokee a series of restrictive and humiliating laws similar to the Black Codes. Then it proceeded to open Cherokee territories to speculation. A Cherokee appeal to the Supreme Court in 1832 was heard by Justice John Marshall. Marshall dismissed the Cherokee claim, ruling that Indians could not sue in federal court. In a decision of the next year, however, Marshall upheld an earlier removal view. He insisted that as "domestic dependent nations," the Cherokee land claim must be treated with respect by the United States and that Georgia could not extend its jurisdiction by setting aside that of the United States or the Indian nation. Jackson refused to enforce the decision and in so doing invited intruders into Indian lands with government blessing.

Following the Marshall decision, the Jackson administration decided that for its legal protection and as an official mandate, the government needed Congressional approval of its policy of transferring Indians west. At Jackson's recommendation, Congress passed the Removal Act in 1830, thus formalizing government policy and providing a firmer framework for tribal relocation. Although it greatly accelerated the pace of resettlement, the law was an incident in the process of removal, not its starting point. What followed in the 1830s was a policy of land purchase, eviction, and resettlement for Indians. In this plan, land titles were extinguished and Indians from all areas of the East were pushed beyond the Mississippi. The policies of Jackson, and after him, Martin Van Buren, coupled with the ambiguity of the Marshall decisions and numerous "overlooked" private encroachments on Indian lands, led to several Indian wars in addition to general removal and to the division and reduction of some of the most "advanced" Indian tribes.

In leaving office, Jackson apparently was tweaked by conscience. He sounded the note that was to dominate the imagery, if not the action, of later presidents. Jackson apologized for the "abhorrent business" of removal, although he admitted that he was pleased that Indian "savages" had been "saved from the degradation and destruction to which they were rapidly hastening." He was certain that the "philanthropist will rejoice that the remnant of that ill-fated race has at length been placed beyond the reach of injury and oppression"[6] The alteration was verbal only. It did not end the removal policy. It indicated only Jackson's sensitivity to liberal opinion in the East. To be sure, the willful deception practiced by the federal, state, and local governments in the 1830s in defrauding Creeks, the slaughters of the Black Hawk War of 1832, and, later, the incredible hardships of the Cherokee, Chickasaw, Choctaw, Creek, and Seminole, who died by the thousands on the "trail of tears" from the southeastern states to Oklahoma, did not go unprotested. Some eastern intellectuals, missionaries, and congressmen, while approving of the principle of removal for the protection of the Indian, were sickened by government excesses. But their protest, no matter how principled, accepted many of the familiar assumptions about the Indian as an obstacle to civilization. Therefore they were ineffective intellectually, and in any case failed to touch the interest motives of the frontier. As stated by Lewis Cass, a territorial governor for eighteen years and Secretary of War under Jackson after 1831, according to the American way, the Indian had a right to be defrauded. His department, Cass explained, could offer the Indian no protection.

The policies of Indian removal were markedly successful for whites in the short run. They eliminated Indians from the states of the Union. But the problem of racial adjustment could not be solved by sending one party to the dispute away. Eventually whites and reds would have to come into contact again. When they did, the Indians would harbor bitter memories and deep hostility. Indians would not be so easily taken a second time. In effect, Indian removal left the problem of white adjustment to the existence of Indians for succeeding generations and administrations to solve.

III

No sudden or dramatic shifts in the white image of Indians occurred in the Civil War era, nor did government policies deviate basically from patterns established in the Jacksonian period. However, the stability in Indian affairs, so desired in Jackson's time, did not endure. The uneasy settlement of the 1830s and 1840s degenerated rapidly into a series of new and more desperate conflicts as the nation approached civil war. Although the typical conception of the Indian did not change in substance, the new outbreak of hostilities intensified the belief in his savagery.

In 1840, when the permanent Indian frontier had been established,

[6] In Edward Pessen, *Jacksonian America: Society, Personality, and Politics* (Homewood, Ill., 1969), p. 322.

the territory of the United States extended to the lines of the Louisiana Purchase. By 1848, almost a million and a quarter square miles of land had been added to the domain of the United States. Within a decade after the completion of the removal of the Indian from the East, the discovery of gold and increasingly liberal settlement laws began to bring a wave of white invaders. The trickle of fortune seekers and speculators of the 1840s soon grew into a torrent of permanent settlers. In the decade of the 1850s, the population west of the Mississippi doubled. With the invasion of speculators, miners, ranchers, and farmers, the process of negotiation with tribal leaders for lands promised Indians *in perpetuum* began anew. On the near frontier and far, under the promises of new cessions and threats of war, Indians yielded up lands. In Kansas in the 1850s, Indians gave up almost nine-tenths of their territory. In California, in 1851 alone, 119 tribes were deprived of half their lands by a series of extortionate treaties.

Land hunger aside, there were other events contributing to the new wave of Indian misfortune before the Civil War. The first of these was disease. Four severe epidemics swept the plains between 1830 and 1860. The depopulation and debilitation they caused at a time when the number of whites in the West was multiplying impaired the ability of Indians to withstand the influx of homesteaders. A second factor was the intertribal rivalry generated among Indians by the relocation of eastern red men. The first invasion of the Plains Indians' territories and those of the more sedentary southwestern Indians in the 1830s and 1840s was by other Indians, not whites. Often the result was increased internal tension among western Indians who were warlike even before the newcomers' arrival. At first, it was white policy, not white presence, that forced Indians into a self-destructive situation.

An additional factor affecting the Indians of the Plains was the technological advance of white civilization. The railroads began to push westward in the 1840s. By the 1850s, the federal government was aiding them through land grants. This caused not only an increase in speculation and pre-emption of property, but also reinforced white convictions regarding the superiority of their civilization in general. Combined with the more nomadic and aggressive qualities of the Plains Indians, the "technology gap" accentuated the differences between white civilization and red "barbarism." White superiority in weaponry also took its toll in the chase after the buffalo. Under the gun of the white hunter, herds began to diminish. Responding to white demand for skins, the Indians themselves contributed to the extinction of the buffalo. With the demise of the buffalo, Indian civilization based upon the herds began to find its existence threatened. And the shortened food supply increased conflicts among Indian tribes and clans.

The press of white migration often split tribes and fragmented the Indian territory into smaller reserves dotted between outposts of white civilization. As a consequence of this latest episode in the long history of the uprooting of Indian society and the transportation to new and often hostile environments, the number of established tribes decreased. In the process of continual migration Indian population declined to about a third its size in colonial times. No less staggering were the human costs of readapting to new modes of living. Each new relocation brought the Indians to more isolated and less productive areas. The dwindling food supply and increased competition for it further eroded tribal independence. White diseases and liquor completed the cycle of destruction. By the time of the Civil War, not only had the territorial integrity of the Indian been threatened, but also his very survival. By the 1850s few tribes could get along without white technology, money, and amenities, so completely had their own cultures been transformed. Large numbers had been reduced to the status of indigent camp followers.

But, if some Indians hovered around the settlement camps and wagon trains to panhandle, others dogged them to kill. This posed a much more serious military problem than had eastern Indian aggression before the presidency of Andrew Jackson, although given the technical, economic, and population inequalities between white and red cultures, the eventual victory of white America was never in doubt. In the East, white population had usually been more dense. Often it was the Indian who was surrounded by hostile whites. Also, the distances necessary to move troops to the areas of conflict were relatively short. In the West, the problem was almost the opposite. The white population was sparse and its lines of communication were often delicate. In the era of the Civil War there were almost as many white settlements as there were available troops to protect them. The question of how to guard settlements was difficult. The best over-all policy for saving lives, as well as the most humane and logical, was federal control of expansion, and the first governmental response to the manifold problems of frontier expansion was a half-hearted attempt to restrain the pace of settlement. It did not work. Whites poured into the West with or without treaties, with or without government sanction, in spite of the warnings from Washington and the lack of legal justification. Unprepared and unwilling to employ force against migrating citizens, the federal government turned to the army, which settled the problem tactically. It devised a system of permanent forts, from which troops conducted periodic punitive raids against the Indians. Still, the awesome mobility of the Plains Indians often reduced the effectiveness of the policy. In the end, the military solution to the problem of racial adjustment of the 1850s and 1860s was no better than the removal policy of the Jacksonian era.

The fragmentation and instability of Indian life increased after the Civil War. With white homesteaders streaming in and more troops free to engage the Indians, the Indian war became a common feature of western history. The conflict between settlers and Indians in the 1860s and 1870s was simply the inevitable outcome of the history of the preceding years. The Indian response was shaped by the original removal, which led toward the annihilation of the Indian once the Mississippi River was crossed by white settlers. It was reinforced by the floods of white migrants who preempted the areas into which retreat was possible. For a half-century Indians had been under the most concentrated form of economic and cultural assault. The uprisings of the powerful southwestern tribes, the raids by the superior Sioux, and the pitiful flight of the sedentary Indians completed the pattern. Threatened with extinction, cut off from retreat, robbed of pride, the Indian assumed the role white men had earlier assigned to him— that of the savage attacker.

Each act of Indian resistance or reprisal was countered by increased force. By the decade of the 1870s, the sporadic outbursts in the mountain areas and farther west escalated into almost total confrontation. But with the exceptions of Indian victories which led to the closing of the Bozeman Trail in Montana in 1868, and the massacre of the troops of George A. Custer in 1876, all major battles were won by the United States Army. Numerous brutal raids by vigilante groups in retaliation for Indian murders and supply thefts magnified the effects of the major military victories. By the end of Reconstruction, the plains had been brought under white control. The year 1877 saw both the death of Crazy Horse, whose feared Ogalala Sioux tribes had formed one of the last, staunchest, and fiercest pockets of resistance, and the resignation of Chief Joseph of the Nez Perce to "fight no more, forever."[7]

Before the outbreak of Indian resistance to the new white encroachments in the 1860s, the humanitarian sentiment of the Northeast was divided and ambivalent. Those who did not favor expansion for political reasons tended to criticize the policy of removal. Missionaries from New England and other areas in the East were often strong supporters of the Indians, urging them to resist removal and clamoring for their rights in Congress and from the pulpit. One of the most active Indian supporters was Bishop M. B. Whipple, who lived among the tribes in Minnesota, oversaw treaties, initiated petitions and inquiries, and wrote of his life with Indians. But his sentiments were by no means widely shared, even among missionary groups. And in the ranks of political liberals concern was something less. For the most part, after removal had been accomplished in the 1840s, humanitarian interest in the East faded and shifted to more pressing social issues such as Negro slavery. In some instances, pro-Indian sentiment vanished entirely. Thus, in Lincoln's campaign for the presidency, William Seward, a leading radical and soon to be Lincoln's Secretary of

---

[7] In Margot L. T. Astrov, ed., *American Indian Prose and Poetry* (New York, 1962), p. 87.

State, called for the removal of the five civilized tribes from Kansas to a more westerly point in order to promote the organization of the territory. Popular attitudes often were not even this enlightened. Easterners eagerly awaited news of excitement along the Indian frontier. Grossly exaggerated stories of clash and gore often received more notice in eastern newspapers than in western ones. Meanwhile the Bureau of Indian Affairs remained ineffectual in controlling events on the borders, despite the organization of a Board of Commissioners to strengthen it administratively and its symbolic shift in 1849 from the War Department to the newly organized Department of the Interior.

Several changes in attitude and policy toward the Indian as a savage could be noted in the period from 1840 to 1870, though they did not substantially alter the image which underlay the established popular, legal, and even humanitarian views. The first involved mostly the southwestern Indians and reflected a tacit recognition of the differences among tribes. Whereas in many ways the Plains Indians fitted the earlier stereotypes of the Indian as hunter and warrior, the Pueblos and other tribes of the Southwest were far more permanent, settled, and territorially oriented than even the "civilized" Cherokee. The differences became reflected in a separation in thought between "civilized" and "savage" Indians. White Americans applied the category of "civilized" to certain kinds of Indians who either did not rebel or were attached to farming and other ways of life which roughly conformed to their own. Such a distinction rarely restrained settlers from invading Indian lands. When the itch of expansion got too strong, civilized Indians, like uncivilized ones, were victimized. Among southwestern Indians, too, missionary efforts were far weaker. The Spanish already had proselytized among them, and with railroads capturing the nations' imagination, Americans more frequently equated their civilizing mission with technological rather than religious activity.

A second change occurring after the Civil War was the reform of federal Indian policy. The government response to escalating border conflict in the Civil War era was a combination of increased troop commitment and, for the first time, serious and persistent inquiry into the causes of tension. The findings of the first major study by a joint committee of Congress, made public in 1867, were unambiguous. The report noted the alarming trend toward the extinction of Indians, placed the blame for Indian wars "in most cases" upon "the aggressions of lawless White men," condemned in strong terms the local administration of policy by agents of the Bureau of Indian Affairs who were political hacks and self-interested speculators, and called for a strong independent board of overseers to visit the Indian territories and make certain that Indian rights were protected.[8] Despite the unequiv-

---

[8] Schmeckbier, *The Office of Indian Affairs,* pp. 50–51.

ocal nature of the report, the government found it possible only to study the problem further. Meanwhile, on all measures of appropriations or Bureau requests, Congress stalled. It was clear that despite the recommendations of the committee, Congress was not in a mood to be "soft on Indians."

In an atmosphere of increasing popular anger over Indian reprisals, of growing concern by a few over the demoralization and destruction of the Indian, and of Congressional equivocation, Ulysses S. Grant was inaugurated. Much impressed by the need to civilize the Indian with missionary rather than frontier methods, he initiated a reform policy. He established an Indian Peace Commission of prominent private and public citizens, began to clean up the local Indian agencies, let more control of Indian affairs at the all-important local level slip into the hands of missionary groups, and increased expenditures for Indian education. Grant was a military man as well as a Christian, however, and as he expanded the role of missionaries, he also made a larger place for the military. He used the army to rationalize local administration, and troops as an arm of policy. His position represented the ambivalence of the era. In the end, Grant's use of missionary groups accomplished little and his support from Congress was so small that he ended up doing too little too late to stop frontier massacres. Nonetheless, the small steps taken by Grant were evidences of a more humane Indian policy than any since the turn of the century.

With border hostilities at a high pitch in 1871, Grant sought again to solve the Indian problem. Reacting to the pressure that Grant and a handful of eastern senators brought to bear, Congress enacted a new Indian Appropriations Act, whose wording officially brought to an end the era of treatymaking. It rejected the notion of independent Indian nations capable of making treaties. While declaring support for all treaties already in effect, it at last recognized the reliance of the Indian on white civilization and undertook to make national policy adhere to it. Although it was an important turning point, the Appropriations Act shared the ambiguity of the previous steps taken by President Grant. On the one hand, it ended treaty negotiations; on the other, by making the Indian a dependent, it reinforced his alienation from the legal processes. The Appropriations Act of 1871 did not indicate a major elevation in the status of the Indian *vis-à-vis* white society. Instead, it was a recognition of the rent fabric of Indian culture and independence, the signal of changing attitudes that hereafter would become more tolerant, and an indication of the widely held belief among whites that assimilation into their culture was the price for the full benefits of citizenship. By 1871, the ideology of preparation for citizenship in white society was replacing that of cultural separation between white and red societies. This theme was to become characteristic of the next period of Indian-American relations.

IV

Although skirmishing in the West continued into the 1880s, belief in Indian victory was not possible. Centuries of white and red conflict had proven that the Indian was not an unbreakable man. Having defeated him, civilization could live with him. For white Americans to continue to conceive of the Indian now as pure savage was inconsistent with the Indian's dependency and might prove frustrating to conciliatory attempts. To find nobility, aloofness, or independence in the shabby remnants of his life was difficult. Both the "noble savage" and "savage beast" had been destroyed. Only the Indian as humbled victim was consistent with Americans' belief in their own power and generosity. Thus the Indian became for many Americans a willful child capable of maturity only through strict upbringing and kindly aid. The battles of the 1860s and 1870s and white possession of the continent had freed Americans once more to romanticize about the Indian, to pity him, and to lay plans for his final enclosure and absorption.

Hence official government policy endorsed protection of Indian interests, by keeping Indian reservations away from the main lines of white settlement; maintenance of complete control over Indian affairs through appointed agents; and treatment of cooperating Indians on reservations as helpless wards. Numerous programs provided food, education, and miscellaneous forms of aid. All were designed to support the Indian in mastering the complexities of white culture as he proceeded toward full citizenship. Detracting from the new policy was the fact that full citizenship was not offered, but only promised. The distribution of rations and subsidies, moreover, still was presided over by local agents, who, with the waning of the original reform impulse, were less frequently missionaries, or men in sympathy with the Indian's plight. In a few years the effectiveness of the system was once more impaired by corruption. Treaties were ended, but agreements over land rights continued in other forms. The Indian still was not given legal recognition, and with few exceptions, tribes and chiefs remained the units with which white Americans bargained and dealt. Since 1854, inducements of land had been offered to individual Indians, but only in exchange for leaving the tribe and abandoning tribal identities. This was a more subtle form of torture than removal, for it made denial of heritage the cost of viable existence. As false as had been the prior view of the tribe as a political unit, the notion that the individual Indian would reject his cultural roots for land was almost equally unrealistic. Yet it was this policy which eventually was extended to all Indians in 1887.

As the 1880s dawned, it was clear that for all of the realism of the government in defining the "Indian problem," the solution based upon the creation of dependent reservations and individual land gifts left much to be desired. Like the policy of removal, this approach simply delayed the reconciliation of red and white. In addition, it was not based on a consistent outlook or a viable future goal. And finally, it still operated within a framework in which the Indian was not accepted by white society.

The changes in attitudes toward the Indian which were reflected in the transition from removal to reservations to allotment of land in severalty were not caused by government action, but rather were reflected in it. The appointment of a Peace Commission and President Grant's conciliatory public stance were occasioned by outbursts of indignation in eastern journals of social criticism and by a rising concern for the destitute Indian in nonfrontier areas. These changes reflected new interests and a new intellectual milieu. Practically, as the Indians were no longer a significant threat, white Americans could afford to be more generous. Politically, the re-emergence of the South and black migration north created new and more absorbing fears and concerns. Intellectually, as America entered an age of urban life and a highly technological culture, the emphasis of scientists, social critics, and intellectuals turned increasingly to the cities and industrialization. As nationality became linked to race, the image of Indians as original Americans began to take on more positive characteristics. And with the West now one focus of general reform agitation, attitudes toward the Indian began to soften.

One of the most important underlying causes of a more favorable government stance was a long-standing scientific interest in Indian life and the increased prestige and power of scientists in influencing government decisions. Just as Indian savagery had been a mode of defining white civilization, so Indian history became a way of illuminating the racial and cultural roots of whites. The development of a consistent racial theory and the preoccupation of white Americans with traits thought to be racially linked resuscitated interest in the Indians.

Long before the Civil War, some Americans had earnestly sought to understand the Indian as something more than a symbol. In 1798, the American Philosophical Society undertook major studies of ancient Indian life, and in 1812, the newly formed American Antiquarian Society devoted much of its meeting time to questions of Indian lore and language. Discussions in the first part of the century were dominated by enlightenment and biblical concepts of the unity of mankind. However such notions were continually altered until interest and science made the Bible fit their interpretations, and the idea of the brotherhood of man fell into question.

Jefferson was a participant in many of these early quarrels over Indian origins, using linguistic evidence to stress the antiquity of Indian cultures, and arguing for the environmentally determined character of the Indian's less esteemed qualities. Jefferson was supported and attacked by the best scientists of the day. Other public political figures, including Presidents Washington, John Adams, and Madison, also took a hand in ethnological studies. Jefferson's Secretary of the Treasury, Albert Gallatin, wrote an important early work on Indian origins based on linguistic evidence and analysis. By the 1830s, intellectuals had broadened their efforts into a search for the origin of the Indian races, with some opting for answers which related Indians to the "Lost Tribes of Israel," rather than Asian civilization. In a time when many condemned the Indians as primitive, others were using their primitiveness as a measure of the antiquity and originality of America.

The growing sectional interests of the period and the transition to a more romantic framework of racial assumptions were reflected clearly in the work of Samuel George Morton. Morton based his influential *Crania Americana*, published in 1839, on an acceptance of the diversity of men — the belief that there was not a single but rather many separate creations — and on the premise that the white race was biologically superior. Although Morton's attack focused more on the black than the red, he collected and measured the brain capacities of many Indian skulls. He supported his theory of various racial families of man with what was thought to be abundant scientific evidence, and his conclusions of the biological inferiority of Indians stuck for many years.

The American Ethnological Society was founded in 1842 to carry on the research and discussion of many of the problems raised by the Jeffersonians and the ethnologists of the South. At the same time, field workers and collector-historians like Hubert Howe Bancroft, artists like George Catlin, and ethnologists like Henry Rowe Schoolcraft and James Hall, began to collect extensive evidence of Indian craft and folklore, establishing sources for future study.

In the prewar decades, the science of Indian study gained prestige under the impetus of the ideas of Lewis Henry Morgan and Charles Darwin. Morgan's work in the 1850s and thereafter became the basis of many modern Indian studies. Morgan used the Iroquois as a model of the culture of an ancient society. In a highly value-free and positivistic way, he traced the intricate Indian system of blood and personal relations to arrive at a model of a universal social growth from primitivism to complexity based on technological advance. Morgan found that Indians, as a primitive people in the midst of a modern society, were an important link in the evidence for the theory of cultural evolution.

The major contributions of the later era were made by scientists who undertook precise field studies, often less ideologically related than earlier ones. Adolph Bandolier's studies of the Indians of the Southwest helped anthropologists gain the respect of other scientists. Daniel G. Brinton's systematic classification of Indian racial groups and his extensive collection of Indian literature provided the scholarly underpinning for newer and more accurate generalizations based on the richness and diversity of Indian life.

Lewis Henry Morgan's work extended into the late 1870s. By the time of his later studies, Morgan had absorbed major doses of Darwinism. Darwin's work aided racial theory in general by allowing for the development of diversity from a single seed by the process of adaptation to particular environments. However, for the most part, the ideas of American Darwinists on race were never made particularly relevant to Indians. The reason was not that such applications were difficult, but rather that they became irrelevant. Just as absorption with the slavery problem drained sentiment among earlier Indian policy reformers, so Darwinism as a racial ideology increasingly fixed attention on the "slavic hordes" which American white Protestants feared were about to inundate them. Unlike Morton, the new racial ideologists were from New England, not the South.

The nearly complete destruction of Indian culture stimulated the concern of some scientists. The work of one man, John Wesley Powell, did much to forward research and to reshape policy in the 1870s and 1880s. Powell revived the dormant Bureau of Ethnology and lobbied for its separation from the Geological Survey with which it was then connected. He accomplished his goal in 1879, when the Bureau of Ethnology, directed by Powell, was placed under the control of the Smithsonian Institution. He used his many field trips to the West to increase Indian collections, and expanded the system of data collection through soliciting gifts and grants. He lobbied in Congress and in the Cosmos Club and other gathering places of the intellectual and political elite for a government policy toward the West and the Indian based on anthropological, archeological, and geological study. Along with several scientific and political friends, he formed one of the most influential lobbies for science in government and for conservation in general.

By the time of the passage of the Dawes Act in 1887, the study of American cultural groups had become an institutionalized part of American life, and expert advice a part of government policy making. With the founding of the American Anthropological Society by a student of Indian culture less than a quarter-century later, scientific interest in the Indian had not only ameliorated internal expansion policy, but had inspired the growth of a major branch of intellectual endeavor in America. Through the work of twentieth-century scientists like Franz Boas, anthropology was to return the favor and aided New Deal intellectuals in developing more positive attitudes toward Indian culture and more humane Indian programs.

As the threat of the Indian receded and detached and "objective" Indian studies appeared, a more favorable literary image of the red man took form, accompanied by an outcropping of moral revulsion at the white destruction of past generations. But the image did not alter overnight.

Many members of the American literati remained unconvinced. Mark Twain's attitude varied from condescending satire in his sketch of the lazy Goshoot Indians to outright hostility reminiscent of Robert Montgomery Bird. However, the changing tone was expressed by Joachim Miller, who

called the Modoc "gentle" rather than noble savages and paraphrased
Charles Dickens in labeling the Indian "the worst and the best of men, the
tamest and the fiercest of beings."[9] Miller believed that the Indian, with
his stoic countenance and long memory for transgressions, had become
the conscience of America. In popular magazine articles reformer and politician Carl Schurz advocated policies which he eventually was able to enforce as Secretary of the Interior. And Helen Hunt Jackson branded the
treatment of the Indian as a *Century of Dishonor* and dedicated the rest of
her career to righting the wrong through moralistic novels and reports of
government activity. She died before her widely respected work could bear
fruit, but "happier for the belief," as she wrote President Cleveland, that
soon he would remedy the history of injustice to Indians and help to lift
"this burden of infamy from our country." Influential as Mrs. Jackson may
have been, Theodore Roosevelt, who had spent two years in the Dakotas
and whose journals report two near-contacts with Indians, contemptuously
dismissed her book, arguing instead that American policy had been too
hesitating, and that he felt nine out of ten Indians were good only when
dead, "and I shouldn't inquire too closely into the case of the tenth."[10]

A similar story could be told of the prints and paintings of the era.
The most popular western paintings and prints in traveling eastern shows
depicted Custer's heroic last stand. The critical and popular acclaim accorded such mediocre and historically inaccurate paintings as John Mul-
vaney's "Custer's Last Rally" cannot be understood short of assuming that
the audience found confirmation of its self-image in the painting. Similar
attitudes were reflected in the popular Currier and Ives' prints of the nineteenth century. On the other hand, several painters expressed sympathy
for the Indian while using him as commentary on white values. The paintings of Henry F. Farny, along with the earlier works of George Catlin, evoke
the grim loneliness of Indian life, its desperation and solitude, and its disintegration at the hands of technological white civilization.

The increase in white humanitarian interest could also be seen in the
substantial increase of reform organizations and benevolent government
policies. Missionaries took the lead in such reform groups, but eastern
women's organizations and liberal politicians followed. President Rutherford B. Hayes even installed Carl Schurz in his cabinet to oversee a thorough
revision and cleanup in the Bureau of Indian affairs. Coalitions of reform
groups began to meet to map out programs of political pressure on congressmen. Indians themselves began to see the situation as sufficiently hopeful
to form an Indian Rights Association in 1882. It was a sign that white
opinion, for whatever reason, was moving toward a less hostile position.

[9] In Albert Keiser, *The Indian in American Literature* (New York, 1933), p. 241.
[10] Helen Hunt Jackson, in Keiser, *The Indian in American Literature,* pp. 250–251;
Theodore Roosevelt, in Thomas F. Gossett, *Race: The History of an Idea in America*
(Dallas, 1963), p. 238.

White sympathy and organizational pressure soon began to bear fruit, although the direction of the changes was sometimes unintentionally retrogressive. Thus in the early 1880s, the Indian began to acquire voting rights and to come under the shelter of the federal court system. But unfortunately, like liberal legislation of an earlier era, instead of helping the Indian achieve self-respect and reducing racial tensions, the legislative and administrative measures of the 1880s forced Indians to accommodate to white values and undercut the judicial functions of the chiefs in the family and band-centered Indian cultures.

In 1885, just before the death of Helen Hunt Jackson, Senator Henry L. Dawes of Massachusetts began to agitate for an act to relieve the guilt Mrs. Jackson found so oppressive. The Dawes proposal sought to regularize the ineffective and partial allotment procedures in effect since 1854. As passed two years later, the Dawes Act stipulated that each Indian head of household was to be allotted a piece of land, which would be held in trust for him by the federal government until he was educated enough to dispose of it without harm to himself or his family. Presumably, the era of Indian dependency was over. Reservation policy had given him time to acculturate and in turn had tempered his savagery. Bolstered by their exposure to white values, Indians were to enter the broader stream of American society as full-fledged citizens. Once more, white assumptions about the good life — hard work, material accumulation, individualism — triumphed over the understanding of cultural differences.

Designed as a humanitarian gesture, the Dawes Act closed the period on a note of irony. The white American could not, even when he wished to, transcend his own values. Although he tried to act upon a premise of hope for the Indian, the Dawes Act, which had been passed with only one dissenting vote, was doomed to failure because the white man's hope was not the Indian's. If the Indian was not savage until the white man made him so, then he was not now white because Congress defined him so. The Dawes Act was based on a misunderstanding of the Indian concept of family, the Indian meaning of land and wealth, and the Indian way of life. It also underrated white hostility toward the Indian. The law resulted in new plunder as the lands originally given individual Indians came in time upon the white market.

The nineteenth century had opened with Americans holding a notion of the Indian as a beast. It was closing with the idea of the Indian as a retarded child. Never were substantial numbers of Americans able to accommodate themselves to a view of the Indian as a human being. Following the Dawes Act, as the Indian population increased and their land supply shrunk, the original Americans were forced not into a new life, but rather into yet another variation of the old one.

Despite Indian protests, neither the specific provisions nor the underlying ideology of the Dawes Act was overthrown until the Wheeler-Howard

Act of 1934. No less than a half-century of studying the Indian's communal traits and actual tribal conditions, combined with shaken faith in the ethic of unbounded individualism brought about by the Great Depression, would be required to restore to Indians a measure of tribal autonomy and to improve educational and medical facilities. Even then, the beginning made was late and small and has often been reversed in favor of policies in the spirit of the 1880s. The political militancy of Indians initiated in the 1880s has advanced in equally desultory fashion, and is only now, perhaps under the impetus of the small successes of blacks, experiencing a renaissance.

5

Race and the House of Labor

ALEXANDER SAXTON

If America has always been a white man's country, it has not been altogether a white workingman's country. Insofar as they have perceived themselves members of an exploited social class, white workingmen have been of divided mind on the matter of race. Class consciousness has cut at right angles to racial identification. Clearly the "Mind of America," fixed through so many generations upon race, has had to accommodate itself to contradictions stemming from the disharmony between its racial practices and concepts and its received notions of Christian religion, traditional morality, egalitarian politics, and liberal economics. But along with these general contradictions, labor has had its unique dilemma, paralleling and sometimes reinforcing the others.

Each of white America's three great racial confrontations—with the Indian, the African slave, and the Oriental contract laborer—has involved economic exploitation of colored peoples by the dominant white society. In all these transactions, and especially in the two that began with systems of enforced labor, white workingmen have played the dual role of exploiters and exploited. On the one hand, thrown into competition with racial minorities (whether slaves or "cheap labor"), they suffered economically; on the other hand, being white, they benefited by that very exploitation which was compelling the racial minorities to work for low wages, or for nothing. Ideologically they were pulled in opposite directions. In one direction they were drawn to advocate unity in defense of the interests of all workers (or *producers,* to use the earlier Jacksonian term) as a class. In the opposite direction, they were drawn to separate themselves from members of racial minorities in the labor force in order to seek special dispensations as members of the white society. This problem of dual identity has affected the organizational practice and infused the thinking of labor in America from the earliest beginnings of a labor movement.

I

Organization of trades can be traced back to the colonial period; but the emergence of a significant American labor movement dates from the early years of the Jacksonian era. Beginning at Philadelphia in 1827, local journeymen's societies sprang up in many cities of the North and Central Atlantic seaboard. Unionization seems to have come in response to pressure upon skilled workingmen resulting from the expansion of the national market. This was in turn an outgrowth of the transportation revolution. As local markets were thrown together by the construction of new, cheap transportation facilities such as the Erie Canal, the merchant capitalist, expert in wholesale buying and selling, came to dominate the system of manufacture. Personal contacts which formerly had linked masters, journeymen, and customers, now gave way to an impersonal hierarchy. The wholesaler at the top squeezed the master; the master passed the pressure along to his workmen; while the customers receded into an unknown and distant mass market.

Against this background of economic growth and sharpening conflict, trade unions flourished briefly. There were strikes — some successful — for wages, and to shorten the hours of labor, which customarily had run from dawn to sundown. Local unions merged into citywide groupings, and these by 1834–1835 had initiated an annual national convention. Workingmen also ventured into politics. They made the shorter workday a political issue (their efforts culminating in President Van Buren's adoption of ten hours as standard on federal public works); and they campaigned for such egalitarian goals as free public education, mechanics' lien laws, abolition of imprisonment for debt, and abolition of prison labor contracting. In several cities they scored independent electoral successes, but the most impressive achievements came in forcing their programs upon the major parties.

The movement was short lived. Unions and parties both disintegrated in the depression of 1837. Yet part of this disintegration was actually a process of absorption into the major parties, Whig and Democratic. The main drift was to the Democratic party, where workingmen formed part of an urban, radical wing of Jacksonianism. They championed the Bank War, hard money, and the crusade against monopoly. Some began to agitate for free land in the West as a cure-all for the nation's economic ills. The political ideas they expressed had been inherited for the most part from Jefferson, Tom Paine, and the Declaration of Independence. However, to the earlier Jeffersonian notion of the yeoman farmer as keystone of society and custodian of its moral values, had now been added an honorable place for city dwellers, provided they were *producers* engaged in some sort of manual toil. "The agricultural, the mechanical and the laboring classes" (to use the words of President Jackson) comprised the "great body of the people of the United States . . . the bone and sinew of the country." Through the next half century workingmen's leaders would echo and re-echo the rhetoric of the Bank War, for this was precisely how they, and their constituents, wished to see themselves: as producers locked in perpetual battle against "great moneyed corporations."[1]

Despite its egalitarian ideology, the labor movement of the Jacksonian period seems to have had room for none but white participants. I know of no evidence that blacks took part either in the unions or in the workingmen's parties. Black population in the North was relatively small, and in many areas was denied the vote. In the South, on the other hand, where the black population was large, and where slave labor performed not only the unskilled but many skilled tasks as well, virtually no labor movement existed. What few scatterings of labor activity did occur in the South were generally focused upon barring Negroes from employment at skilled jobs. The net result of all this—though for rather different reasons in the North and South —was to foster an exclusionary outlook on the part of white workingmen. Exclusion seemed the natural order of things. From this it was no very long step to an acceptance of slavery itself as part of the natural order.

Slavery, however, was clearly incompatible with any social order in which all men were held to have been created equal. To reconcile this contradiction for free workingmen required an elaborate process of rationalization. In the North, the task was undertaken mainly by spokesmen for the urban radical wing of the Democratic party, since the political careers of these leaders hinged upon party victories in national elections; and such victories depended in turn on the preservation of unity between the northern and southern sectors of their party. Slavery (so the argument ran) was doubtless undesirable in itself; yet it existed and might not be altogether evil in practice. At least for the present, the African race—inherently childish and improvident—required protection within some paternalistic structure. Those self-evident truths of the Declaration, while abstractly valid for all mankind, ought not to be applied literally to the Africans. Antislavery agitation could only worsen their plight, and, moreover, would divide the ongoing movement of Democratic reform and halt or destroy its great

---

[1] President Jackson's Farewell Address in James D. Richardson, ed. *et al., A Compilation of the Messages and Papers of the Presidents* (10 vols.; Washington, D.C., 1896–1899), IV, p. 1524.

progressive work. Thus Ely Moore, former president of the General Trades Union of New York and subsequently president of the short-lived national labor convention which stemmed from it, took the floor while a Democratic congressman in 1839 to denounce antislavery petitions as subversive of the republic. The petitions, he charged, were part of a Federalist-Whig conspiracy to consolidate power in the central government, undermine state sovereignty, and sink the white workingman into "virtual bondage." "Yes sir, for the especial purpose of humbling and degrading the Democracy have the Federal party of the North and East joined in the Abolition crusade; and whenever their object shall be attained, and the Southern negro shall be brought to compete with the Northern white man, the moral and political character, the pride, power and independence of the latter are gone forever. . . ."[2]

Fifteen years later Michael Walsh, another Democratic "workingmen's" congressman from New York, still pursued approximately the same argument. After first establishing his proletarian credentials—"I happen to know something about the people of this land in the position of cabin boy, and of deck hand upon the Mississippi, of fireman working bareheaded and barefooted. I am in the position of a man who never had a dollar from the earnings of any human being but myself"—Walsh went on to demonstrate the enviable situation of the slave in contrast to that of the wage laborer:

> the only difference . . . is that the one has a master without asking for him, and the other has to beg for the privilege of becoming a slave. . . . I would ask the particular advocates of Abolition upon this floor to point me to one single solitary degradation heaped on the head of the negro of the South that a white man at the North is not liable to have imposed on him for the time being through poverty.[3]

Walsh was speaking in defense of Senator Douglas' Kansas-Nebraska bill. His position, as he made clear, was determined by his desire to avoid disruption of the Democratic party. Meanwhile, however, northern workingmen, like many other northerners, were turning with increasing favor toward free soil, not so much from hatred for slavery as because they wished to exclude blacks (slave or free) from the new territories. The argument in this respect had already been set forth by David Wilmot, another latter day Jacksonian, when he defended his famous proviso as a means of preserving to "free white labor a fair country . . . where the sons of toil of my own race and color can live without the disgrace which association with negro slavery brings upon free labor."[4] Thus the Declaration had been harnessed in tandem with white supremacy—in the interest of egalitarianism.

[2] *Congressional Globe,* 25 Cong., 3 Sess., Appendix, p. 241.
[3] *Congressional Globe,* 33 Cong., 1 Sess., p. 1232.
[4] *Congressional Globe,* 29 Cong., 2 Sess., Appendix, p. 317.

II

The decade of the 1850s, during which the nation reached the threshold of industrial maturity, brought a resurgence of organizational activity among workingmen. The Civil War, with its resultant labor shortage accompanied by rising wages and more rapidly rising prices, further stimulated unionization. Local unions merged into city centrals, and these once again began planning a general convention. The result was the first session of the National Labor Union, held at Baltimore in 1866. Among the leaders of this new organization were many who had grown up as young radicals during the Jacksonian period. As they viewed the circumstances before them, barely more than one year after Appomattox, they must have supposed that the American labor force stood upon the brink of extraordinary changes. "One eighth of the whole population"—those black slaves whom Lincoln in his Second Inaugural had described as "somehow the cause of the war"—had been converted, nominally at least, into free laborers. "Unpalatable" though this fact might be, it nonetheless seemed clear to the authors of the National Labor Union's introductory *Address . . . to the Workingmen of the United States* that the African race was "destined" to play a new role in the future:

> That it will neither die out nor be exterminated, is now regarded as a settled fact. They are there to live amongst us, and the question to be decided is, shall we make them our friends, or shall capital be allowed to turn them as an engine against us? . . . we are of the opinion that the interests of the labor cause demand that all workingmen be included within its ranks, without regard to race or nationality.[5]

Here was an unequivocal statement of one of the two ideological alternatives open to white workingmen in America.

The other alternative—that of exclusion—was not long in finding expression. At the second NLU convention, opposition to the views set forth in the *Address* quoted above forced a deadlock on the matter of Negro participation. The committee entrusted with discovering a solution found instead "the subject involved in so much mystery, and upon it so wide a diversity of opinion among our members, we believe it is inexpedient to take action. . . ." In his own locality (New Haven), the committee chairman reported, were "a number of respectable colored mechanics, but they had not been able to induce the trades' unions to admit them. He asked, was there any union in the states which would admit colored men?"[6]

[5] Andrew C. Cameron, *The Address of the National Labor Congress to the Workingmen of the United States* (Chicago, 1867) in John R. Commons, *et al., A Documentary History of American Industrial Society* (New York, 1958), IX, pp. 158–160.

[6] In Commons, *A Documentary History of American Industrial Society,* IX, pp. 185–187.

It may be taken for granted that spokesmen for both sides in this controversy believed in the inherent superiority of the white over the black race. Their divergent positions on Negro membership in the NLU stemmed, not from differing attitudes on race, but from different concepts of labor strategy. Those who had drafted the opening *Address,* and through the subsequent debates favored interracial unity, formed what might be described as an *old left* within the labor movement of the 1860s. While some were in fact trade union leaders, they were not fully committed to trade unionism. Divisions based upon occupation or skill seemed of secondary importance compared to the overriding common interest of "all on our side of the line." What was crucial was the achievement of cooperation among workingmen, among the *producers* broadly defined in the old Jacksonian style as "the agricultural, the mechanical and the laboring classes."[7] The road ahead, as indicated by the *Address,* was a political road. Improvements of all sorts, not only in wages, hours, conditions of labor, but in currency, credit, tariffs, land policy, education, might all be achieved through the voting power of the producers—once those producers mobilized themselves in the cause of labor reform. The type of organization dictated by this concept would be *in*clusive: no producers could safely be left out. Given the apparent transformation of former slaves into citizens, voters, and independent economic agents, the rational self-interest of white producers would best be served by cooperation with black producers.[8]

That was one side of the controversy. The other side was supported by men more consciously trade unionists, and probably younger. They represented the new craft locals which had sprouted in the 1850s, burgeoned during the war years, and which were moving toward national craft organization. Economically rather than politically oriented, these men sought to maximize the bargaining power of skilled workers through union control over competition for skilled jobs. To this purpose they would strive to define the limits of each craft, to restrict entry by means of rigorous apprenticeship programs, and to establish union supervision over apprenticeship and hiring. The type of organization dictated by the craft concept of labor strategy was necessarily *ex*clusive: optimum membership for each craft union would be that which took in all trained practitioners of the craft, while excluding all others. Since the black contingent of the labor force remained generally unskilled and inexperienced at industrial occupations, it was certain to fall largely within the excluded portion. Quite apart, then, from any racial attitudes actually held by craft unionists, the *logic* which flowed from their concept of labor strategy tended to reinforce the exclusion of nonwhites.

[7] Commons, *A Documentary History of American Industrial Society,* IX, p. 159; Richardson, *A Compilation of the Messages and Papers of the Presidents,* IV, p. 1524.

[8] No such transformation, of course, occurred until the twentieth century. But in 1868, when this debate was held, the failure of radical Reconstruction in the South was not yet apparent to labor leaders or to most other Americans.

Craft unionism at the end of the Civil War represented a wave of the future. The skill-based, exclusive principle of organization, already widespread, would become dominant in the American labor movement before the end of the century. Needless to say, the corollary of that principle, as it applied to black labor, prevailed in the NLU. A handful of Negro delegates gained admission to the national conventions, but nothing was done about membership in local unions. Negro workers were allowed to go unorganized, or to form their own associations. In 1869, a National Colored Labor Convention set the following memorial before the United States Congress:

> The exclusion of colored men, and apprentices, from the right to labor in any department of industry or workshops, in any of the states and territories of the United States, by what is known as "trades' unions" is an insult to God, injury to us, and disgrace to humanity.[9]

III

The annual assemblies of the NLU dwindled off during the depression of 1873–1878 and were never resumed. Craft unionism, however, survived the depression and by the 1880s was entering a phase of renewed growth. Lloyd Ulman, in his study of *The Rise of the National Trade Union,* has taken the drive of skilled workingmen to improve their collective bargaining potential as the chief dynamic factor in the growth of national unions. Here was the determinant, Ulman argues, in the drawing of boundaries around particular skills. And, given the mobility of American society, it was this same factor which impelled craftsmen, grasping for some means of control over entry into the various trades, to unite their separate local unions into national organizations; then to permit the transfer of effective power from the local to the national level. Capstone to this structure was the American Federation of Labor, founded in 1881, which provided an annual convention and an executive to speak for, and serve, its constituent organizations.

Essentially the American Federation of Labor (AFL) was not a unified labor center, but an alliance of national craft unions. The AFL's long jurisdictional struggle against its chief rival, the Knights of Labor, can best be understood as a conflict between craft unionism and an opposite, or *inclusive*, tendency of labor strategy. Established in 1869, the Knights of Labor had grown slowly until the 1880s when they began suddenly to expand. The Knights comprised a mixed grill of organizational and ideological types. Among these were to be found several predecessors of modern industrial unions, as well as cooperatives, educational societies, Jacksonian assemblies of workers, farmers, and small businessmen—and a

---

[9] Commons, *A Documentary History of American Industrial Society,* IX, p. 250.

number of locals of the strictly skilled craft form. Yet insofar as the Knights differed from the AFL, it was through the espousal of *producer* rather than craft loyalty. Their declared aim—closely akin to what would later be termed *industrial* unionism—was to organize workers regardless of trades or degrees of skill; and regardless also, of sex or race. They endeavored with some success to recruit both women and Negroes into the labor movement.[10] Partly from internal dissension, partly from the assaults of employers on the one hand, and the rival AFL on the other, the Knights of Labor disintegrated during the early 1890s, leaving the national craft unions to assume, more or less unchallenged, the leadership of American labor.

Thus triumphantly institutionalized, craft unionism continued to display much the same ambivalence with respect to race that had characterized the earlier debates of the National Labor Union, as well as the somewhat contradictory undertakings of the Knights of Labor.

At the highest level, the AFL executive and the national conventions spoke the old egalitarian language of labor unity. The convention of 1894, for example, pledged itself to the unionization of workers "irrespective of creed, color, sex, nationality, or politics." During the early 1890s, the executive board refused charters to organizations of machinists, boilermakers, and shipbuilders which insisted upon explicit anti-Negro clauses in their constitutions. Samuel Gompers, president of the AFL for all but one of its first forty-three years, regularly denounced racial exclusiveness. Labor could never achieve its goals, he asserted, unless it struggled to "eliminate the consideration of a color line. . . ." "If we fail to make friends of [Negro workers], the employing class won't be so shortsighted. . . . If common humanity will not prompt us to have their cooperation, an enlightened self-interest should."[11] Gompers, an immigrant English Jew, had ample reason for standing against racial discrimination. His rise to labor leadership in America had been through the skilled trade of cigar making. Several of his early associates were of Marxist political background; and while Gompers as an official of the American Federation of Labor vigorously rejected socialist politics, he tended to express his organizational concepts—drawn mainly from the model of British skilled unionism—in a language of working-class identification.

Gompers and his colleagues, in fact, leaned more on British and Euro-

---

[10] The principle of industrial organization is to bring all the workers of any particular industry, regardless of their trades or levels of skill, into a single union. This contrasts with the principle of craft organization, which is to bring all practitioners of any particular craft, regardless of what industry they work in, into a single union. In their racial attitudes the Knights of Labor were not consistent. While they took in Negro members in the East, they maintained a ferocious opposition to Chinese in the Far West.

[11] American Federation of Labor, *Procedings of the 14th Annual Convention* (Washington, D.C., 1894), p. 25. Samuel Gompers to James H. White, September 14, 1889, and to H. M. Ives, November 10, 1892, in Philip S. Foner, *History of the Labor Movement in the United States* (New York, 1955), II, p. 196.

pean labor precedents than on native Jacksonian radicalism. In the European tradition, the term *working class* conveyed a precise meaning assigned to it by both Marxist and classical economists. It meant wage laborers thrown into the commodity market with nothing to sell but their labor power. This differed sharply from the loose Jacksonian concept of *producers* which might include farmers, laborers, craftsmen, small businessmen, and entrepreneurs.

Yet since the idea of common interest, of the prime need for unity, remained central to both definitions, Gompers and other AFL spokesmen could employ a language similar to that of their Jacksonian predecessors. And just as in the earlier period, their verbal constructions tended to part company from organizational reality. The real point of conflict, for example, in the case of the machinists mentioned above was not acceptance of Negroes into the union (which was later admitted to the AFL upon simply transferring its discriminatory rule from the constitution to the initiation ritual), but public expression of exclusionist policy in the union constitution. Semantics rather than substance was at issue. What was developing was an arrangement by which the national craft unions made their practical decisions in the field, while the Federation, created by the nationals, but lacking real coercive power over them, continued to speak of (and to) Negroes in the language of working class unity. Gompers apparently felt that so long as the image of a racially inclusive labor movement could be honored in words, it would remain possible sometime, under more favorable circumstances, to readjust the reality.

Circumstances, however, were turning less rather than more favorable. It had been the crisis of Civil War—the desperate defense of the Union, the ideological excitement surrounding emancipation, the bold egalitarian promises of radical Reconstruction—which had forced upon labor leaders of the 1860s and 1870s their belief that black freedmen were on the verge of becoming citizens. And to be citizens then had seemed to mean that they would become voters and independent economic agents as well. Largely from that belief had stemmed the invocation of racial unity in the National Labor Union's *Address* of 1867. But these expectations had not materialized. They were aborted by the failure of radical Reconstruction. The emancipated blacks, contained within the South, had been rendered politically impotent and reduced to semipeonage. Thus any real need even for a rhetoric of racial unity appeared to be fading from the historical scene. During the 1880s and 1890s, despite the neo-Marxian scruples of some of its officers, the Federation swung toward a more open avowal of the exclusionist practice of its constituent unions.

Restrictions, whether simply by long custom or written into constitutions and rituals, came to be accepted without protest by the federation. In a report prepared for Atlanta University in 1902, W. E. B. DuBois estimated that some 40,000 Negroes belonged to unions affiliated to the AFL;

but of these nearly 30,000 were in three organizations of heavy black membership and semiskilled status. That left approximately 10,000 black craftsmen forming a modest 3 percent of the remaining AFL membership. The bulk of these were in the South, in segregated locals, often receiving lower hourly pay than whites doing the same work. As of 1900, the U. S. Bureau of Labor Statistics listed eighty-two unions affiliated with the AFL. DuBois reported that thirty-nine of these had no Negro members, and another twenty-seven contained only a scattering. While some of the figures cited above are estimates subject to considerable question, there can be little doubt as to the accuracy of the general picture they suggest.

Nor can there be much doubt that the situation in the labor movement paralleled that of the nation at large. These were the years when the legal and institutional structure of Jim Crow was brought to final perfection in American society; when lynching reached a statistical apex; when racist thinking had taken possession not only of American politics and popular culture, but of the churches, and the social and scientific mind as well. Gompers and his AFL colleagues, while still proclaiming the unity of all workingmen, endorsed special segregated locals for blacks which controlled their competition and collected their dues money, while denying them any effective voice in union policy. "Well, we must hold on and hope for a time," Gompers counseled. He, and other Federation leaders, now blamed exclusion upon the Negroes themselves, charging that their willingness to be used as strikebreakers was at the root of the matter.[12]

IV

To understand the supremacy within organized labor of the white-only alternative over its opposite, we will have to turn to a closely related but parallel sequence of events which occurred largely in the Far West. This involved the relation of white Americans, not to black slaves or freedmen, but to Orientals. Ten years before the American Civil War, as news of gold at Sutter's Mill spread across the world, a stream of migrants converged upon California. Among them were large numbers of Chinese. Most of these came from the overpopulated and hunger-stricken region around Canton; and many came not as free agents but as contract laborers. The export of Chinese contract labor — the so-called coolie trade — had already been highly developed by Chinese merchants, and by British, Dutch, Spanish, and Portuguese entrepreneurs, as a substitute for the African slave trade which had gradually been closed off during the preceding half cen-

---

[12] Gompers in *American Federationist,* X (1902), p. 709, in Foner, *History of the Labor Movement in the United States,* II, p. 360. Ray Marshall, *The Negro and Organized Labor* (New York, 1965), pp. 15–18.

tury. Chinese coolies provided a cheap, virtually enslaved, labor force for the planting and extractive enterprises of the Pacific islands, as well as for the west coast of South America, and for the Caribbean.

After Sutter's Mill, the coolie traffic flowed into California. The majority of Chinese migrants during the early 1850s joined the rush to the gold fields. There they found themselves in competition with white miners, who, despite the multiplicity of their own languages and nationalities, generally managed to resolve their differences sufficiently to join in evicting the Chinese from the camps. But the rich surface deposits were scraped off quickly, the white miners drifted to other pursuits, and the Chinese returned to work over the low yield diggings and tailings. They moved also into heavy construction. From 1866 to 1869, the Central Pacific Railway kept some 10,000 Chinese at work boring the Sierra tunnels and building the transcontinental line across Nevada and Utah. Others found employment on California's ranches which were requiring enormous supplies of manpower for clearing, diking, ditching, draining, irrigating, and harvesting their new crops.

Employment of coolie labor offered several advantages to American entrepreneurs. In the first place it was cheap. Records of the Central Pacific construction indicate that the railroad was able to obtain unskilled (and some skilled) Chinese laborers for roughly two-thirds the cost of unskilled white labor. Second, it was readily available. At a time when white workingmen from the East were in short supply, British and American vessels, fitted with barred cargo holds like the old Atlantic slave ships, poured a continuous stream of Cantonese immigrants into San Francisco. Finally, and perhaps most advantageous of all, this labor force could be held under close control. The newcomers generally were bonded for passage and other debts to Chinese merchants living in California. They were then rented out in gangs of fifty to a hundred, each under the direction of an agent, usually an English-speaking Chinese. Neither state nor federal law provided any legal means of enforcing labor contracts. Yet for the individual Chinese laborer—ignorant of American law as he was of the English language—escape from this system became virtually impossible. In effect he was at the mercy of the American employer, and of the Chinese merchant associations, agents, or contractors, who had arranged his passage from Canton, who hired him out, received his wages, provided food and protection, and determined when, if ever, he would return home again. To complete this circle, an extralegal but firm understanding between the Chinese merchant associations and Pacific ship operators hindered any Chinese from booking return passage until he had been cleared by the merchant associations. It was a tight system, not exactly the same as slavery, but not altogether different.

In 1870, 8.6 percent of all Californians were Chinese. Ten years later, despite the influx of population from the eastern United States and Europe, the Chinese percentage still stood at 7.5. This fraction of total population, however, represented a vastly higher proportion of the actual labor force since virtually all Chinese migrants were male wage laborers. Approximately one quarter of all workers available for hire in California in the 1870s must have been Chinese.

How were these Chinese laborers received by the white population — especially by white workingmen? The answer is that they were received with hostility from the beginning. In part this was due to the economic problem posed by the coolie labor system. Available in seemingly unlimited supply from south China, forced under semibondage to work for pitifully small remuneration, Chinese threatened to undercut wage levels and living standards of all other workers. The point was made clear in 1869 when a commercial and agricultural convention at Memphis, Tennessee, proposed to solve the South's difficulties with its newly liberated freedmen through importation of coolie labor; and even more dramatically in that same year by the use of Chinese for strikebreaking in several New England and Pennsylvania factories. In this respect of course the situation of the Chinese scarcely differed from that of most immigrants. Irish, Italians, Slavs, and many others were also imported as contract laborers, also undercut wage levels, and were often forced to become strikebreakers. They incurred hostility from both native born and earlier immigrants. Yet the hostility directed against European immigrants, whether in the East or the Far West, never approached the virulence of the hatred reserved for Orientals.

The reason for this was that resentment stemming from economic competition coincided with and reinforced already established patterns of racial hostility. Previous essays have traced the long history of white supremacist thought in America; and we have already noted how that line became tangled during the Jacksonian era with ideas of radical egalitarianism. Americans moving westward on their journey to the Pacific slope carried this ideological baggage along with them. As for the European immigrants, they seemed to assimilate the native style in racial attitudes more readily than almost any other characteristic. Generally near the bottom of the job ladder, insecure economically and psychologically, they would attempt to drive off competition and at the same time declare their newfound Americanness through manifestations of hostility toward nonwhites. The New York draft riots of 1863, as described in an earlier essay, exemplify this tragic dynamic.

These, then, were some of the patterns transplanted during the 1850s and 1860s to the Pacific coast. How whites, especially those who entered the labor force, responded to the Chinese was shaped largely by adjustments previously registered with respect to Negroes, or, more precisely, to the *concept* of the Negro enslaved. Doubtless the first impression of the Chinese was one of amazement at their strange ways. Yet almost immediately came an emphasis upon inferiority. They were perceived as repulsive.

To the reporter for a San Francisco gazetteer, writing in 1856, it seemed astonishing "that nature and custom should so combine to manufacture so much individual ugliness." Chinese women he described as "the most degraded and beastly of all human creatures." Only thirteen years later the hard rock miners of Virginia City, Nevada, warned their fellow workingmen of impending disaster:

> Capital has decreed that Chinese shall supplant and drive hence the present race of toilers. . . . Every branch of industry in the State of California swarms with Chinese. . . . Here, then, upon the threshold of a conflict which, if persevered in, will plunge the State into anarchy and ruin, we appeal to the working men to step to the front and hurl back the tide of barbarous invaders.[13]

Chinese, as noted above, comprised at this time about one quarter of all wage laborers on the Coast. The remaining three quarters, though nearly all white, formed in themselves an extraordinarily heterogeneous grouping. Among them were men of different languages and religions, of diverse national, ethnic, economic, and social backgrounds. While in other areas of the nation such a mixture might have separated along its various cleavage lines, in the West it was knit more tightly together by what its members shared in common: first, their experience of displacement and relocation; and second, the fact that, whatever else they might be, they were not Chinese. Upon the base thus amalgamated, there emerged in California during the last three decades of the nineteenth century a labor movement which both in its political and economic endeavors was perhaps more effective than any other in the United States.

In California before the Civil War, the Democratic party generally had commanded a comfortable majority. While a number of party leaders turned out to be Confederate sympathizers, the bulk of Democratic voters opposed secession and many swung over to the Union Republican ticket. In 1867, struggling to recover from its wartime collapse, the Democratic party adopted anti-Orientalism for its central slogan. This coincided with the party's national focus upon white supremacy and speedy readmission of the seceded states, in contrast to the radical Republican program of egalitarian reconstruction of the South. California Democrats found additional reinforcements, meanwhile, in a crop of new trade unions which during the war years had been able to win improvements in wages and hours for their skilled membership. Squeezed by the postwar recession, these unions turned to politics, hoping to protect their economic gains by procuring favorable enactments from the state legislature. They allied themselves with the Democratic party upon the anti-Chinese platform.

---

[13] Colville's *San Francisco Directory and Gazetteer* (San Francisco, 1856), p. xv. San Francisco *Daily Alta,* June 17, 1869.

The San Francisco *Examiner,* chief Democratic organ in the state, summed up the gist of the entente as follows:

> The Democracy are and ever have been, the party of the Constitution, the party of the people. They are for a white man's government constitutionally administered, against a great Mongrel military despotism, upheld by a union of the purse and the sword, and sought to be perpetuated through negro and Chinese votes.

Focal point for the entire campaign was this linking together of Chinese in the West with black ex-slaves in the East. Thus the *Examiner* predicted that "colored Senators" would soon be welcomed into the United States Senate and went on to suggest that for a body already so "reeking with treason, perjury and robbery," the addition of a few black men would scarcely lower the tone. "The champions of 'universal brotherhood,'" however, would never be satisfied with "making Senators of Negroes alone of the colored races. The Chinamen of the Pacific Coast should have a chance." A letter to the editor, prominently featured and signed by "a workingman and a Democrat," spelled out the full logic of the appeal to labor voters. The Central Pacific Railroad, largest importer of Chinese coolies, dominated the Republican party (so the argument ran), and was seeking absolute control of the state government. Should it succeed, the state would certainly be "overrun with Chinamen and negroes." What then would become of white laborers? "They will starve of course. My fellow working men, rally, rally . . . and defeat the railroad monopoly and Chinese labor. Now is your time—now or never. . . ."[14]

The result was victory at the polls and rehabilitation of the Democratic party in California. This outcome made clear that anti-Chinese politics, in the Far West at least, were likely to be winning politics. As such they came to be diligently cultivated, especially by politicians seeking the votes of white workingmen. At the time of the first nationwide railroad strikes in 1877, a mass meeting called in San Francisco to support the railroad strikers was taken over by anti-Chinese agitators. Riots and the looting and burning of Chinese shops and wash houses followed. From this chaotic background emerged the Workingmen's party of California, led by Denis Kearney, an Irish immigrant, former ship's officer and boss drayman. During the next several years the Workingmen's party dominated San Francisco voting. It elected a massive bloc of delegates to the 1878 state constitutional convention which wrote several violent (but unenforceable) anti-Chinese clauses into the constitution. While the central problem may have been that of economic competition, the rhetoric in which this problem was discussed took a far turn from the normal language of economic

[14] San Francisco *Examiner,* July 1 and 13, 1867.

suasion. "Are you ready to march down to the wharf and stop the leprous Chinese from landing?" Kearney demanded of his listeners. "Judge Lynch is the judge wanted by the workingmen of California. I advise all to own a musket and a hundred rounds of ammunition."[15]

Although the Kearney movement disintegrated and was absorbed rapidly back into the two major parties, its spectacular success furthered that institutionalization of race hostility which had begun with the election of 1867. Through the next half-century, anti-Orientalism furnished a channel of political protest for white labor west of the Rockies. It soon became impossible for any western political leader, regardless of his party affiliation, to oppose the principal goal of the crusade, which was to pressure the federal government into shutting off Chinese immigration. This was accomplished by the Exclusion Act of 1882, which banned entry of Chinese "laborers," nominally for a ten-year period. The crusade then focused upon campaigns to make the act permanent, to extend it to Japanese and other Asians, to segregate them in public schools, to deny them ownership of real property in California, and to prevent their coming to the mainland from the Hawaiian Islands or the Philippines after the United States acquired those island territories. All these campaigns, to a large extent successful, contributed to establishing precedents for the racial restrictions which would dominate American immigration policy from World War I to the middle of the twentieth century.

Nor was the utility of anti-Orientalism confined to the political sphere. It became a building block for labor organization. Both the union label and the shop card made early appearances in American labor history as means for differentiating the product of white labor from that of Chinese. The consumer boycott, familiar in earlier days to Sam Adams and the Sons of Liberty, was pressed into service by western workingmen as a weapon against Chinese competition. These complex ramifications of anti-Orientalism come most clearly into focus when they are viewed in connection with the long-continued effort by West Coast labor to create a permanent labor council at San Francisco—that location being crucial because the city remained, at least until the end of the nineteenth century, the single great metropolis and manufacturing center on the Pacific slope.

The first such attempt, coinciding with the National Labor Union in the East, occurred at the close of the Civil War. During the brief postwar recession, a council was established to lobby for state legislation that would protect the favorable conditions gained during wartime by San Francisco trade unionists. The necessary bid for mass political support was made upon the basis of anti-Orientalism, and on this same basis, the trade unionists (as noted above) allied themselves with the Democratic party in

[15] Hubert Howe Bancroft, *Popular Tribunals* (2 vols.; San Francisco, 1887), II, p. 722; *History of California* (7 vols.; San Francisco, 1884–1890), VII, p. 357, note 21.

the electoral campaign of 1867. Yet though successful at the polls, labor gained nothing from the legislature which could serve as a bulwark against deteriorating economic circumstances. The long depression of the 1870s wiped out the union gains, as well as most of the new trade unions; and this first council itself soon went out of existence.

The second attempt—the San Francisco Trades Assembly—grew directly from the anti-Chinese riots of 1877 and the Workingmen's party. The Trades Assembly flourished through the brief prosperity of the early 1880s, then wilted under the return of hard times. Union leaders in 1882 endeavored to recoup its fortunes through sponsorship of an anti-Chinese boycotting program known as the League of Deliverance. Ironically, however, the league was destroyed by the very success of the cause it espoused. After Congress passed the Chinese Exclusion Act of 1882, there seemed little reason for continued activity (or fund raising) on the part of the league. It then disintegrated; and the Trades Assembly, which it had been intended to resuscitate, perished soon afterward.

One might have supposed, from the emphasis placed by anti-Chinese leaders on the economic aspects of their argument, that hostility toward Chinese would have slacked off after the congressional victory of 1882 which checked the influx of coolie labor. Precisely the opposite was the case. The year 1885–1886 marked a crescendo of rhetorical and physical violence against Chinese in the West. From Seattle to southern California, from the Pacific to the Rocky Mountains, Chinese ghettos were mobbed or burned out, their residents dispersed or even murdered. White organized labor played a leading part in many of these attacks. At the end of 1885, a coastwide labor convention assembled at San Francisco to consider means for the final and complete expulsion of Chinese remaining on the West Coast. During its deliberations, only one delegate rose to speak in behalf of Chinese laborers. This was a Polish immigrant named Sigismund Danielewicz, a Marxist and pioneer organizer of West Coast sailors. According to the account of a contemporary newspaper, Danielewicz

> tried the patience of the convention by reading several pyramids of words about the equality of men. He said that he belonged to a race which had been persecuted for hundreds of years and was still persecuted—the Jews; and he called upon all of his people to consider whether the persecution of the Chinese was more justifiable than theirs had been. And he left it upon the Irish to say whether it was more justifiable than their persecution had been; and upon the Germans to make similar comparison. . . .[16]

Danielewicz might perhaps have gone on to argue that with further importation of coolie laborers halted by the Exclusion Act the time had come for

[16] San Francisco *Daily Report,* December 3, 1885, in Ira B. Cross Labor Notes, Carton IV, folder 148, Bancroft Library, University of California, Berkeley.

a new strategy toward the Chinese—a strategy of aiding them to break out of their contract bondage, and at the same time bringing them into the unions. But Danielewicz did not finish his speech; he was laughed at, howled at, and booed from the podium.

Already by 1885, it was too late for white labor to sort out the dual aspects, economic and racial, of its Chinese problem. The political uses, the organizational utility, the unifying power, the mass emotional satisfaction to be derived from the cultivation of racial hostility had become indispensable. Out of that San Francisco convention in 1885 sprang the first permanent labor council on the West Coast. Remodeled in the 1890s, with its name changed to San Francisco Labor Council, it has continued a robust existence to the present day. That is not to say that its racial attitudes have remained unchanged. Yet the fact is that these attitudes showed little if any modification until after World War I. As trade unionism expanded on the Pacific Coast during the early years of the twentieth century, other councils and federations developed out of and alongside the San Francisco Labor Council. Together, they created in 1905 the Asiatic Exclusion League, aimed primarily against the Japanese (Chinese exclusion having been made permanent by Congress in 1902). Business and farm organizations supported this movement, as did spokesmen for the Democratic, Republican, Progressive, and Socialist parties. Yet no historian could deny the claim— as it was put forward by labor politicans and trade union leaders in those days—that anti-Orientalism was in large part labor based. The Asiatic Exclusion League operated out of union offices, and its secretary was the full-time secretary of the AFL's Building Trades' Council.

V

Organized labor in the West had played the role of defender of the national integrity against an alien incursion. Organized labor nationally took to itself the prestige of this performance. At its founding convention in 1881, the American Federation of Labor endorsed the western stand against Chinese immigration and for the succeeding thirty years not only repeated that endorsement at regular intervals, but campaigned for exclusion of all other Orientals as well. While in its earlier years the federation had stressed, verbally at least, the theme of interracial unity with respect to black labor, it showed no such ambivalence in the case of the Chinese. Through the 1890s and on into the twentieth century, it kept up a barrage in openly racist terms against all varieties of "Mongolians."

Thus the convention of 1893 resolved that Chinese brought with them "nothing but filth, vice and disease"; that "all efforts to elevate them to a higher standard have proven futile"; and that Chinese immigrants were to blame for degrading "a part of our people on the Pacific Coast to such a degree that could it be published in detail the American people would in their just and righteous anger sweep them from the face of the earth." Samuel Gompers in his presidential report informed the convention of 1901 that "every incoming coolie . . . means so much more vice and immorality injected into our social life." In a pamphlet published by the federation for mass distribution, Gompers and Hermann Gutstadt, a West Coast trade union official, quoted with approval a memorial sent to Congress by citizens of San Francisco in which they warned the lawmakers to beware especially of the offspring of miscegenation between Americans and Asiatics, for these proved "invariably degenerate."[17] It is hardly necessary to extend this recitation in order to make the point that the language is that of race hatred, not of economic reasoning.

When the theme of anti-Orientalism was introduced in this essay, an argument was proposed that patterns of thought and behavior with respect to blacks, which had taken shape in slaveholding America before the Civil War, had fixed the white response to Chinese in the West. The argument may now be completed by suggesting that the long crusade against Oriental immigration fixed for organized labor nationally its exclusionary policy toward nonwhites, and imparted to that policy the prestige of high patriotism. How easily the language of the Federation, and of its leading officials, could adjust to these changing viewpoints! In 1898, an article featured in the *American Federationist,* official organ of the AFL, explained that blacks were not suitable for trade union membership because they were "of abandoned and reckless disposition," lacking "those peculiarities of temperament such as patriotism, sympathy, sacrifice, etc., which are peculiar to most of the Caucasian race." The best solution would be to export them to Liberia or Cuba. Gompers not only endorsed this article; he went on to expand upon it in his own speeches. "But the caucasians," he told a presumably Caucasian audience at St. Paul, Minnesota, in 1905, "are not going to let their standard of living be destroyed by negroes, Chinamen, Japs, or any others."[18]

The phrase "any others," tacked on seemingly as an afterthought to the main sentence, actually contained a major significance. It referred to the so-called new immigration from southern and eastern Europe. The linking of these "any others" in Gompers' formulation to "negroes, Chinamen, Japs," suggests the degree to which racist patterns of thought had infused labor's response to European immigration. This connection has generally been underestimated by historians of labor and immigration.

There had been, since the end of the Civil War, occasional demands

---

[17] AFL, *Proceedings* (1893), p. 73; (1901), p. 22. AFL, *Some Reasons for Chinese Exclusion. Meat vs. Rice. American Manhood against Asiatic Coolieism. Which Shall Survive?* (Washington, D.C. 1901), p. 34.

[18] *American Federationist,* IV (February 1898), pp. 269–271; XII (September 1905), pp. 636–637.

from labor groups for federal action to halt contract labor importation, but little discussion as to the desirability of general immigration restriction. Labor—including organized labor—had traditionally favored an open door to European immigrants. Not only did this express the spirit of Jacksonian egalitarianism, one of the earliest and most enduring components of labor ideology; it was also in harmony with the loyalties of first and second generation immigrants who were coming to form an increasingly large proportion of membership and leadership of the Federation. It is true, of course, that most of these unionists belonged to the "old immigration" from the British Isles and northwestern Europe, and could therefore see themselves as distinct from those more recent immigrants, the bulk of whom were of south and east European origin. Nonetheless, the open-door viewpoint was deeply held and would not readily be set aside.

Industrial conflict in the 1880s and the depression of the 1890s forced the labor movement to turn its attention to the immigration problem. Labor leaders and journalists began to insist that unrestricted entry was a prime cause of unemployment and falling wages. Gompers in 1891 warned the AFL of these dangers and in subsequent years proposed the preparation of legislative proposals for submission to Congress. He encountered angry opposition. The question was debated, sometimes bitterly and publicly, at annual conventions. The intensity of this conflict is apparent from the fact that Gompers and his executive board pressed the issue for six years before winning a grudging acquiescence from the 1897 convention.

How were the proponents of general restriction able to overcome the traditional Jacksonian scruples and ethnic loyalties of the open-door advocates? A large part of the answer seems to be that an analogy was developed, building upon the exclusion of Chinese, which labor (and probably the majority of white Americans) by this time accepted as a law of nature. Superior races *naturally* could be expected to resist amalgamation, economically or in any other way, with inferior races. Inferior racial stocks were therefore "unassimilable" into a white democratic society like that of the United States. While Slavic and Mediterranean peoples might generally be classified as European, and presumably white, they resembled Orientals in their slavelike disposition. Had they not (like the Chinese) passively endured through many centuries barbaric depotisms which had ground out the last sparks of initiative, intelligence, self-respect, and progress? Whether this abject disposition resulted from long social conditioning or from the penetration of inferior racial strains was a question best left to scholarly investigation. For practical purposes, however, since they behaved like Orientals, they could be set down as equally "unassimilable." The next step was to move by analogy to the conclusion that Slavs, Greeks, Turks, Armenians, Sicilians, and all the rest of that clamoring horde deserved to be rejected for the same good reasons as Chinese.[19]

[19] For examples, see Gompers, AFL, *Proceedings* (1894), p. 12; (1902), pp. 21–22.

VI

What made this analogy possible was the series of identifications formulated and passed down through the historical experiences and responses of the white labor force. Out of the Jacksonian background had come the egalitarian tradition, deeply flawed by long acceptance of slavery. In its earliest organizations, then through the development of national craft unionism after the Civil War, white labor had pursued two contradictory policies with respect to black labor. One was *in*clusive, a policy of working-class (or *producer*) unity; the other was *ex*clusive, a policy of race segregation. The latter, though not necessarily corollary to skilled craft organization, fitted logically within it, since the organizational strategy of each craft was exclusive with respect to all other workers, and especially unskilled workers. Blacks, for obvious historical reasons, were largely among the unskilled. Thus for skilled white craftsmen there was a potential advantage in discrimination against blacks, since they would thereby strengthen their ability to limit supply through controlling entry into the skilled group. Although AFL leaders often spoke as representatives of all workingmen, and liked to describe the federation as the "House of Labor," blacks generally were closed out at the effective level of local union membership.

Meanwhile white population moving to the West Coast had come into conflict with Chinese immigrants. The economic problem—that of competition between free wage labor and contract labor held in semibondage—was a real and pressing one. The wage laborer's grievance against contract labor, however, merged with earlier patterns of thought and behavior fixed long since with respect to Indians and blacks, but especially to black slaves. Chinese and other Orientals were equated to blacks as nonwhite—and therefore inferior. Within this wider context, the economic aspects of the problem were subsumed and engulfed. Hatred for Orientals proved a powerful unifying factor among whites of diverse religious and ethnic backgrounds. Soon this factor became indispensable. It furnished building blocks for party organization as well as trade union structure; and out of this mix of ingredients was generated the anti-Oriental crusade which dominated West Coast politics and deeply affected the course of national affairs through three quarters of a century.

Organized labor, nationally, enlisted in the crusade. Its public pursuit of exclusionary measures against nonwhite aliens imparted a sense of principle and patriotic purpose to its already exclusionary membership practices toward minority citizens. Moreover, the successful campaigns to restrict immigration from Asia furnished an analogy by which labor was able to rationalize a shift of position from its traditional open-door policy to advocacy of general restriction. Since this analogy was founded upon racist assumptions, the result was that labor gave its support, not to impartial general restriction, but to selective and discriminatory measures.

After World War I, the AFL helped to win enactment of an immigration system based upon national quotas which was heavily biased (within a vastly reduced total) to favor immigrants from northern and western Europe. Asian immigration was closed off completely.

Internally, during these same years, white labor faced another sort of immigration problem. World War I, while marking the end of large-scale European immigration, speeded the movement of Negroes out of the rural South to northern and western cities where many entered the ranks of un-skilled industrial labor. Yet the racial exclusiveness of the trade unions remained virtually undented. In 1924, the National Association for the Advancement of Colored People found that "Negro labor in the main is out-side the ranks of organized labor" because "white union labor does not want black labor, and . . . black labor has ceased to beg admittance. . . ."[20] Warning that the division would prove disastrous both to white and to black labor, as demonstrated by the use of Negro strikebreakers in the 1919 steel strike, the NAACP proposed a joint commission to seek ways of bringing black workers into the unions. This proposal was brushed aside by the Federation, as were the frequent criticisms and suggestions of A. Philip Randolph, leader of the all-black Brotherhood of Sleeping Car Porters, and for years the only Negro member of the AFL's executive council. In 1933, according to estimates of two contemporary labor historians, blacks comprised 2.3 percent of the membership of the American Federation of Labor. Half of these were in Randolph's union. Nine years later, Gunnar Myrdal wrote in his *American Dilemma* that "the discriminatory attitude of the organized building crafts," which were in a position to "dominate the American Federation of Labor," was a key factor "behind the reluctance of this organization to take any definite action against the exclusionist and segregational practices."[21] Thus, through the Depression and to the very eve of World War II, racial exclusion continued to play a central role in the organizational and political functioning of the labor movement.

Yet that cannot be quite the last word on the matter. While the tendency to exclude nonwhites was clearly dominant during the period under con-sideration, the other tendency, the *in*clusive tendency, was never totally destroyed. In fact it always found advocates within the labor movement. Nor was such advocacy due solely to sentiment or opportunism, for the inclusive approach to membership was logically inseparable from any con-cept of labor strategy which emphasized industrial as opposed to craft organization, or which looked toward long-range social change through

[20] In Charles H. Wesley, *Negro Labor in the United States, 1850–1925* (New York, 1927), pp. 275–277.

[21] Gunnar Myrdal, *An American Dilemma: The Negro Problem and American Democracy* (New York, 1944), p. 1102, in Herbert Hill, "The Racial Practices of Orga-nized Labor: The Contemporary Record," in Julius Jacobson, ed., *The Negro and the American Labor Movement* (New York, 1968), p. 293.

political action. Efforts to organize on the inclusive basis characterized the Knights of Labor in the early period, as well as certain long-established industrial unions such as the United Mine Workers. Scatterings of radical unionists, among them Socialists, members of the IWW, and Communists, pushed sporadically in the same direction. Nearly always such efforts at inclusive organization were restricted as subversive by the craft union leaders of the Federation. Indeed it required the great Depression and the advent of Franklin Roosevelt's New Deal, combined with a veritable explosion of organizational enthusiasm *outside* the perimeter of established unionism, to break open the rigidly conservative control exercised by the old leadership.

When that breakthrough finally did occur in the mid-1930s, organized labor added 5 million recruits, more than doubling its size within four years. The vast majority of these new members worked in previously unorganized mass production industries such as steel, automobile, electrical equipment, rubber, chemical, and packinghouse. For the most part they were unskilled or semiskilled, and among them were substantial numbers of nonwhites. This explosive increase brought dramatic changes both in structure and racial composition to the American labor movement. New unions sprang up, modeled not along the old craft lines, but industrially, so as to include all persons, regardless of craft or skill, who worked in a particular industry. Breaking away from the parent AFL, these new unions formed their own Congress of Industrial Organizations (CIO), inscribing upon their banner not only industrial organization but its logical corollary: mass membership without discrimination on account of race or sex. Mass membership generated political power. Labor became an indispensable part of the New Deal coalition, and by its support for such reforms as social security, federal guarantees of collective bargaining, public housing, and wages and hours legislation, helped to build the foundations of the American welfare state.

To many observers at the time, certainly, and to many participants, it seemed that the inclusive principle of labor organization had at last prevailed. Yet immediately after World War II the dynamic of union growth tapered off. Blue-collar jobs declined relatively within the labor force, and so too did union membership. Efforts to unionize the South proved generally unsuccessful. Those new unions which had skyrocketed before and during World War II shifted gradually to a defensive posture. Meanwhile the old craft organizations of the AFL had demonstrated an extraordinary survival power. They too had expanded vigorously in the period of upsurge and had adopted many methods and techniques of industrial unionism. They too suffered from relative membership loss after World War II. Thus by the 1950s, both the members and the leadership bureaucracies of organized labor were turning their energies to the preservation of gains already won for themselves, rather than to pioneering further innovations for society at large. Any differences of principle between the two wings of the labor movement now receded to a vanishing point. In 1955, they reunited to form the AFL-CIO—with the AFL assuming the role of dominant partner.

In retrospect, then, the transformation of the labor movement which occurred during the rapid growth years of industrial unionism may appear somewhat less fundamental than at the time it was generally taken to be. As unionism after World War II failed to expand into new regions or new fields of employment, the infusion of nonwhite membership diminished. At the same time labor's increasingly defensive stance tended to bring forward old ways and old attitudes. This was especially true in the matter of race. Patterns of thought, behavior, and organizational practice, built up through more than a century of racial exclusiveness, could not readily be set aside. Such contributions as have been made by the labor movement to the humanizing of race relations in America since the end of World War II have been relatively meager. The minority labor force today, remains for the most part unskilled, bears a disproportionate burden of unemployment, is underrepresented in union membership, and virtually excluded at the leadership level of organized labor.

6

Racism in the Era of Industrialization

RICHARD WEISS

By the latter part of the nineteenth century, racism had long become a generic cast of mind in the United States. As the previous essays have shown, no racial minority group in the United States, whether Indian, African, or Asian in origin, was immune from the effects of this racism. Neither the American Revolution, the era of Jacksonian democracy, the Civil War, nor the abolition of slavery had made any significant inroads on the racist assumptions of white Americans — assumptions which translated themselves into social exclusion, political powerlessness, and economic exploitation so far as minority groups were concerned.

I

The presuppositions underlying a racist classification of people were well established by the second half of the nineteenth century, and like a latent germ could be activated with regard to almost any group. In the most general sense, these assumptions were that particular groups possessed distinguishing qualities, that all members of these groups possessed these qualities, and that little in the way of environment could alter them. Here one encounters one of the central paradoxes of nineteenth-century thinking. On the one hand, the national ideology posited the dictum that every person

121

should be judged as an individual. Notions of class, caste, and ancestry which in other cultures conferred distinction were rejected in America. Presumably men were to be judged only by their accomplishment. At the same time, the idea that individuals were fragments of collectivities had equal currency. Men, it was argued, were in large part prefigured by the characteristics of the race they happened to spring from; irrespective of environmental differences, blood would tell. Despite the clash of logic, both sets of ideas coexisted comfortably in the popular mind.

From the 1870s onward, the categorization of people along racial lines was applied over a broader spectrum than in the past. Racial designations had been used in America, as in other countries, to distinguish people of different color and to discriminate against them. But now they were extended to cover virtually every group in the nation. Racist thinking, always a part of the American scene, intensified greatly. It carried both positive and negative connotations. While the idea of race was used to impute inferiority to some, it also was used to prove the superiority of others. At the same time that negative racial attributes were ascribed to blacks and immigrants, the cult of Anglo-Saxon superiority flourished as never before.

Antagonism toward immigrants on racial grounds evolved from nativistic antecedents which had deep historical roots in the United States. Traditionally, American nativism had focused on two presumed enemies: the radical and the Catholic. As early as the 1790s the new nation had suffered from fears of externally inspired subversion. The French Revolution sent out shock waves that reverberated on this side of the Atlantic. Bowing to popular fears, Congress passed the Alien and Sedition Acts, the first attempt to guarantee political conformity through legislative fiat. Since that time, the country has periodically experienced fear of subversion by "alien" peoples and ideologies.

The two decades just prior to the Civil War witnessed another eruption of nativist feeling which had as its focus anti-Catholic rather than anti-radical sentiment. Under the stress of tensions growing out of intensive economic growth and the political conflicts which were to culminate in the Civil War, American Protestants saw in Roman Catholicism a threat to the nation's institutions. To many, the large influx of Catholics into the country in the 1840s and 1850s appeared as a potential "fifth column," the first step in a plot to place America under Popish rule. The hierarchical structure of the Roman church was seen as antithetical to democracy. Catholic opposition to the use of the King James' Bible in public schools was interpreted as an attack on the religious principles upon which the republic presumably rested. Protestantism was changing from a mere religious designation to an integral part of the conception of American nationality. Just as Catholicism was identified with Irish nationalism, so in the United States Protestantism came to be identified with the "American way of life."

Outcroppings of nativist feeling, however, were the exception rather than the rule. Along with strains of a parochial nationalism, there existed in the United States a strong cosmopolitan tradition. National policy had always encouraged immigration, and the ideal of a melding of peoples, if not religions, on the North American continent dated back to the colonial period. The Civil War had the effect of diminishing nativist feeling and bringing American cosmopolitanism to the fore. The call to arms for defense of the Union lessened antagonism toward foreigners as all joined in the common effort of keeping the nation together. Disunion, the most severe threat to the American nationality, came not from aliens but from natives. The North, which contained the bulk of the nation's immigrants, was in the position of protecting the integrity of the body politic. It is not surprising that in this context fears of alien subversion declined.

Acceptance of the foreigner was furthered by the tremendous expansion in transportation and industry which followed the Civil War. Rapid industrial growth required muscle, and immigration was welcomed as necessary and beneficial to the country's development. Indeed, one heard echoes of Crèvecoeur's notion expressed in 1782, that "here individuals of all nations are melted into a new race of men, whose labours and posterity will one day cause great changes in the world."[1] In the years immediately following the Civil War, as the reunited country faced the future with confidence, the assimilating power of the nation was not seriously questioned. Indeed, the cosmopolitan tradition continued to find voice even as nativism mounted again in the late 1870s and 1880s. As late as 1888, Walt Whitman declared:

> America must welcome all—Chinese, Irish, German, pauper or not, criminal or not—all, all, without exceptions: become an asylum for all who choose to come. We may have drifted away from this principle temporarily, but time will bring us back. The tide may rise and rise again and still again and again after that, but at last there is an ebb—the low water comes at last. Think of it—think of it! how little of the land of the United States is cultivated—how much of it is still untilled. When you go West you sometimes travel whole days at lightning speed across vast spaces where not an acre is plowed, not a tree is touched, not a sign of a house is anywhere detected. America is not for special types, for the castes, but for the great mass of people—the vast, surging, hopeful, army of workers. Dare we deny them a home—close the doors in their faces—take possession of all and fence it in and then sit down satisfied with our system—convinced that we have solved our problem? I for my part refuse to connect America with such a failure—such a tragedy, for tragedy it would be.[2]

[1] J. Hector St. John de Crèvecoeur, *Letters from an American Farmer* (New York, n.d.), p. 43.
[2] In Horace Traubel, *With Walt Whitman in Camden* (2 vols.; New York, 1915), II, pp. 34–35.

By this time, however, nativism was again running at high tide. The nation's historic open-door policy toward immigrants had been seriously compromised by the Chinese Exclusion Act of 1882. Through the next four decades, the clamor against immigration grew until general restriction was adopted in the 1920s.

II

The resurgence of nativism from the late 1870s onward was related to the social transformation that changed America from a mercantile society to a modern industrialized state. American industrialization progressed rapidly, redrawing the face of the nation within scarcely a generation. The tensions that accompanied social reorganization resulted in a general sense of insecurity which found one focus in the immigrants who came in droves to man the nation's new factories and people its cities. While the ratio between foreign- and native-born remained fairly constant over the half-century following the Civil War, the immigrant in these years attained a heightened visibility. The "new" immigrants came from different areas of Europe than the "old." In 1860, more than 80 percent of the foreign-born came from Ireland, Great Britain, and Germany; by 1910, the proportion from these countries had dropped by more than half. The new sources of foreign population were Russia, the Austro-Hungarian empire, Italy, and other countries of southern and eastern Europe. In appearance, language, manner, and custom, these groups seemed more alien than the earlier comers. This was attested by the report of the Dillingham Immigration Commission of 1910 which in its introduction stated:

> The old and the new immigration differ in many essentials. The former was . . . largely a movement of settlers . . . from the most progressive sections of Europe. . . . They mingled freely with the native Americans and were quickly assimilated. On the other hand, the new immigration has been largely a movement of unskilled laboring men who have come . . . from the less progressive countries of Europe. . . . They have . . . congregated together in sections apart from native Americans and the older immigrants to such an extent that assimilation has been slow.[3]

The accuracy of this description may be questioned but it doubtless reflects the dominant sense of the time.

More important in understanding the fears aroused by the new immigrants is the timing of their arrival in the midst of an industrial revolution. Industrialization causes severe dislocation in all societies and the United States was no exception. Socially and economically, the Gilded Age was a

---

[3] In Oscar Handlin, *Race and Nationality in American Life* (New York, 1957), p. 81.

period of extreme instability. While great fortunes were made, the rate of business failure rose sharply. The movement from farm to city accelerated. Labor unrest accompanied by violence became commonplace. Corruption, both public and private, reached new dimensions. Science and scholarship challenged traditional beliefs. The pace of change in all areas of the national life became bewilderingly swift. Expressing a widespread feeling, Reverend Josiah Strong lamented: "When would these changes cease? How much of the old structure of society and belief would they leave standing? Were there any great certainties left?"[4] The fear was realistic enough. Society was undergoing fundamental transformation. What was irrational was focusing the anxiety over change on people who in a causal sense had little to do with it. The new immigrant became the living symbol of the new order. For those who resented the disappearance of the hallowed and familiar, the foreigner became a scapegoat.

Americans were ill prepared for the heightened class antagonism that industrialism brought in its wake. Surrounded by two oceans, favored with immense resources in land and minerals, the United States had an historic experience which it believed set it apart from the societies of Europe. Unburdened by the inequities which in Europe caused class warfare and violent social upheaval, Americans cultivated the illusion that theirs was a society without "down-trodden masses." The "riotous poor" were associated with the monarchies and aristocracies of the old world. No basis for class division existed in the United States, where labor and industry brought just rewards. The only qualification Americans admitted to this general picture was the South, where slavery had in fact created a class structure. Otherwise, ours was regarded as a classless society. This image was rudely shaken in the decades following the Civil War. Large-scale industrialization created a massive proletariat much of which barely eked out a subsistence living. Conflict between workers and owners reached unprecedented dimensions and the faith in American immunity from class warfare began to crumble. In this connection, the great strikes of 1877 mark a turning point in the American consciousness.

The Panic of 1873 was the start of a series of cyclical depressions which rocked America for the next three decades. As the effects of the depression deepened, employers discharged large numbers of workers who could find no other means of subsistence. Thousands of unemployed demonstrated in cities throughout the nation to convince authorities of the urgency of their need. Seen as a possible threat to the peace, demonstrators were ordered to disperse. Often in despair at official indifference to their plight, they refused, and clashes between police and unemployed demonstrators became common. In 1875, in the wake of these disturbances, violence broke out in the coal fields of eastern Pennsylvania. Miners attempted to unionize

[4] Josiah Strong, *The Times and Young Men* (New York,: 1901), p. 14.

for better wages but the operators refused to compromise over grievances. A strike was called which the workers were ill equipped to support. With vastly greater resources, the operators were much better able to weather the storm. Many workers were forced by cold and hunger to return to work. Strikebreakers were called in to replace the rest and pitched battles broke out between remaining strikers and forces hired by the companies to protect the strikebreakers. This and other violence in the region held the public's attention for months.

Capping these almost continuous manifestations of labor unrest were the railroad strikes of 1877. Wage cuts on the major lines precipitated a series of spontaneous strikes that spread throughout the railway network of the nation. They began on July 1, 1877, when the workers on the Baltimore and Ohio walked off their jobs. Other lines followed. Workers attempted to prevent strikebreakers from taking their places and were determined to keep the trains from moving. The operators were equally determined to get the trains going and called on state authorities for aid. Rioting broke out in Baltimore, Pittsburgh, Chicago, St. Louis, and other railroad centers. State militias were often unequal to the task of quelling the outbreaks and federal troops finally were used. As President Hayes sent federal forces into city after city, the country witnessed its first labor upheaval on a national scale. The strikes, as the *Nation* remarked, put to rest the notion that the United States had "solved the problem of enabling labor and capital to live together in political harmony, and that this was the one country in which there was no proletariat and no dangerous class, and in which manners as well as legislation effectually prevented the formation of one." Noting this challenge to the national image, the magazine ventured an explanation of the causes. While acknowledging that legitimate grievances might exist, it could not condone violence which it found distinctly un-American. As usually happens in such situations, attention focused on the bloodshed rather than the grievances. Violence, the magazine editorialized, was attributable to the vast increase of foreigners in the population "to whom American political and social ideals appeal but faintly, if at all."[5]

The association of immigrants with violence and radical ideology intensified in the following decade, reaching its apex in the response to the Haymarket Square Riot of 1886. In the spring of that year, a movement spread across the country calling for demonstrations in support of an eight-hour day. The call received a particularly strong response in Chicago, then considered the center of radical labor sentiment in the country. The eight-hour demonstration on May 1 passed without incident. Two days later, however, strikers and strikebreakers clashed outside the McCormick Harvester plant. Police were called in and four men were killed. An anarchist group called for a protest meeting in Haymarket Square for the following

[5] *The Nation,* 25 (Aug. 2, 1877), p. 68.

evening. A crowd of about 3000 gathered. Speakers went on interminably. It began to rain and the bulk of the crowd dispersed. As the meeting was breaking up, 200 police arrived. A bomb was thrown. A melee ensued in which both police and protesters were injured and killed. Cries of anarchy immediately were raised as the press encouraged fears of imminent social catastrophe. One newspaper announced that "if civilization is not to be plunged into chaos, the supremacy of law must be vindicated and maintained at whatever cost."[6] Eight anarchists were arrested and convicted of inciting—not committing—the crime. The state's attorney argued that the safety of the nation's institutions demanded that examples be made of these men so that all could see that America would not tolerate anarchy. While the incident was minor as a symptom of radicalism and while anarchist and socialist groups had scant influence in the labor movement as a whole, its effect was to fan public hysteria. Note was taken of the large numbers of Poles and Bohemians in Chicago's population. Radical doctrines were held to be foreign imports carried into the country like germs by such immigrant groups. An article in the *Atlantic* explained the labor unrest in the country as follows:

> We have agreed to open the door wide to all the world, and all the world accepted our invitation. We have relied confidently upon the tendency of our institutions, and above all upon our educational system, to counteract the disturbing effect of a continual influx of foreign ignorance. . . . Under the circumstances, we ought not to be surprised that the public schools fail to keep pace with the immigration; that we acquire every year many thousands of citizens who cannot speak English, and who have not the faintest apprehension of American institutions and governmental theories; that, in effect, the country is being colonized from Europe with people who bring here complete theories of life, many of which are utterly opposed to our form, or to any form, of civilization.[7]

Unable to perceive the weaknesses in the social structure which made violence an almost inevitable part of the adjustment to industrialization, Americans searched for reasons extrinsic to themselves and their society. Immigrants provided the needed explanation. In the simplistic logic of prejudice, this could lead to only one conclusion. If foreigners were the cause of disorder, then their exclusion was the cure. Illusory as this was, it served as an outlet for the anxieties of many caught in the dislocations of an economic revolution.

Another sore on the body politic for which immigrants were blamed was the increase in political corruption that characterized the period. The

[6] In Frederic C. Jaher, *Doubters and Dissenters: Cataclysmic Thought in America 1880–1918* (New York, 1964), p. 40.

[7] George F. Parsons, "The Labor Question," *Atlantic Monthly,* 58 (July 1886) pp. 98–99.

growing exploitation of the nation's resources meant that the government, as dispenser of the national domain, had a capacity for largesse on a grand scale. The power of Congress to make land grants and pay subsidies to railroads made the business of bribing legislators for government favors a profitable one. On the local level, government also became an important object in the considerations of businessmen. Rapid urbanization created needs that were readily exploitable by politicians and businessmen with their eye on the main chance. Growing cities needed gas and water facilities, public transportation, sewage systems, and other services. Municipal legislatures, having the power to grant franchises for these purposes, could bestow fortune on the lucky bidder. In these circumstances, the growth of corruption is not surprising. Public morality reached a low ebb in the decades following the Civil War. In the South, corruption was linked with the blacks; in the North, it was linked with the immigrants. E. L. Godkin, editor of the *Nation,* expressed a widely held sentiment when he decried the corrosive influence of foreigners on American politics.

> The harm they do the country as additions to the voting population is undoubted, notorious, and undeniable. . . . Nearly all the economical absurdities produced on the stump or embodied in legislation are due to a desire to "capture the foreign vote." The degradation of our city government is largely due to the readiness of the natives to let the immigrants sack the cities in return for their support in the Federal arena. In truth, there is no corner of our system in which the hastily made and ignorant foreign voter may not be found eating the political structure, like a white ant. . . .[8]

The fact that many bosses of political machines were of foreign extraction only helped to prove the point. To be sure, the role of immigrants in the growth of machine politics was an important one. What critics failed to perceive, however, was that politicians of foreign extraction also served to mediate between the masses of recently enfranchised immigrants and the established and respectable elements of society. Furthermore, whatever impulse for corruption came from the new arrivals was more than matched by that emanating from the urban economic elites. It was not until the twentieth century, however, that investigations like Lincoln Steffens' *Shame of the Cities* brought the connection between businessmen and urban machine politicians to light. Thus the immigrant served as a convenient scapegoat for the nation's shortcomings. This is not meant to imply a conscious manipulation of antiforeign feeling for purposes of social control. But the question of intention apart, the focus on the immigrant as the great subverter of American institutions helped to deflect analysis from the more realistic and more threatening sources of the trouble.

[8] *The Nation,* 56 (Jan. 19, 1893), p. 43.

III

As the nation entered its most severe industrial crisis in the depression which rocked the country from 1893–1897, anti-immigrant feeling intensified and cries for restriction became more shrill. At the same time, preservers of American purity grew restless and aggressive. The decade saw the growth of patriotic organizations, membership in which was akin to a pedigree. The Daughters of the American Revolution embarked on intensive Americanization campaigns to prevent the erosion of national traditions. Less exclusive, the American Protective League set out to save the country from Catholic subversion. In 1893, under the impact of the worst depression the country had ever known, it enrolled more than half a million members. Superpatriots were on the march, and spoke as if the fate of civilization hung in the balance. The national genius was identified with the racial stock of the early colonial settlers. The cult of the Anglo-Saxon was the order of the day.

Taking their cue from the English historian, Edward A. Freeman, American scholars and popularizers had for some years argued that the political genius of the English-speaking peoples was traceable to the tribal councils of the ancient Teutons. In America, this tradition found expression in the New England town meeting, the seed bed of American liberty. The Anglo-Saxons were an offshoot of the Teutonic racial tree, hence their peculiar political genius. Positive racists had their disagreements. Some, like Henry Cabot Lodge, preferred to emphasize the Norman component in the English racial make-up. Others, like John W. Burgess, argued that the Normans corrupted the Anglo-Saxon bloodstream in England which explained British aristocracy and decadence. Somehow the American forests had purged our early settlers of this impurity and there had been a reversion to the earlier pure Teutonic mold. The cult of Anglo-Saxonism found its way into the highest repositories of culture. Editors, political leaders, and scholars, in varying degrees, succumbed to the myth of a super race. Anglo-Saxon language and literature were introduced into college and high school curricula, finding greater vogue here than in England. The national greatness was inextricably linked to the national bloodstream.

The cult of the Anglo-Saxon fit well with the expansionism of the 1890s and served as a convenient rationale for American imperialism. Racism had its role in earlier expansionist movements but by the 1890s had the added force of Darwinian theory. In posing the theory of evolution, Darwin argued that some species survived, while others perished, through a process of natural selection. Herbert Spencer, the British sociologist, applying evolutionary theory to societal development, stated that natural selection operated through a struggle for existence among competing species in which only the fittest survived. Progress came about through a process of continuing struggle with the weak succumbing to the strong. In the context of such a world view, imperialist expansion took on the force of a biological imperative. Social Darwinism gave the dominance and growth of the superior races the sanction of nature.

Josiah Strong—a Congregational minister, and one of the country's foremost propagandists for expansionism—popularized this argument in his influential book, *Our Country* (1885). Strong's book drew the concerns of nativists and expansionists under a single cover. He worried over immigration, describing the typical foreigner as "a European peasant, whose horizon has been narrow, whose moral and religious training has been meager or false, and whose ideas of life are low." Their presence here in large numbers lowered the moral and intellectual tone of American society. Strong also warned of the dangers of Popery, declaring that there was an irreconcilable difference between the principles of Roman Catholicism and "the fundamental principles of our free institutions." Along with these classic nativist themes, he waxed eloquent on the Anglo-Saxons' unique mission in fulfilling the divine will. The Anglo-Saxon race was representative of two great ideas, civil liberty and "pure spiritual Christianity." The fulfillment of these ideas was mankind's greatest need in hastening the coming of Christ's kingdom. "It follows, then, that the Anglo-Saxon, as the great representative of these two ideas, the depository of these two great blessings, sustains peculiar relations to the world's future, is divinely commissioned to be, in a peculiar sense, his brother's keeper." Furthermore, there was no doubt that "North America is to be the great home of the Anglo-Saxon, the principal seat of his power, the center of his life and influence."[9] Consequently, the Anglo-Saxon destiny and the American destiny were one. As the world was filling up, as there were no new continents to be discovered, as the usable arable lands throughout the globe were limited, a new era was dawning.

> The time is coming when the pressure of population on the means of subsistence will be felt here as it is now felt in Europe and Asia. Then will the world enter upon a new stage of its history—*the final competition of races, for which the Anglo-Saxon is being schooled.* . . . Then this race of unequal energy, with all the majesty of numbers and the might of wealth behind it—the representative, let us hope, of the largest liberty, the purest Christianity, the highest civilization—having developed peculiarly aggressive traits calculated to impress its institutions upon mankind, will spread itself over the earth. If I read not amiss, this powerful race will move down upon Mexico, down upon Central and

[9] Josiah Strong, *Our Country* (New York, 1885), respectively pp. 40, 53, 161, and 165.

South America, out upon the islands of the sea, over upon Africa and beyond. And can any one doubt that the result of this competition of races will be the "survival of the fittest"?[10]

To be sure, there were those who balked at these cosmic predictions. They reminded the nation of its commitment to liberal principles of self-government and cautioned against aggressive expansionist policies abroad. But the current of jingoism ran strong. Theodore Roosevelt sneeringly referred to the anti-imperialists as "futile sentimentalists of the international arbitration type." If they prevailed, they would produce "a flabby, timid type of character, which eats away the great fighting features of the race."[11] For racial determinists, American expansion was foreordained. To thwart it was to thwart the will of God. Senator Beveridge of Indiana, addressing the Congress during the debate over the annexation of the Philippines declared:

> God has not been preparing the English-speaking and Teutonic peoples for a thousand years for nothing but vain and idle self-contemplation and self-admiration. No! He has made us master organizers of the world to establish system where chaos reigns. He has given us the spirit of progress to overwhelm the forces of reaction throughout the earth. He has made us adept in government that we may administer government among savage and senile peoples. Were it not for such a force as this the world would relapse into barbarism and night. And of all our race He has marked the American people as His chosen nation to finally lead in the regeneration of the world.[12]

Aggressiveness abroad was matched by fears for the deteriorating national character at home. Many of the international muscle flexers were in the forefront of nativistic agitation. Racism, never entirely absent from nativism, became more marked in the 1890s. Focus shifted from radicalism and Catholic plots to fears of corruption of the national bloodstream. At the same time, restrictionist sentiment became more organized. The year 1894 saw the formation of the Immigration Restriction League under the leadership of a group of upper-class New Englanders. Members of this elite segment of American society suffered acutely from a sense of displacement. Long accustomed to leadership, they now found themselves relegated to subsidiary roles in national affairs. Once a dominant group, they were now being pushed to the periphery of power.

The loss of social power was compounded by a growing concern over

[10] Strong, *Our Country,* p. 175.
[11] *Selections from the Correspondence of Theodore Roosevelt and Henry Cabot Lodge,* Henry Cabot Lodge, ed. (2 vols.; New York, 1925), I, p. 218.
[12] In Claude G. Bowers, *Beveridge and the Progressive Era* (Cambridge, Mass., 1932), p. 121.

the fecundity of old stock Americans. The great families seemed to be dying out. Among the most prominent New Englanders to give credence to fears of race suicide was Francis A. Walker. A distinguished social scientist, he served as Professor of Political Economy and History at Yale and later as president of the Massachusetts Institute of Technology. As early as 1870, when he was Superintendent of the Census, he noted a decline in the birth rate among Americans of native stock. He also observed that Americans of recent arrival reproduced at a much higher rate than natives. This disparity had begun with the arrival of immigrants in large numbers in the 1840s and 1850s. From 1870 to 1890 the trend intensified. Furthermore the decline in the fecundity of old-stock Americans occurred in precisely those areas where immigrant settlement was most dense. Walker dismissed the notion that there had been any decline in the virility of native Americans. The problem was not physical but social and psychological. He argued that old-stock Americans would have retained a high rate of increase were it not for the fact that immigrants provided a "shock to the principle of population among the native element."[13] The reason for this was the trauma to community structure and values brought about by large incursions of foreigners whose standards of living and of social decency were offensive to descendants of the early settlers. They shrank from economic competition with such groups and were unwilling to bring children into a world where they might be subjected to such competition.

Walker further argued that prior to large-scale immigration labor was respected everywhere but in the South. Immigrants divided the social structure of the rest of the country into two classes—native and foreign. This resulted in a stigma attaching to certain kinds of work, causing the older families to shun having many children. Thus the cause for the decline of the older stock was not "physiological nor climatic" but "social and economic."[14] The threat was clear. Foreigners were replacing native Americans. If nothing were done, the latter would gradually disappear. It was this kind of thinking that caused national leaders like Theodore Roosevelt to worry about racial extinction.

> Any man who studies the statistics of the birth rate among the native Americans of New England . . . needs not to be told that when prudence and forethought are carried to the point of cold selfishness and self-indulgence, the race is bound to disappear. Taking into account the women who for good reasons do not marry, or who when married are childless or are able to have but one or two children, it is evident that the married woman able to have children must on an average have four or the race will not perpetuate itself.[15]

[13] Francis A. Walker, "Immigration and Degradation," *Discussions in Economics and Statistics,* D. R. Dewey, ed. (2 vols.; New York, 1899), II, p. 423.

[14] Walker, "Immigration and Degradation," p. 426.

[15] Theodore Roosevelt, *An Autobiography* (New York, 1927), pp. 161–162.

While some concerned with preservation of the race encouraged women of good stock to have many children, others stepped up their efforts to slow or stop the influx of foreigners. The Immigration Restriction League propagandized throughout the country on the need for some kind of restriction and finally came to focus on a literacy requirement as the best means of accomplishing this end. This would not stop immigration altogether but would introduce a principle of selectivity into the process. People of less desirable stock usually came from areas of Europe where literacy was low. Immigration from northern and western Europe would not be seriously impeded. As one political scientist explained: "We must preserve our Aryan nationality in the state, and admit to its membership only such non-Aryan race elements as shall have become Aryanized in spirit and in genius by contact with it, if we would build the superstructure of the ideal American commonwealth."[16]

The chief political spokesman for restriction was Henry Cabot Lodge, New England Brahmin and senator from Massachusetts. Throughout the 1890s, Lodge sought Congressional enactment of a literacy test. His bill would have excluded from entry into the United States all persons over fourteen years of age who could not read and write some language. He presented two basic reasons for restriction: the first was economic, the second racial. He held that large-scale immigration adversely affected the American worker by providing too much cheap competition for his services. This, however, was not the primary consideration. More important to Lodge than the quantity of people entering the country was their quality. His bill would permit unrestricted immigration of desirable types. Though the literacy test would technically apply uniformly, its chief impact would be on people from southern and eastern Europe. Candidly, Lodge declared before the Senate:

> It is found . . . that the illiteracy test will bear most heavily upon the Italians, Russians, Poles, Hungarians, Greeks, and Asiatics, and very lightly, or not at all, upon English-speaking emigrants or Germans, Scandinavians, and French. In other words, the races most affected by the illiteracy test are those whose emigration to this country has begun within the last twenty years and swelled to enormous proportions, races with which the English-speaking people have never hitherto assimilated, and who are most alien to the great body of the people of the United States.[17]

This could be counted on because the nations of eastern and southern Europe were generally backward and had weak educational systems. One could of course argue that illiterates could be taught to read and

---

[16] John W. Burgess, "The Ideal of the American Commonwealth," *Political Science Quarterly*, 10 (September 1895), p. 407.

[17] *Congressional Record*, 54th Congress, Session 1, pp. 2050 ff.

write, but for Lodge this was not the essential concern. Literacy testing was merely a device to put a good face on racism. Low rates of literacy were most prevalent in those parts of Europe which were peopled by inferior racial stocks. To permit such peoples continuing entry was to invite "a great and perilous change in the very fabric of our race."[18]

It is important to examine Lodge's concept of race. Well-educated, a scholar and historian, he was aware of the theoretical writings on race then in existence. He acknowledged that movements and mixtures of races on the European continent had resulted in the amalgamation of different human stocks. In an absolute sense, there was no such thing as pure blood. Nonetheless, he contended that there were peculiarities that attached to peoples and that these had been forged over such long periods of time as to make them virtually fixed. He defined racial characteristics comprehensively as

> the moral and intellectual characters, which in their association make the soul of a race, and which represent the product of all its past, the inheritance of all its ancestors, and the motives of its conduct. The men of each race possess an indestructable stock of ideas, traditions, sentiments, modes of thought, an unconscious inheritance from their ancestors, upon which argument has no effect. What makes a race are their mental, and above all, their moral characteristics, the slow growth and assimilation of centuries of toil and conflict. These are the qualities . . . which make one race rise and another fall. . . .[19]

Strictly speaking, this was not biological determinism; but, in a functional sense, its implications were much the same.

Next, Lodge addressed himself to the problem of race mixture. During a trip to Europe in 1895, he discovered Gustave Le Bon's recently published *The Psychology of Peoples.* Citing the French social psychologist as his authority, Lodge warned against amalgamation. He maintained that history taught that when unequal races mixed, the inferior prevailed.

> There is a limit to the capacity of any race for assimilating and elevating an inferior race, and when you begin to pour in unlimited numbers people of alien or lower races of less social efficiency and less moral force, you are running the most frightful risk that any people can run. The lowering of a great race means not only its own decline but that of human civilization.[20]

IV

Extrapolating from Lodge's speech, it is possible to discover many of the assumptions which governed thought about race toward the end of the nineteenth century. The concept of race for Lodge, and most of his con-

[18] *Congressional Record,* 54th Congress, Session 1.
[19] *Congressional Record,* 54th Congress, Session 1.
[20] *Congressional Record,* 54th Congress, Session 1.

temporaries, carried complex connotations. It was not simply a biological concept. It did not encompass only physical and anatomical differences such as color, brain size, and facial features. It included these, to be sure, but it covered much more. When Lodge referred to the mental and moral characteristics of peoples, he was ascribing to race qualities which we would refer to as cultural. Differences in language, the arts, social organization, and aspiration were part of the "souls" of peoples, and soul was as much a part of a person's inherited propensity as was size or skin color. Physical and cultural attributes were linked under the heading of race and both were passed from generation to generation through a kind of mystic inheritance. Almost all the qualities which make men what they are were considered racial. Thus even the well-educated could speak in terms of the American's inborn love of freedom, or the eastern European's inborn preference for autocracy. Implicit in this reasoning is the assumption of a kind of cultural Lamarckianism. Characteristics acquired in the process of adapting to experience and environment were passed on through the germ plasm.

In discussing race, social scientists did not seriously disagree over the inheritability of cultural capacities. They only differed over the question of how many generations this process took. Almost all shared the premise that the "new" immigrants and the blacks were racially inferior. Those sympathetic to these groups argued that education and exposure to a new environment would bring about changes very quickly, even physical changes such as increased brain size. Those hostile to these groups argued that the qualities which distinguished races were developed over centuries or even millenia and that for all intents and purposes they were fixed relative to any time span that made sense in terms of formulating social policy. Thus even the reform economist, John R. Commons could write: "Race differences are established in the very blood and physical constitution. They are most difficult to eradicate, and they yield only to the slow processes of the centuries."[21] Racist assumptions, then, were the property of reformers and conservatives alike. Assimilationists and exclusionists both attached central importance to race in the development of civilization.

As Lodge's Senate speech indicates, the question of the effects of race mixture also very much agitated men's minds. The debate over the harmfulness of interbreeding had raged since the late eighteenth century. Here the question of the origins of different human types was crucial. Prior to the publication of Darwin's *Origin of the Species* in 1859, two schools of thought prevailed over the nature of ultimate human origins. Monogenists argued that all the different groupings of mankind were descended from a common set of parents. This carried implications for the essential oneness of mankind. Polygenists argued that the differences among various human groupings were so fundamental they could only

---

[21] John R. Commons, *Races and Immigrants in America* (New York, 1915), p. 7.

be explained in terms of different sources of origin. For the monogenist, mixture was not unnatural. For the polygenist, it was akin to crossing a horse with a donkey and coming up with a mule. They argued that crosses between races would have the same effect as crosses between species — weakness, infertility, and general debility in offspring. Darwin's theory of evolution, in ascribing a common ancestor to all humans, put the debate between monogenist and polygenist to rest. In the context of evolutionary theory, the question of unitary or multiple creations became meaningless. By the late nineteenth century, virtually all educated opinion accepted Darwin's explanation of human evolution in formal terms. Nonetheless polygenist assumptions continued to operate. Scarcely anyone would deny an ultimate common ancestry for all men. In a proximate sense, however, this often was disregarded. Whatever the nature of origins in the distant past, the different paths of development among different racial groups had gone on for so long as to be virtually primordial. Lodge's fear of pollution of the national bloodstream by mixture with inferior stocks reflects the continuing vitality of polygenist assumptions.

The revival of genetic studies toward the turn of the century provided fresh fuel for racial determinists in their campaign to save the nation's germ plasm. The rediscovery of the Mendelian laws of heredity focused attention on the genetic transmission of characteristics from generation to generation. Here was further proof that environmentalists were merely deluded sentimentalists. The science of genetics inspired the eugenics movement which got under way in the United States in the early 1900s. Aspects of the movement's message gave it a reformist and humanitarian air. Its concern for preventing the reproduction of persons with such congenital defects as feeble-mindedness seemed motivated by humane sentiment. At the same time, however, the emphasis the movement gave to unalterable hereditary qualities had reactionary implications. Eugenicists ascribed deviancy to the genes rather than to social forces. For example, the eminent biologist Charles B. Davenport, who spearheaded the movement in America, attributed prostitution to inherited predisposition. Most prostitutes, he claimed, were born of mothers of like occupation. This, he explained, was due to congenital hypereroticism, not to socio-psychological causes. Various forms of criminality were explained similarly. A broad range of social deviance was treated as genetically determined. The solution eugenicists offered was the prevention of propagation among such types. Incarceration, sterilization, and stricter marriage laws were among the solutions posed at various times.

Organized eugenics got its immediate impetus at a meeting of the American Breeders Association in 1904. Hearing reports of great success with the selective breeding of plants and animals, delegates asked why such techniques could not be applied to humans. Three years later, the association established a committee on human heredity. Mrs. E. H. Harriman was impressed enough with the need for such a project to subsidize it. With her generous financing, the Eugenics Record Office was established in 1910 with Davenport at its head.

Speaking at the first National Conference on Race Betterment in 1914, Davenport sought "to awaken an interest in heredity among our best stock, so that in marrying, the old ideals of marriage into good stock may be restored." Echoing Walker and Roosevelt, he bemoaned the dying out of the old New England families through their failure to reproduce and implored good Americans to realize the "importance of marrying, marrying well and having healthy effective children—and plenty of them." At the same conference, Harvard professor Robert DeC. Ward, stressed the need for keeping certain foreigners outside our borders. He noted that the country was more selective in the breeds of cattle it imported than in choosing the immigrants to whom it opened its doors. He urged "every citizen who wants to keep the blood of the race pure" to support enactment of a literacy qualification.[22] Such legislation did finally become law over President Woodrow Wilson's veto a few years later.

By the eve of World War I, American racism had achieved as much refinement as an ideology as it would ever develop. The most systematic exposition of racism to come from the pen of an American appeared in 1916 with the publication of Madison Grant's, *Passing of the Great Race.* Grant was a New York patrician whose family had been prominent in Knickerbocker society since the colonial period. Of independent means, he was something of a scientific dilettante. He was well read in zoology, ethnology, and anthropology, and had wide contacts within the scientific community. Grant was also regarded as an expert genealogist, an interest which probably reflected the same insecurity which had led to the formation of so many exclusivist organizations in the 1890s. Pushed from the center of the national stage, American aristocrats were at pains to document their identities. Grant was also active in the restrictionist movement, serving for twenty-five years as a vice-president of the Immigration Restriction League, and was closely associated with the American Eugenics Society. His social and intellectual concerns converged to produce one of the classic statements of the racist viewpoint.

In a preface to Grant's work, Henry F. Osborn, Professor of Zoology at Columbia University, struck the keynote of the book.

> If I were asked: What is the greatest danger which threatens the American public today? I would certainly reply: The gradual dying out among our people of those hereditary traits through which the principles of our religious, political and social foundations were laid down and their insidious replacement by traits of less noble character.[23]

---

[22] *Proceedings of the First National Conference on Race Betterment* (Battle Creek, Mich., 1914), respectively pp. 454, 456, and 545.

[23] Madison Grant, *The Passing of the Great Race* (New York, 1923), p. ix.

Racial and social disintegration went hand in hand. In this formulation, racism acquired a significantly new dimension. Always a rationale for oppression, it now was used to explain all of society's ills. Problems took on a tantalizing simplicity in such a reductionist world-view. All social issues, however complex, could be ascribed to racial causes. By the same token, the need for racial purity became more urgent. Grant attacked the melting pot theory as dangerous sentimentalism. Mixture only brought reversion to inferior type. The "cross between any of the three European races and a Jew is a Jew." If Americans wanted to preserve their institutions, they must learn that social systems had their racial correlates. "The Nordics are, all over the world, a race of soldiers, sailors, adventurers and explorers, but above all, of rulers, organizers and aristocrats in sharp contrast to the essentially peasant and democratic character of the Alpines." The Nordics as early settlers had framed our institutions; the Alpines who were flooding into the country by the millions would overrun them if something were not quickly done to prevent it. Grant attacked the assimilationists who argued that southern and eastern Europeans could be made into good Americans. "There exists today a widespread and fatuous belief in the power of environment, as well as of education and opportunity to alter heredity, which arise from the dogma of the brotherhood of man, derived in its turn from the loose thinkers of the French Revolution and their American mimics. . . ."[24] Grant, then, was attacking not only the "racial abyss" toward which the United States was moving, but the whole democratic tendency of the previous century. Racism, however, moved across the whole of the political spectrum. Reform thinkers would balk at Grant's arch-conservatism and were less rigidly deterministic on the nature of racial differences, but scarcely any would have denied the central importance of race as a factor in human development.

The most important voice to challenge seriously the assumptions that linked race and civilization was that of Franz Boas. This equation, he noted, rested on the assumption that a civilized society was based on the natural aptitudes of its members. The higher the civilization, the higher the aptitudes of those who composed it. "We must investigate," he wrote in *The Mind of Primitive Man* (1911), "in how far we are justified in assuming that achievement is primarily due to exceptional aptitude. . . ." He argued that there was scant justification for such a conclusion. History rather than ability accounted for the different paths of development followed by various peoples. "In short, historical events appear to have been much more potent in leading races to civilization than their faculty, and it follows that achievements of races do not warrant us in assuming that one race is more highly gifted than the other." In a career extending over fifty years as one of America's leading anthropologists, Boas brought one

[24] Grant, *The Passing of the Great Race,* respectively pp. 18, 228, and 16.

after another racist assumption under question. Physical differences between races were small, he noted, compared to their similarities. Furthermore, most of the obvious physical differences among races seemed to have no functional significance whatsoever. Blond or dark hair, brown or blue eyes, smooth or hairy skin, bore no demonstrable relation to faculty or capacity for achievement. With regard to brain size, Boas noted, even granting that more people of one race had larger brains than people of another, the vast majority of brain sizes of all races fell within a common measurement. That is, if brain size was indeed a determinant of intelligence, the faculty of the average in all races was roughly the same. With reference to the Negro, Boas wrote: "As it is, almost all we can say with certainty is that the differences between the average types of the white and of the negro, that have a bearing upon vitality and mental ability, are much less than the individual variations in each race."[25] Boas, however, was in a small minority, and belief in the innate inferiority of the nation's largest oppressed minority continued to dominate both popular and scientific thought.

V

The history of the black man in America after emancipation was one of repeated frustration and disappointment. Racist attitudes helped insure that the promise of freedom and equality for the emancipated slaves and their descendants would go unfulfilled. Economic, political, and social arrangements in the South after the Civil War effectively prevented blacks from realizing the fruits of citizenship. Most of the country's blacks remained attached to the land. While many of the South's plantations had been broken up into smaller units after the Civil War, ownership continued to be highly concentrated. Blacks, for the most part, did not own the land they worked. They tilled the soil on a rental basis. Some were cash tenants but the vast majority were sharecroppers. Under this system, an individual was given a plot of land to work; in return he guaranteed the landlord a share of his crop, while at the same time landlords advanced to tenants the necessary implements and supplies to begin farming. Southern legislatures passed lien laws which gave the landlord-merchant first claim on the tenant's crop for any outstanding indebtedness. Rarely able to escape debt, sharecroppers were caught in a system which reduced them to a position of virtual peonage.

After the withdrawal of federal troops from the South, the rights granted to blacks during Reconstruction were gradually eroded. Even

[25] Franz Boas, *The Mind of Primitive Man* (New York, 1911), respectively pp. 5, 17, and 269.

before disfranchisement was written into law, various techniques were developed to limit or control the black vote. Negro districts were gerrymandered to render the black vote ineffectual. Often polling places were established at distances which made accessibility by blacks difficult, or polling places were changed without black voters being notified. Where the vote was not eliminated, it often was controlled. Blacks were alternately cajoled or threatened, reminded of their economic dependence, and then taken to the polls where they voted according to instruction.

For a period during the 1880s and early 1890s, it appeared that this political powerlessness might change. The Panic of 1873 inaugurated a severe depression in southern agriculture that was to continue for the rest of the century. Thousands of poor whites lost their land and like blacks became ensnared in the crop-lien system. Under severe economic distress, farmers began to rebel against the Bourbon leadership of the southern Democracy. Furthermore, by the 1880s, fear of "black domination" had receded. Poor whites were no longer willing to adhere to the regular Democratic party out of fears of black takeover. For a time, it appeared that poor blacks and whites might unite politically for the redress of common grievances. Both conservatives and agrarian radicals began to vie for the black vote, often restoring suffrage where it had for some time been denied. This created situations in which blacks held the political balance of power between competing white groups. Confronted by the political resurgence of the Negro, conservatives once again began to raise cries of "Black Republicanism" and to exhume the presumed horrors of black rule during Reconstruction.

Where the conservatives could not control the black vote, they sought disfranchisement. Similarly, agrarian radicals, disappointed in many areas by the conservatives' ability to manipulate the black vote, became disillusioned with the possibility of an effective political coalition with blacks along lines of common economic interest. For the poor white, racism took precedence over self-interest. A consensus emerged in the South to eliminate the black man as a factor in southern politics and to let the competing elements within the white community fight it out among themselves. From 1889 to 1908, the southern states revised their constitutions to facilitate denial of the suffrage to Negroes. Poll taxes, "grandfather clauses," literacy tests, and white primaries were among the legal techniques used to disfranchise the black. At the Virginia constitutional convention of 1901, Carter Glass declared:

> In the midst of differing contentions and suggested perplexities, there stands out the uncontroverted fact that the article of suffrage which the convention today will adopt does not necessarily deprive a single white man of the ballot, but will inevitably oust from the existing electorate four-fifths of the Negro voters. That was the purpose of the convention; that will be its achievement.

Asked if the Negro was not being denied the vote by fraud and discrimination, he replied:

> By fraud, no; by discrimination, yes. But it will be discrimination within the letter of the law, and not in violation of the law. Discrimination! Why, that is precisely what we propose; that exactly is what the convention was elected for—to discriminate to the very extremity permissible under the limitation of the Federal Constitution with a view to the elimination of every Negro who can be gotten rid of, legally, without materially impairing the numerical strength of the white electorate. . . . As has been said, we have accomplished our purpose strictly within the limitations of the Federal Constitution by legislating against the characteristics of the black race and not against the "race, color, or previous conditions" of the people themselves. It is a fine discrimination indeed, that we have practiced in the fabrication of this plan.[26]

Such bluntness was possible only because racism had such legitimacy in the American value structure. No attempt was made to discriminate among Negroes as to real qualification for the suffrage. Disfranchisement was intended to be absolute. As J. K. Vardaman of Mississippi put it: "I am just as opposed to Booker Washington as a voter, with all his Anglo-Saxon re-enforcements, as I am to the coconut-headed, chocolate-colored, typical little coon, Andy Dotson, who blacks my shoes every morning. Neither is fit to perform the supreme function of citizenship."[27]

By the turn of century, whatever inhibitions northern sentiment had placed on the excrescences of southern racism had been removed; the North had been converted to the southern point of view. An editorial in the *New York Times* in 1900 noted that "Northern men . . . no longer denounce the suppression of the Negro vote in the South as it used to be denounced in the reconstruction days. The necessity of it under the supreme law of self-preservation is candidly recognized."[28] Similarly, the federal government, in all its branches, was content to leave the destiny of blacks in the hands of southerners. Congress failed to take effective measures to guarantee Negro rights and the Supreme Court in a series of decisions from 1876 to 1896 nullified the Fourteenth Amendment as a means for guaranteeing judicial protection to blacks. Abandoned by northern sentiment, Congress, and the courts, blacks were left defenseless against the onslaught of discriminatory legislation and practice. Along with disfranchisement came a spate of Jim Crow laws which wrote discrimination into the statute books. Laws requiring segregation in parks, hospitals, public toilets, and eventually in virtually all public facilities were passed throughout the South. At the same time, the racist consensus among the white population could

[26] In R. Grann Lloyd, *White Supremacy in the United States* (Washington, D.C., 1952), pp. 10–11.
[27] In John Hope Franklin, *From Slavery to Freedom* (New York, 1967), p. 341.
[28] In C. Vann Woodward, *The Strange Career of Jim Crow* (New York, 1966), p. 73.

be counted on to ensure the same treatment in private facilities. While the Progressive reform movement of the early twentieth century was seeking to enlarge democratic perspectives for white society, the Negro was being pushed to the nadir of his experience since emancipation.

Even reformers troubled by the plight of the nation's blacks operated on assumptions of racial inferiority. With a myopia that seems remarkable in retrospect, they perceived the period after emancipation as one in which great vistas were opened to blacks who were not able to profit by them. The reform economist, John R. Commons, writing in 1907, remarked on the opportunities and educational advantages that had been given to the Negro over the past forty years. These opportunities and advantages had been offered, he wrote, "not only on equal terms, but actually on terms of preference over the whites, and the fearful collapse of the experiment is recognized even by its partisans as something that was inevitable in the nature of the race at that stage of its development."[29] Even the well-intentioned, then, saw the continuing degradation of the Negro as inherent in his race rather than in the oppressive practices of American society. Liberals seasoned their sympathy with a heavy helping of condescension.

In this climate of opinion violence against black people could proceed relatively free of moral censure. Between 1900 and the outbreak of World War I, more than 1100 Negroes were lynched throughout the country. Little was done in North or South to protect the black from "lynch law." Often victims of lynch mobs were subjected to the cruelest torture before being killed. The conservative sociologist, William Graham Sumner, remarked in 1907 that: "It might have been believed . . . that torture could not be employed under the jurisdiction of the United States, and that, if it was employed, there would be a unanimous outburst of indignant reprobation against those who had so disgraced us."[30] No such outcry was forthcoming.

Another form of social intimidation which intensified after the turn of the century was the race riot. These tended to follow a common pattern: some altercation between a black and a white would inflame racial feelings; then white mobs would descend on black communities, wreaking havoc. Such riots multiplied in both the North and South during the first decade of the new century. The increasing urbanization of the Negro after 1900 made him a convenient target for the tensions of urban maladjustment.

One of the worst of these riots occurred in Springfield, Ohio, in 1904. The precipitating event was the killing of a white policeman by a Negro. A mob broke into the jail where the suspect was being held for trial. He was killed, his dead body hung from a telegraph pole and riddled with bullets. Following the lynching, the mob proceeded to the Negro section

[29] Commons, *Races and Immigrants in America,* pp. 3–4.
[30] In Thomas F. Gossett, *Race: The History of an Idea* (New York, 1965), p. 273.

of the city burning and beating at random. Nothing was done to mete out punishment to the rioters. Four years later the bloodiest riot of the decade took place in Springfield, Illinois. A white woman identified a black man as the one who had entered her home one night and assaulted her. Subsequently, she testified before a grand jury that her assailant had been white. By this time, however, race feeling was at a fever pitch and the fact that the case against the Negro had been completely fabricated made little difference. He was removed to another locality for safekeeping. When this became known, a mob formed and began rampaging through the city. Two blacks were lynched, one of them an eighty-four-year-old man who had been married to a white woman for more than thirty years. Scores more were injured. Municipal authorities were unable to control the rampaging whites and it took more than 5000 of the state militia to restore order. There was a tragic irony in such a spontaneous outpouring of race hatred occurring in the home city of the Great Emancipator and on the centenary of his birth.

The systematic denial of Negro rights reached its culmination when the administration of Woodrow Wilson inaugurated Jim Crow policies in the federal civil service. Thus the pattern of segregation which had been worked out over the past two decades on the state level was extended to the national government. During the first year of Wilson's tenure, segregation of toilets, lunchroom facilities, and working areas was begun in a number of federal departments, reversing a fifty-year policy of an integrated civil service. Wilson defended the policy of segregation as conducive to the comfort and best interests of both races.[31] Thus as the Progressive movement reached its peak, and the nation prepared to embark on a war to save the world for democracy, the black man found himself more threatened, more despised, and more discriminated against in his own land than at any time since emancipation.

[31] See Nancy J. Weiss, "The Negro and the New Freedom: Fighting Wilsonian Segregation," *Political Science Quarterly,* 84 (March 1969), pp. 61–79.

7

The Failure of the Melting Pot

STANLEY COBEN

During the late nineteenth and early twentieth centuries Americans and western Europeans carried out an insidious type of conquest throughout the world; tearing apart established religious, economic, and political relationships, attempting to replace them with Western cultural forms. Minority ethnic groups in the United States were subjected to similar cultural assaults, usually more subtle, but in many respects more effective than attacks on cultures in foreign lands. Only the United States, among the Western powers, contained among its population large elements of many races generally believed in the West to be inferior. No where else were nativist organizations and official policies directed against internal minorities which together formed such a substantial portion of the population. Only the United States, therefore, suffered massive counterattacks analogous to the revolts of colonial races elsewhere. There was an element of reality, then, in the terror experienced by millions of Americans when revolution swept eastern and central Europe during 1919 to 1920, and propagandists among hitherto subservient races threatened similar rebellion in the United States.

I

A series of short-term, postwar dislocations further disturbed the psychological equilibrium of large numbers of Americans. Some of these events—runaway prices, a brief economic depression, and a stock market crash—could be connected to racial minorities only by the most prejudiced. But thousands of returning soldiers were disgruntled when they found their old jobs occupied by Negroes and recent immigrants. And other disturbances—race riots, labor strikes, formation of Communist parties, widespread bomb explosions and bombing attempts, and an outpouring of arch-radical propaganda—were easily linked in the public mind with alien races and peoples. The formation of the Comintern in Moscow in 1919 and the revolutions then raging in eastern Europe seemed to give credence to the fear that a new revolutionary force was loose in the world that threatened to overwhelm American institutions. The result was an intensification of nativist patterns of thought. These found expression in a quasi-religious nativist movement aimed at unifying an apparently disintegrating culture against an onslaught by darker, inferior races. Americans who took part in this crusade for "100 percent Americanism," as it was popularly called, hoped to eliminate the intrusive influences felt to be the chief cause of contemporary anxieties, if they could not eliminate the intruders themselves.[1]

A similar movement, less frenzied, perhaps, but with the same objectives, probably would have taken place even without the stimulation provided by postwar disturbances. The real foundation of the movement for 100 percent Americanism was a long-term crisis for the nation's dominant cultural groups: the urbanization of America and the peopling of its great cities by black migrants from the southern states, and by other dark immigrants from Italy, eastern Europe, Mexico, and the Caribbean. These were regarded by white native-born Americans as dangerous, immoral people, easily associated with the immorality they read about and believed they saw all around them in the nation's urban centers.

The dimensions of the problem facing native-born white Americans can be indicated by a few demographic statistics. Of a total population of 106 million in 1920, 54 million lived in urban areas, the first time in the nation's history that the urban exceeded the rural populace. In 1860, only 20 percent of all Americans had lived in towns and cities. Of 106 million Americans in 1920, 23 million were immigrants or the children of immigrants, and over 10 million of these had migrated in the fifteen years before World War I, the height of the exodus from Italy and eastern Europe. In the year before the war, immigrants from southern and eastern Europe outnumbered those from northwestern Europe by six to one. The majority of these "new" immigrants settled in the metropolitan centers.[2]

---

[1] These events are described and an attempt made to link them theoretically with similar movements at other times and places, in Stanley Coben, "A Study in Nativism: The American Red Scare of 1919–1920," *Political Science Quarterly,* 79 (March 1964), pp. 52–75.

[2] U.S. Bureau of the Census, *Historical Statistics of the United States, Colonial Times to 1957* (Washington, D.C., 1960), chapter C.

Even more alarming to white Americans was the concurrent movement of southern Negroes to the cities, especially the large northern cities. There they congregated, or were forced to concentrate, in huge ghettos. Of 11 million Negroes in the United States, 2 million lived in the North by 1920, and, like the influx of Europeans, the migration showed signs of continuing if not increasing its pace. Tired of low pay, mistreatment, and a losing battle against the boll weevil, at least 600,000 Negroes moved north during the 1920s, and tens of thousands more came from the Caribbean Islands, especially Jamaica, after World War I. The 1930 census revealed that 273,000 Negroes lived in New York City alone, only 9000 of whom had been born in any of the North Atlantic states. Most had come from Virginia and the Carolinas. Harlem, a white, middle-class area in 1910, was inhabited almost entirely by 106,000 blacks in 1930. By that year, also, 232,000 Negroes were settled in Chicago, most of them from states of the Deep South. Another 118,000 Negroes lived in Detroit by 1930. The same kind of movement away from the tenant farms and rural villages took place within the South. According to the 1930 census, 96,000 Negroes lived in Memphis, 35,000 of whom had come from Mississippi alone; 99,000 Negroes lived in Birmingham; 90,000 in Atlanta; 63,000 in Houston; and 38,000 in Los Angeles, only 6700 of whom had been born anywhere in California.[3]

White leaders attempted to check the shift in Negro population both at its source and its destination. Mississippi employers, facing a labor shortage, formed an association and hired agents to woo blacks back to the pleasant land they had left. Advertisements promising jobs and transportation were placed in northern newspapers, agents made personal pleas, and even intimidation was tried. Some tactics closely resembled kidnapping. But nothing worked. Those Negroes who did return to the South often acted as labor agents for northern employers, and soon returned to northern cities accompanied by friends and relatives. The most common attitude was that periodic unemployment and freezing weather in the North was preferable to certain peonage and possible lynching in the South. A contemporary folk tale, frequently repeated in northern ghettos, describes an unemployed Negro migrant, cold, wet, and hungry, appealing to God for advice. "Go back to Mississippi," the Lord told him. "You don't mean it, Lord," the poor man replied, "You're jesting." The Lord repeated, "Go back to Mississippi!" Finally, the man relented: "Very well, Lord, if you insist, I'll go. But will you go with me?" The Lord answered: "As far as Cincinnati."

Most of the Negro migrants were young, and, at first, predominantly

[3] U.S. Department of Labor, Division of Negro Economics, *Negro Migration in 1916–17* (Washington, D.C., 1919); Louis V. Kennedy, *The Negro Peasant Turns Cityward* (New York, 1930); Bureau of Census, *Historical Statistics of the United States,* chapter C.

single men. The Department of Labor's Division of Negro Economics, established primarily to find the causes and probable duration of the black exodus, gave as a typical example of the process at work, this account by a rural Negro preacher:

> My father [said he] was born and brought up as a slave. He never knew anything else until after I was born. He was taught his place and was content to keep it. But when he brought me up he let some of the old customs slip by. But I know that there are certain things that I must do, and I do them, and it doesn't worry me. Yet in bringing up my own son, I let some more of the old customs slip by. He has been through the eighth grade; he reads easily. For a year I have been keeping him from going to Chicago; but he tells me that this is his last crop; that in the fall he's going. He says, "When a young white man talks rough to me, I can't talk rough to him. You can stand that; I can't. I have some education, and inside I has the feelins of a white man. I'm goin'."[4]

Most northerners were not pleased by their new black neighbors, and thousands organized either to keep Negroes out of their residential areas, or to ensure that the newcomers acted as Negroes were supposed to act — subserviently. A letter sent to a Lenox Avenue, New York City, realty company warned, "We have been informed of your intention to rent your house . . . to Negro tenants. This is wholly un-American, and is totally against our principles. We ask you in a gentlemanly way to rescind your order, or unpleasant things may happen." The note was signed: Ku Klux Klan, Realm 7, Chapter 3. In Chicago, twenty-four bombs were thrown at the houses of Negroes who moved into previously all-white neighborhoods, or at the offices of the real estate agents who sold or rented them the houses. No arrests were made as a result of these bombings.[5]

The extent of residential and school segregation varied widely from city to city. A study published in 1930 found the least segregation in Minneapolis, Buffalo, and New York City, where over 100,000 Negroes lived outside Harlem. In Chicago, the city administration held office by grace of Negro votes, so official racist policies were opposed at the highest level. Nevertheless Chicago's citizens proved adequate to the task of confining Negroes to certain slum areas, and keeping the better schools limited to white children. In Philadelphia, twelve schools had 100 percent Negro student bodies. Other schools in the city contained separate entrances for Negroes. Chester, Pennsylvania, operated parallel school systems for Negroes and whites through junior high school. Segregationists also enjoyed wide success in such midwestern cities as Gary, Dayton, and Indianapolis.[6]

[4] Department of Labor, *Negro Migration in 1916–17,* p. 33.

[5] Clyde Vernon Kiser, *Sea Island to City* (New York, 1932), p. 22. Chicago Commission on Race Relations, *The Negro in Chicago* (Chicago, 1922; reprinted, New York, 1968), p. 3.

[6] Kennedy, *The Negro Peasant Turns Cityward,* pp. 193–200.

Nevertheless, schools in all the northern cities were far superior to those operated for Negroes in the South. This was an important reason why the harassment mentioned above, and even the race riots described below, tended to stimulate withdrawal into the Negro ghettos and into Black Nationalist organizations, rather than a mass return to the South.

The hostility these demographic shifts provoked among thousands of whites can be seen most vividly in the pattern of violent racial disturbances which shook a dozen northern urban centers following the end of World War I. Chicago was typical. A teen-aged Negro boy, Eugene Williams, swimming off a Lake Michigan beach on a hot Sunday afternoon, July 27, 1919, accidentally wandered over the traditional line separating white and black swimming areas. Whites on the shore began throwing rocks at him. Some apparently found their target for the boy sank and drowned. Blacks insisted that a policeman at the scene arrest one of the white rock-throwers, but the officer refused and tried to arrest a Negro instead. Groups of blacks then attacked the policeman; whites came to his rescue, and a wild battle began on the beach. Accounts of the fighting on the Lake Michigan shore quickly spread through the sweltering south side of Chicago.

That night, white teen-aged gangs captured Negroes who worked in white areas of the city, and beat, stabbed, or shot them. Two died and over fifty reported their injuries to hospitals or the police. For the next twelve days, law and order almost disappeared from Chicago as armed white gangs in automobiles invaded black districts, shooting from their cars into Negro homes and setting some of them on fire. Snipers fired from rooftops on these cars and on others driven by whites. Negroes working in white areas continued to be attacked on the streets and in buses and streetcars. Black gangs retaliated against whites who made the mistake of venturing into the Negro ghetto (where hundreds of them worked) on foot. Eventually the state militia restored relative peace; but by then 23 Negroes and 15 whites were known to have died in the fighting, at least 520 were seriously injured, and over 1000 were left homeless by fires set in the Negro district.

Perhaps the most significant statistics from the Chicago race riot were the number of whites killed and injured. These indicated that from the Lake Michigan beach to the south side ghetto Negroes were fighting back. In all, six major race riots and about twenty other racial conflicts erupted in American cities during the summer and fall of 1919. Some, like the battles in Washington, D.C., and Knoxville, Tennessee, were only slightly less violent than the conflict in Chicago. A race war in and around Elaine, Arkansas, was the bloodiest of all. In every case, whites were the aggressors in the large-scale fighting; but blacks fought back, which helps account for the ferocity of the riots. Negroes shed most of the blood everywhere, and black spokesmen termed the months of race riots the "Red Summer" of 1919.[7]

II

Although the major riots took place in the eastern and central sections of the nation, Americans in the southwest also were gripped with severe racial fears, though they could hardly have been alarmed by the comparatively small number of Negroes and "inferior breeds" of European immigrants in their section. The role that these groups played in the East and Midwest was filled instead by Orientals and Mexicans. With their yellow and brown skin color, their tendency to speak languages other than English, and their willingness to work hard for low wages, these peoples clearly established their cultures as inferior in the view of the white majority.

Chinese immigration to the United States was negligible after passage of the Exclusion Act of 1882; but Japanese entrants increased sharply at the turn of the century, setting off demands for further exclusion legislation aimed at this new source of Oriental immigration. "The Japanese are starting the same tide of immigration which we thought we had checked twenty years ago," complained San Francisco's Mayor James Duval Phelan in 1900. "They are not the stuff of which American citizens can be made. . . . Let them keep at a respectful distance." Phelan would continue to inveigh against the presence of Japanese in America for the next thirty years, including a period when he served as United States senator.[8]

Japanese armed forces annihilated the Russian fleet and mangled the Russian army in 1905. Californians, alarmed by this powerful "yellow peril" in the Pacific, joined labor representatives fearful of economic competition and nativists from all classes terrified of "racial mongrelization," to form the influential Asiatic Exclusion League. Under pressure from the league, the San Francisco Board of Education barred Japanese-American children from all but special "Oriental" schools in 1906, creating a major diplomatic issue. To avoid further strife, President Theodore Roosevelt and Secretary of State Elihu Root negotiated the Gentlemen's Agreement with the Japanese government, ending the migration of Japanese laborers to America.

---

[7] The best account of the Chicago riot can be found in Chicago Commission on Race Relations, *The Negro in Chicago.* The other riots of the period are described in Arthur I. Waskow, *From Race Riot to Sit In* (Garden City, N.Y., 1966), chapters 1–9. As indicated in earlier chapters, race riots were not a new phenomenon in United States history. But never had riots been even remotely as widespread or as violent on *both* sides as in 1919.

[8] In Roger Daniels, *The Politics of Prejudice,* University of California Publications in History, Volume 71 (Berkeley and Los Angeles, 1962), p. 21.

Nonlaborers, especially wives of Japanese men already resident in the United States, continued to enter the country, however. As Japanese families bought land, mostly in the fertile California valleys, demands for anti-Japanese legislation spread from San Francisco throughout the state. An Alien Land Law, passed in 1913, limited Japanese ownership of farms; but in most cases it was evaded easily.

In conformity with the national pattern, the most virulent phase of the agitation against Japanese began in 1919. In September of that year leading California politicians of both parties responded to public clamor for action by meeting "to consider the Japanese question." After the conference, the politicians issued a report stating: "All agreed that their [Japanese-American] loyalty was first to Japan and second, if at all, to America; that they were here in large part in pursuance of a plan to populate the Pacific Slope of America and that they were a peril, economically, politically, and socially."[9]

The California American Legion fought the "peril" by producing a movie, *Shadows of the West,* circulated in 1920. Japanese-American characters in the film were revealed as spies and sex fiends. At the tale's climax, two innocent white girls were rescued from the Oriental fiends by brave Legionnaires—just in time.

The political highlight of this California campaign was an initiative measure placed on the state ballot in 1920, forbidding further purchase of California land by Japanese or their agents. The measure passed by a vote of 668,483 to 222,086. National endorsement of the California position came with the passage of the Immigration Act of 1924, which excluded all Japanese immigration to the United States. California nativists, working for a Constitutional amendment which would deprive American-born Orientals of their citizenship, continued to warn about the menace posed by the "little brown men." But until World War II they were unable to convince even southern congressmen that such drastic action was necessary.

The great fear in the Southwest after the mid-1920s was occasioned by the movement of more than a million Mexicans into that area—at least one-tenth of Mexico's total population. The basis for this migration was the federally financed irrigation of vast stretches of desert land in the area from California to Texas. A series of laws, beginning with the Reclamation Act of 1902, made possible this government action. Then, during the 1920s, Americans drastically shifted their eating habits, consuming a much greater quantity of fruits and vegetables. New canning methods and refrigeration cars made it possible to carry perishable crops long distances and to store them for lengthy periods. The irrigated southwestern lands were ideally suited for production of fruits and vegetables; but these required enormous numbers of laborers with special characteristics to prepare the land and harvest the crops.

[9] In Daniels, *The Politics of Prejudice,* p. 84.

Growth and harvest of an acre of wheat during the 1920s required 13 man hours; an acre of lettuce, however, took 125 man hours; and an acre of strawberries took 500 man hours. Very cheap labor, therefore, was a necessity in the Southwest. Furthermore, these low-paid workers would have to farm a reclaimed desert, where temperatures frequently rose above 100 degrees, clearing and planting a terrain that few white Americans understood.

By 1925, the southwestern states produced 40 percent of the nation's fruits, vegetables, and truck crops, almost all on farms developed during the twentieth century. Only an enormous influx of Mexican labor made this production possible. The Mexicans, who could withstand the heat, who knew how to clear the many varieties of desert brush, and who would work for infinitesimal wages at a time when American farm help was scarce, provided about 75 percent of the labor that cultivated the new southwestern crops. They also contributed most of the labor that created cotton fields on irrigated land in Arizona, Texas, and California; as well as 60 percent of the mine workers and approximately 80 percent of the railroad laborers employed in the western states between 1910 and 1930.[10]

Immigration from Mexico, and other Western Hemisphere countries, was not limited by the 1921 and 1924 Immigration Acts, which set quotas for other nations. In 1923 and 1924, Mexican entrants comprised over 12 percent of total immigration to the United States, and in 1927 and 1928 about 20 percent. Almost half a million Mexicans entered the country during the ten-year period from 1920 to 1929, according to official records. However, Labor Department officials estimated illegal entries from Mexico at two to five times the number who passed through immigration stations. Most of these immigrants crossed the border into Texas and the majority remained there; but at least 200,000 moved to California during the 1920s alone.[11]

Until the late 1920s, the Mexicans were almost universally welcome. They seemed content to live in their own communities, and to exist in squalor, while earning the contempt of native Americans by working at the most menial labor for wages which seldom rose above an average of $100 a month for an entire family.[12] But the passivity of the Mexican laborers was coming to an end.

A suggestion of what was to come occurred in Arizona during 1920 when 4000 cotton field workers—all migrants from Mexico—struck for

[10] Carey McWilliams, *North from Mexico* (New York, 1948, 1968), chapter 9.

[11] Bureau of the Census, *Historical Statistics of the United States,* chapter C.

[12] McWilliams estimated the average wage at $600 annually per family; but outside of the beet sugar industry the majority of Mexican-American families seem to have earned slightly over $1000 a year. In any case, the average was well below that set by the Bureau of Labor Statistics as the minimum for subsistence. For incomes of large samples of Mexicans in a variety of California agricultural and nonagricultural industries, see *Mexicans in California, Report of Governor C. C. Young's Mexican Fact-Finding Committee* (San Francisco, 1930), chapters 4–5.

higher wages. Scores of workers were arrested, the leaders deported, and the strike broken. Mexican-American farm laborers in Texas and California began organizing on a large scale in 1927. To some observers it seemed that they were protesting against social subordination and humiliation as much as they were attempting to improve their economic condition. The *Confederación de Uniones Obreras Mexicanas,* established in southern California in 1927, was able to call out on strike as many as 5000 Mexican-American field workers in the Imperial Valley. Mexicans also comprised three-quarters of the farm workers' union in the lower San Joaquin Valley.

From Texas to California, the pattern was the same. Strikes were broken with large-scale violence, including the use of tear gas, clubs, and guns. Strikers were arrested by legal authorities or kidnapped and beaten by growers' private armies. The leaders were deported. Starting in 1931, California officials resorted to mass deportations. During 1932, over 11,000 Mexicans were "repatriated" from Los Angeles alone. [13]

This series of events, beginning in the 1920s changed for decades to come the dominant attitude of western Americans toward the Mexicans who had built the foundations of their agricultural economy. Creation of labor organizations and consequent strikes ended the myth of the docile Mexican laborer. Machinery invented late in the 1920s began to replace human labor in fruit and vegetable harvesting. Then the depression halted the steady rise in demand for those crops.

In response to the unrest among agricultural laborers, the governor of California appointed a "Mexican Fact-Finding Committee" which reported in October 1930. The committee employed as investigators social scientists sympathetic with the Mexicans. Nevertheless, as often happens, the group's final report reflected the prejudices of the government officials named to head the project. Its conclusions provided a rationale for the treatment accorded Mexican-Americans during the following decades. The committee estimated that whites comprised less than 10 percent of Mexico's population. It quoted George P. Clements, Director of the Agricultural Department of the Los Angeles Chamber of Commerce, who stated that 13 of the 15 million inhabitants of Mexico were Indians, "as primitive as our own Indians were when the first colonists arrived in America." These barely civilized Indians, the committee concluded, now were inundating California. Forty percent of all alien immigrants enter-

[13] The report compiled for the Mexican Fact-Finding Committee on the formation of the chief California unions and their treatment by growers and local officials was both detailed and fair. When the committee's chief investigator showed a copy of his account of the cantaloupe pickers' strike to the district attorney of Imperial County, the official complained that "while the report was on the whole correct and accurate as to details, it gave the erroneous impression that the district attorney's office was unreasonable in its conduct during the labor troubles." Actually the report indicated that the county sheriff, not the district attorney, was arresting strikers indiscriminately. *Mexicans in California,* chapters 6, 7; also McWilliams, *North from Mexico,* chapter 10.

ing the state came from Mexico; and the proportion of Mexican migrants who gave California as their eventual destination when they crossed the border increased annually. The committee reported also that Los Angeles police department records "indicate an increasing proportion of arrests of Mexicans in the city." About 40 percent of the Mexican-Americans in California already lived in Los Angeles.[14]

As in the case of Oriental-Americans, California's treatment of Mexican immigrants and their descendents is among the more dismal chapters in the national history. Mobilized by newspapers, politicians, and official publications like the Mexican Fact Finding Committee report, Californians resorted to violent means of ridding their state of racial minorities. Almost immediately after Japanese-Americans had been dispatched to "relocation" camps in March 1942, police, servicemen, and other citizens in southern California started a campaign of terror against Americans of Mexican origin, especially Mexican-American youths. Beginning in August 1942, police dragnets in Mexican sections of Los Angeles periodically stopped all cars entering or leaving the districts. As many as 600 persons were arrested in one night for possession of dangerous weapons that included jackknives and equipment for changing automobile tires.

In June 1943, young Mexican-Americans and some Negroes were the victims of what California newspapers and police called "zoot-suit riots." Less prejudiced observers termed these events mob violence, and even mass lynching. For almost a week, mobs of hundreds and even one of several thousand roamed those areas of Los Angeles and nearby cities that were inhabited or frequented by Mexicans, savagely beating and stabbing Mexican-Americans and Negroes. Los Angeles police sometimes followed the mobs, arresting the bleeding or unconscious victims on charges ranging from assault to inciting a riot. In no reported cases did the police intervene, except to help beat Mexicans.[15]

The anxiety generated in native Americans by migrant Negroes, Orientals, and Mexicans closely resembled the panic created at the same time by the vast flow of Italian and Slavic immigrants. Some of the country's politicians, editors, and polemicists made the association explicit. Speaking in favor of immigration restriction legislation, Oscar W. Underwood of Alabama, the most influential Democrat in the House of Representatives, contrasted the pure white blood of those who had made America great with the mixture of African and Asian blood that fixed the character of southern European immigrants. In the Senate, while debating the same issue, Fernifold M. Simmons of North Carolina warned that Anglo-Saxon civilization in America was in danger of destruction from immigrants who "are nothing more than the degenerate progeny of the Asiatic hordes which, long cen-

---

[14] *Mexicans in California,* pp. 20, 25, 43, 49, 59.

[15] McWilliams, *North from Mexico,* chapters 12, 13. McWilliams led efforts first to prevent, then to end, these events.

turies ago, overran the shores of the Mediterranean . . . [and] the spawn of the Phoenician curse." Thomas Abercrombie of Alabama also pointed to *prima facie* evidence of the new immigrants' inferiority: "The color of thousands of them differs materially from that of the Anglo-Saxon."[16]

A torrent of literature expressing this sense of white racial superiority flowed from the presses in the 1920s. The most popular polemic on the subject was Theodore Lothrop Stoddard's *The Rising Tide of Color Against White World Supremacy,* which appeared in 1920. In this and a score of other books, Stoddard parroted the theme developed in prewar racist literature, that progress and civilization were products of "Nordic" blood. This magnificent breed had "clean, virile, genius-bearing blood, streaming down the ages through the unerring action of heredity, which, in anything like a favorable environment, will multiply itself, solve our problems, and sweep us on to higher and nobler destinies." Stoddard warned of the danger to Nordic supremacy from less civilized eastern and southern European, as well as Oriental and other "colored" peoples. Another popular author on the same topic, Henry Pratt Fairchild, a former president of the American Sociological Society, wrote in 1926 that "if America is to remain a stable nation it must continue a white man's country for an indefinite period to come." Fairchild's statement was part of a plea, not for Jim Crow laws in the South, but for immigration restriction directed largely against "inferior" European races.[17]

The alleged relationship between darker peoples and urban problems was made to seem even more menacing during 1919–1920 by those who attempted to associate these groups with the specter of international communism. By mid-1919 almost every nation in eastern and central Europe had undergone a communist revolution, several of them successful, although only the Bolshevik government in Russia retained power. Russian and Baltic language organizations in the United States moved—or were moved by their leaders—into the new American communist parties, partly out of pride in the Bolshevik achievements. Probably 90 percent of the parties' members in 1919 were eastern European immigrants. Several men who became Bolshevik leaders in Russia during the Revolution, including Leon Trotsky, sat out most of World War I in New York City. Therefore,

[16] John Higham, *Strangers in the Land: Patterns of American Nativism 1860–1925* (New Brunswick, N.J., 1955), pp. 164–165, 168.

[17] Theodore Lothrop Stoddard, *The Rising Tide of Color Against White World Supremacy* (New York, 1920), p. 89; Thomas F. Gossett, *Race: The History of an Idea in America* (Dallas, 1963), pp. 387, 395–396. A recent survey of anti-Negro literature in the United States concluded that "By 1925 a marked change was occurring in the attitude of scientific circles toward the subject of race . . . By 1930 the amount of scientific literature purporting to prove the Negro's alleged inferiority had precipitously declined." A conspicuous reduction in the amount of popular anti-Negro writing followed immediately afterward. I. A. Newby, *Jim Crow's Defense: Anti-Negro Thought in America 1900–1930* (Baton Rouge, La., 1965), pp. 50–51.

there was some slight basis in fact for Attorney-General A. Mitchell Palmer's assertion in 1920 that the Bolshevik triumph was led by "a small clique of outcasts from the East Side of New York. . . . Because a disreputable alien—Leon Bronstein, the man who now calls himself Trotsky—can inaugurate a reign of terror from his throne room in the Kremlin; because this lowest of all types known to New York can sleep in the Czar's bed . . . should America be swayed by such doctrines?"[18]

Palmer's alert antiradical division, directed by J. Edgar Hoover, discovered that American Negroes were deeply involved in the communist conspiracy. Hoover, an avid reader of dissident books, journals, and newspapers, hardly missed an expression of seditious propaganda. Although there is no evidence that Negroes took part in founding the communist parties in September 1919, or that any joined soon afterward, dozens of black propagandists sounded enough like revolutionists to convince the Justice Department experts that they constituted an authentic menace. The antiradical division's collection of this inflammatory literature was published in the fall of 1919 in a pamphlet entitled "Radicalism and Sedition among the Negroes as Reflected in Their Publications." Among the black radicals cited were A. Philip Randolph, a moderate socialist best known as president of the Pullman Car Porters; and Marcus Garvey, one of the country's more enthusiastic champions of capitalism. Both men had written powerful diatribes against contemporary American white culture, especially its racist aspects, which sounded to Hoover like calls to revolution.[19]

Theodore Lothrop Stoddard also warned his fellow countrymen that the world-wide movement to undermine the Nordic's natural superiority was being encouraged if not directed from Moscow: "In every quarter of the globe . . . the Bolshevik agitators whisper in the ears of discontented colored men their gospel of hatred and revenge. Every nationalist aspiration, every political grievance, every social discrimination, is fuel for Bolshevism's hellish incitement to racial as well as to class war."[20]

Almost all the racial fears felt by white Americans after World War I were distilled and promulgated by one organization: the Ku Klux Klan. The Klan gave voice also to the traditional culture—such as the dangers carried by new ideas and moral standards. The KKK of that period was started by a small group in Atlanta during 1915. The time and place were chosen to

[18] Palmer is quoted more fully on this subject in Stanley Coben, *A. Mitchell Palmer: Politician* (New York, 1963), p. 198, and chapters 11 and 12, *passim.*

[19] A. Mitchell Palmer, "Radicalism and Sedition among the Negroes as Reflected in Their Publications," Exhibit 10, *Investigation Activities of the Department of Justice,* Volume XII, Senate Document 153, 66 Cong. 1 Sess. (Washington, D.C., 1919), pp. 161–187. By far the best account of Negroes' role in the American communist movement after World War I can be found in Theodore Draper, *American Communism and Soviet Russia* (New York, 1960), chapter 15.

[20] Stoddard, *The Rising Tide of Color Against White World Supremacy,* p. 220.

coincide with excitement generated by the showing of the motion picture "The Birth of a Nation." In that tremendously popular epic, white-hooded Klansmen of the post-Civil War era were depicted redeeming the South and its most cherished values from the clutches of black Reconstruction.

Until the cultural crisis of 1919–1920, however, the twentieth-century Klan remained a small, southern organization. When it expanded, the professional publicists who managed the membership drive discovered that the largest potential source of Klan dues lay not in Georgia or South Carolina, nor even in Alabama and Mississippi, those traditional strongholds of vigilante justice for Negroes. The greatest response to the Klan's brand of racism appeared in growing cities of the Southwest and Midwest: Shreveport, Dallas, Youngstown, Indianapolis, Dayton, and Detroit; and in smaller cities like Joliet, Illinois; Hammond, Indiana; Oklahoma City; San Antonio; Babylon, New York; Camden, New Jersey; and Anaheim, California.

In areas where Klan organizers—or Kleagles, as the invisible empire called them—were most successful in recruiting, they entered towns instructed to discover the prejudices of prospective members, then to exploit these peoples' complaints. At first it was assumed that the Klan once again would be chiefly a device for keeping southern Negroes and their white friends in place. When he called together the first small group of Klansmen in 1915, William J. Simmons explained that Negroes were getting "uppity." Klan recruiting efforts played cleverly on the Reconstruction Klan's reputation for punishing ambitious Negroes and for protecting white women against threats to their purity. A Klan recruiting lecturer promised: "The Negro, in whose blood flows the mad desire for race amalgamation, is more dangerous than a maddened wild beast and he must and will be controlled."[21]

However, when questions and applications from all over the country poured into Atlanta headquarters during 1920, Imperial Wizard Simmons readily conceded that Negroes were not the only enemies of 100 percent Americans. Furthermore, he announced: "Any real man, any native-born white American citizen who is not affiliated with any foreign institution (that is, not a Catholic) and who loves his country and his flag may become a member of the Ku Klux Klan, whether he lives north, south, east, or west."[22] The only other requirement for membership was a man's willingness to part with a $10 initiation fee, of which $4 went to the Kleagle, $2 to Simmons, $2.50 to the publicists in Atlanta, and the rest to the local Grand Goblin. Further payments were extracted later for membership dues and for uniforms (sheets), which were supplied from Atlanta.

[21] In Kenneth T. Jackson, *The Ku Klux Klan in the City, 1915–1930* (New York, 1967), p. 22.

[22] In Charles C. Alexander, *The Ku Klux Klan in the Southwest* (Lexington, Ky., 1966), p. 9. The prejudice of Klan leaders against women, who were segregated in separate organizations, deserves more exploration by historians than it has received.

Throughout the nation, Kleagles discovered a fear of Catholics, Jews, and recent immigrants, as well as Negroes. They also found native Americans worried about the erosion of moral standards, and angry about widespread lawlessness. Frequently this laxity was associated with foreign or colored races. Violation of prohibition statutes especially was blamed on urban minorities. Established governmental institutions seemed incapable of handling these elements—incapable of protecting white, Anglo-Saxon Victorian civilization. So Kleagles received a warm welcome when they came to town and gave native Americans an opportunity to fight back. One of the most effective pieces of Klan recruiting literature read:

> Every criminal, every gambler, every thug, every libertine, every girl ruiner, every home wrecker, every wife beater, every dope peddler, every moonshiner, every crooked politician, every pagan Papist priest, every shyster lawyer, every K. of C., every white slaver, every Rome-controlled newspaper, every black spider—is fighting the Klan. Think it over, which side are you on?[23]

Local chapters took action against what they considered indecent motion pictures and books. They destroyed stills, and attacked prostitutes and gamblers. Groups of hooded men even invaded lovers' lanes and beat up the occupants of cars, in one case beating a young couple to death. This work was considered no less important than political efforts to destroy parochial schools, to enforce Bible reading in classrooms, and to defeat Catholic and Jewish candidates for public office.

Although membership figures remain largely shrouded in secrecy, available records indicate that the hooded empire probably enrolled over 5 million members during the 1920s, with a peak membership of about 2 million in 1924. Because members were concentrated so heavily in certain northern and western areas, the Klan won considerable political power in at least six states, and in large sections of about ten others.

In the great cities, however, and eventually in the country as a whole, the Klan discovered that the time had passed when an organization devoted to the supremacy of white Anglo-Saxon Protestants could operate both violently and safely. In some respects the whole movement for 100 percent Americanism was an anachronism in the post World War I era; but the Klan especially depended upon a widespread delusion that this was still the world of Wade Hampton and the young Rudyard Kipling.

The Klan's fate in New York City was pathetic—and illustrative. In the world's wealthiest city, the nation's largest by far, with a million native-born white Protestants among its inhabitants, the KKK was treated like a band of shabby criminals. The great majority of New York's population of 6 million were Catholics and Jews; and the Irish Catholics who dominated the city's politics and police force were especially offended when the

[23] Jackson, *The Ku Klux Klan in the City,* p. 19.

Klan dared organize in New York. The city seethed with bigotry against Negroes, Catholics, and Jews, including considerable distaste within these groups directed at members of the others. But even among white Protestant New Yorkers eligible for Klan membership, few were so foolhardy during the 1920s as to identify themselves publicly with an organization so clearly marked for disaster. It was not an absence of racial prejudice that doomed the Klan in New York, but rather the fact that in most respects the city already was controlled by the "minority" groups which the Klan aimed to suppress.

A year after Kleagles entered the city, two grand juries commenced investigations of the secret order. Special legislation, directed at the KKK, forced all unincorporated associations to file annual membership lists. New York Mayor John F. Hylan denounced Klan members as "anarchists," and the city police force was ordered to "ferret out these despicable disloyal persons who are attempting to organize a society, the aims and purposes of which are of such a character that were they to prevail, the foundations of our country would be destroyed."[24]

In most of New York City, the customary march of hooded Klansmen, carrying banners with messages that were so popular in Kokomo and Anaheim, would have been a feat of amazing courage. In certain sections—the lower east side and Harlem, for example—such a march would have been the most foolhardy event since General Custer's seventh cavalry left a day early for the Little Bighorn. New York's borough of Queens, however, remained predominantly suburban and Protestant in the 1920s. Although subject to hostile laws and unsympathetic policies there as in the rest of New York City, a Klan chapter continued to operate in Queens. In 1927, it received permission to take part in the Queens County Memorial Day Parade to the local Soldier's Monument.

Both the Boy Scouts and the Knights of Columbus withdrew from the patriotic celebration rather than march in the same line as the KKK. The New York police did their best to stop or divert the Klan members, but something less than their best to hold back angry crowds determined to halt the hooded patriots. After 1500 Klansmen and Klanswomen—including a 100-man paramilitary unit—broke through several police barricades, the police simply left the KKK to the parade audience. According to the *New York Times*: "Women fought women and spectators fought the policemen and the Klansmen, as their desire dictated. Combatants were knocked down. Klan banners were shredded. . . ." Five Klansmen were arrested during the melée. Finally the police ceased holding back traffic as the remnant of the Klan cavalcade passed, and motorists tried to run the white-robed marchers down. The Klan parade disintegrated, although three Klansmen in an automobile managed to reach the war memorial monument and

[24] Jackson, *The Ku Klux Klan in the City,* p. 177.

placed a wreath with the KKK signature upon it. The wreath promptly was stolen.[25]

Throughout the Northeast, the Klan found only mild support, and even that sometimes aroused the kind of mob violence for which the Klan itself was so well known in the South. In Boston, Mayor James Michael Curley incited crowds by speaking before flaming crosses—the Klan's favorite symbol—and pointing to the cross while he shouted to his predominantly Irish Catholic audiences: "There it burns, the cross of hatred upon which Our Lord, Jesus Christ, was crucified—the cross of human avarice, and not the cross of love and charity. . . ." Curley declared Klan meetings illegal even in private homes, and in Boston he obtained support in his crusade not only from the City Council, but also from city's Catholic and Jewish leaders. It was just as well for the Klan that they did not meet in Boston; houses of people only suspected of being Klan members were attacked with bricks and stones.[26]

In Pittsburgh, another center of Catholic population, Kleagles enjoyed great success in recruiting members. Ten thousand Klansmen from the area, led by the national Imperial Wizard, Hiram Wesley Evans, gathered outside the nearby town of Carnegie for an initiation rally in August 1923. When they marched into town, however, they were met not with cheers, but with angry shouts and a hail of rocks and bottles. The Klansmen continued until a citizen started shooting and a Klan member fell dead. There were no further Klan parades in the Pittsburgh area. The Klan chapter in Perth Amboy, New Jersey, obtained substantial police protection for its meetings; but guards availed little in that heavily Catholic and Jewish industrial and resort area. The entire city police and fire department, protecting a meeting of 500 Knights of the Secret Order, were overwhelmed by a mob of 6000 on the evening of August 30, 1923, and the Ku Kluxers were beaten, kicked, and stoned as they fled.

When the Klan reached its peak strength in 1924, less than 4 percent of its members lived in the Northeast—the entire area from Portland, Maine, through Baltimore, Maryland—despite strenuous organizational efforts. The Klan itself claimed that over 40 percent of its membership lived in the three midwestern states of Indiana, Illinois, and Ohio. Even in that hospitable area, however, the Klan's brand of racism was not welcome everywhere.

For a while it appeared that white Protestants in Chicago, disturbed by a rapid influx of Negroes and immigrants, and by the city's infamous lawlessness during the 1920s, might make it the hub of the Klan empire. By 1922, Chicago had more Klan members than any other city, and initiation fees continued to flow from the midwestern metropolis into Atlanta.

[25] *New York Times,* May 31, 1927, pp. 1, 7.

[26] Jackson, *The Ku Klux Klan in the City,* p. 182. The Klan's activities in northern cities like Boston, Pittsburgh, and Chicago are described in Jackson's volume.

When Imperial Kleagle Edward Young Clarke visited the city in June 1922, he announced that 30,000 Chicagoans already belonged to the Klan, and implied that the branch soon would be large enough to help enforce the law in Chicago, thus reducing the city's alarming crime rate. In smaller communities, where violators of Klan mores were easier to intimidate, bootleggers were forced to obey Prohibition laws, and gamblers and other sinners were punished by the secret order. When a major civic association started investigating crime in Chicago, however, the group's leader—a prominent clergyman—was found shot to death in Cicero, Illinois, then the center of Al Capone's operations. After Clarke returned to Atlanta, the Chicago Klan wisely continued to leave the war against crime to the police, the FBI, and the Treasury Department, even though these organizations were overwhelmed by the task.

As soon as the Klan's strength in Chicago became known, powerful enemies sprang up to protect the threatened minority groups. Mayor "Big Bill" Thompson, elected with crucial aid from Negro votes, denounced the Klan. The City Council opened an investigation of the society, and made its findings available to other state and local political bodies. One consequence was a bill prohibiting the wearing of masks in public, that passed the Illinois House of Representatives by a vote of 100 to 2, and the State Senate by 26 to 1. The City Council itself resolved by a vote of 56 to 2 to rid the city's payroll of Kluxers. Within a week, two firemen were suspended and the Klan's attorney had to be rushed from Atlanta to take legal steps halting the purge. Meanwhile the American Unity League, dominated by Catholics, started publishing the names of Klan members, concentrating on those in business and the professions. Salesmen, milkmen, and even a bank president were forced out of their jobs when their customers refused to deal with Klan members. The disheartened bank president, complying with his board of directors' request that he resign, explained, "I signed a petition for membership in the Klan several months ago, but did not know it was anything else than an ordinary fraternal order."[27] He may not have realized either how many Jewish, Irish, and Negro depositors had placed their money in his bank.

A counterattack was also launched in the press. In a front-page editorial headlined "To Hell with the Ku Klux Klan!" the Chicago *Defender,* the nation's leading Negro newspaper, advised readers to get ready to fight "against those who now try to win by signs and robes what their fathers lost by fire and sword." A prominent rabbi warned that "Protestantism is on trial. Protestantism must destroy Ku Kluxism or Ku Kluxism will destroy Protestantism."[28]

Political candidates backed publicly by the Klan fared badly in Chicago.

[27] Jackson, *The Ku Klux Klan in the City,* p. 104.
[28] Jackson, *The Ku Klux Klan in the City,* p. 102.

Enough excitement was generated during the city election of 1924 to bring forth a series of threatening letters from the Klan. Some of these went to Chicago's largest Negro church, which was completely destroyed one night by fire. On the other hand, bombs demolished a shop just vacated by the Klan journal, *Dawn,* and other bombs were exploded against offices of Klan members and of advertisers in Klan periodicals.

The accumulation of outside pressures on the Klan in Chicago—political, economic, and physical—served to increase internal dissension in the order. Although the Klan enrolled well over 50,000 members in Chicago by 1924, at the end of that year the organization was practically dormant in the city. For similar reasons it already was on the way to destruction as a major political and social force throughout the United States. The failure of the KKK, after temporary success in the immediate postwar years, should not be interpreted as a sign that racism was waning. The Klan simply had tried to take on too many enemies. The "minorities" which the Klan was organized to suppress possessed far more members, votes, wealth, and almost every other kind of power than the Klan itself. The order's fate should have served as a warning to the American people of the changes taking place in a world in which white Protestants were far outnumbered; but it did not.

IV

Another ominous development for the future of "Nordic" supremacy in America was the creation after World War I of an impressive movement for black nationalism and black power. Although dozens of organizations devoted to those ends were formed during the postwar period, by far the largest was the Universal Negro Improvement Association, sometimes called the Garvey movement after its founder Marcus Garvey. The history of the UNIA, and of black as well as white reaction to it, illuminates many qualities of the ferment that arose forty years later when Negro protest again tended to move in the direction of black separatism.

The societal dislocations which gave rise to the movement for 100 percent Americanism, affected Negro Americans also. The shift from the rural South to densely populated northern cities, despite the obvious compensations, left even the most adaptable migrants somewhat disoriented. Not only were familiar and loved friends and relatives left behind, but so were southern customs, games, climate, landmarks, and to some extent even language. For those who made the move directly from the farm, all these difficulties were magnified. Certain aspects of the white nativist response—the great increase in lynchings and Klan membership beginning in 1919, the ferocious race riots, the organized hostility of white property owners—also helped make black Americans susceptible to a movement similar, in some respects, to that of the Klansmen. They differed drastically, however, in one crucially important respect: Garvey's movement attempted to uplift a long-exploited people; whereas the Klan intended to continue suppression of racial minorities.

Marcus Garvey repeatedly stated: "I believe in a pure black race, just as all self-respecting whites believe in a pure white race."[29] He scorned attempts at integration and ridiculed Negro leaders who worked in any way toward that objective. Whites respected nothing but power, he insisted, and Negro equality could come only from black unity in America combined with a strong black nation in Africa.

Garvey, a stocky, intense, black-skinned man, born on the West Indian island of Jamaica, was a dynamic orator with all the charismatic qualities of the successful visionary, including an inability to handle administrative details. His speeches, and to a lesser degree his essays in his newspaper, *Negro World,* awakened a pride in their race and color among millions of Negroes throughout the world. Garvey delighted in telling his audiences: "I am the equal of any white man." A black skin, he declared repeatedly, far from being a badge of shame, was a glorious symbol of racial greatness, even superiority; a reminder of the African past when, he claimed, black civilizations were the most advanced in the world. These could be thrilling words to Negroes born and raised in the North as well as the South, who had been trained never to think such thoughts, much less express them publicly.

The 1920 UNIA convention, held in New York, was a memorable event for American Negroes, and a disturbing experience for whites accustomed to Negro subservience. Black delegates attended from almost every nation in the Western Hemisphere, as well as from several African states. The convention opened with a silent march by thousands of delegates through the streets of Harlem. The parade, and all subsequent activities connected with the convention, were pervaded by a fervent spirit of black nationalism.

At the convention's climax, Garvey addressed an overcapacity crowd of 25,000 jammed into Madison Square Garden: "We are the descendents of a suffering people. We are the descendents of a people determined to suffer no longer." In another speech during the convention he warned that Negroes never again would fight in the service of whites, as they had during World War I: "The first dying that is to be done by the black man in the future will be done to make himself free."[30]

Black Americans were far from unanimous in accepting Garvey's leadership. Among New York's Negro intellectuals—vitally involved in creating their own image of the "new Negro"—hostility to Garvey's style if not the content of his message, was common. Garvey's disdain for the

[29] Amy Jacques Garvey, ed., *Philosophy and Opinions of Marcus Garvey* (New York, 1923), p. 37.

[30] In Edmund David Cronon, *Black Moses, the Story of Marcus Garvey and the Universal Negro Improvement Association* (Madison, Wis., 1955), p. 65.

intellectuals, and for all light-skinned Negroes, his enthusiasm for capitalism, and his emphasis on action in Africa rather than in the United States, displeased the men who led the Harlem literary and artistic renaissance of the 1920s. Established Negro politicians in major cities also criticized Garvey and his program, although some important Negro dissident political organizations in Chicago and New York were more sympathetic. This criticism became more intense when Garvey's plans for a steamship line, and then for an industrial corporation, failed.

As Garvey and his lieutenants spoke increasingly of violence, they further antagonized the Negro intellectuals and worried the politicians. The UNIA leader even appeared willing to reach some agreement with the Ku Klux Klan, defending this attempt by explaining: "I regard the Klan, the Anglo-Saxon Clubs and White American Societies as better friends of the race than all other groups of hypocritical whites put together." Garvey's ambassador to the League of Nations, William Sherrill, unsettled some Americans by stating in 1922: "Black folk as well as white who tamper with the Universal Negro Improvement Association are going to die."[31] Not long afterward, one of Garvey's most vociferous critics, James W. H. Eason, was shot and murdered in New Orleans where he had gone to address an anti-Garvey rally. Two of Garvey's henchmen had arrived in New Orleans about the same time as Eason; however, the men were acquitted of complicity in the crime. Nevertheless, the murder, and the growing paramilitary element in Garvey's organization, turned Negro intellectuals increasingly toward open opposition.

A week after Eason's murder, eight of the most highly respected Negro leaders in the country protested to the Justice Department that Garvey's trial for mail fraud already had been postponed for a year and a half. They asked why this "unscrupulous demagogue" was being treated differently than ordinary citizens. Garvey responded by charging that the "Committee of Eight" were almost all octoroons or quadroons, or married to quadroons, and were enemies of the black race. Nevertheless, Garvey soon was tried, convicted, sentenced to prison, and a few years later deported to the West Indies.

Garvey's organization disintegrated after his removal from the scene. By the mid-1920s, however, Garvey's was not the only movement unable to sustain the high promise of 1919–1920. Dozens of smaller black nationalist groups also were fading, including W. E. B. DuBois's Pan African movement. The African Blood Brotherhood, a propagandistic society whose members included some of the most intelligent and able black leaders in the country, merged and practically disappeared into the Communist Party during this period. A meeting in 1924 of representatives from sixty-four Negro organizations—ranging in the political spectrum from the NAACP

[31] In Cronon, *Black Moses,* pp. 190 and 109.

to the Blood Brotherhood—seemed to foreshadow unified action on some issues, at least; but the movement toward unity soon faltered.[32]

At about the same time, membership in the Ku Klux Klan began falling rapidly, despite a temporary recovery during the crusade against Al Smith's presidential candidacy in 1928. The massive "Americanization" campaign directed at recent immigrants lost its urgency after passage of immigration restriction legislation in 1924. A marked decline in the publication of pseudo-scientific racist literature was noted about 1925. Even efforts to enforce prohibition, and to spread and protect the doctrines of fundamentalist religion, were reduced in fervor after the mid-1920s.

It would be an exaggeration to state that "normalcy" had returned; that the movement for 100 percent Americanism was successful enough to obviate the need for organizations like the Klan; that dissident groups like Garvey's and the communists were doomed by that success. Too many other factors were involved; such simple statements provide only partial explanations. However, they *are* partial explanations. The movement to protect the established culture, which included the maintenance of attitudes and institutions based on the concept of white racial superiority, did accomplish many of its objectives. Nevertheless, it left the major problems facing modern American society basically unsolved, especially those involving racial and cultural differences within the society. The holding action conducted by 100 percent Americans from 1915 to 1930 handed these problems to future generations, who would have to deal with them in even more acute forms, at a time when temporary expedients would not suffice.

[32] Alain Locke, "The Negro Speaks for Himself," *The Survey* (April 15, 1924), pp. 71–72; Draper, *American Communism and Soviet Russia,* chapter 15.

8

Sambo

The National Jester
in the Popular Culture

JOSEPH BOSKIN

"The subtlest and most pervasive of all influences," wrote Walter Lippmann "are those which create and maintain the repertory of stereotypes. We are told about the world before we see it. We imagine most things before we experience them."[1] Once implanted in popular lore, a stereotype attached to a group, an issue, or an event pervades our senses and affects our behavior. A standardized mental picture representing an oversimplified opinion or an uncritical judgment, a stereotype is tenacious in its hold over rational thinking. Its power is gained by repetitive play, so that the image it projects becomes firmly imbedded in reactive levels of thought and action.

Although images can serve a positive function, many are deleterious in their effect. As an integral part of the pattern of culture, a stereotype, by its very nature, will operate within and at most levels of society. It will affect the thoughts and actions of those who are aware of its existence; more importantly, it influences those who are not. Indeed, stereotypes are often so powerful that they can be dislodged only after a series of assaults on them.

[1] Walter Lippmann, *Public Opinion* (New York, 1922), pp. 89–90.

I

In the history of race relations in the United States, stereotypes have been particularly pernicious. Of the various images assigned to darker-skinned persons by whites, two were developed and flourished almost simultaneously for more than three centuries: Sambo and the Brute. Their functional presence and constant refurbishment in the face of vast social and economic changes attests not only to their tenacity but to the deeply rooted prejudices of those who had developed them in the first instance. Both images were originated by white Americans and were utilized as a means of maintaining their superior position in society.

To a considerable extent, the concepts of Sambo and the Brute complemented each other. Both derived from the view of other racial groups as inferior—either for religious, biological, anthropological, or historical reasons. With respect to the Brute, it was contended that the black man was a primitive creature given to fits of violence and powerful sexual impulses. It was argued, often with quasi-scholarly data, that such dark-skinned peoples as the Africans were stunted in their intellectual capacities because of physical limitations or their slow ascent up the evolutionary ladder. This argument gave rise to myths about the characteristics of black men. Most whites spoke and wrote of the Negro's "natural rhythm," his sexual prowess, "flashy" dress habits, and proneness to rioting and fighting.

The Negro as a Brute, albeit an integral part of the fiction of whites, was not always explicit in the popular culture. Movies such as D. W. Griffith's early classic, "Birth of a Nation," portrayed Negroes as ignorant legislators and sexual violators, but the image of the black as a violent man was usually implicit. This was partly due to the fear of whites that constantly to portray the Negro as the Brute was to affect a possibility of its realization. Not wishing to encourage black violence and retaliation, white society generally stressed the other side of the stereotype. By emphasizing the Sambo image, white America hoped to minimize black hostility and develop a character amenable to the institution of slavery and, after emancipation, to second-class citizenship.

Although the name of Sambo predominated in the mass culture, other folk expressions were used over the centuries. At various times, the Negro was referred to as "Tambo," "Rastus," "Sam," "Pompey," "Mammy," and "Boy." In popular songs, he was called "Old Black Joe" and "Uncle Ned." He could be found in advertising in the form of "Uncle Ben's Rice," "Aunt Jemima's Pancakes," "Ben the Pullman Porter," and the "Gold Dust Twins." In literature, the most famous expression of the character was developed by Joel Chandler Harris in "Uncle Remus" and his stories. In the development of the mass media in the twentieth century he became "Stepin Fetchit," "Amos 'n Andy," "Rochester," and a host of other characters.

What were the essential features of the Sambo stereotype which became so deeply imbedded in the popular culture? A southern novelist and poet, Robert Penn Warren, summed up the various aspects of the personality type:

> He was the supine, grateful, humble, irresponsible, unmanly, banjo-picking, servile, grinning, slack-jawed, docile, dependent, slow-witted, humorous, child-loving, childlike, watermelon-stealing, spiritual-singing, blamelessly fornicating, happy-go-lucky, hedonistic, faithful black servitor who sometimes might step out of character long enough to utter folk wisdom or bury the family silver to save it from the Yankees.[2]

The Sambo figure had two principal parts. In the beginning he was childish and comical. Given to outlandish gestures and physical gyrations, he was the buffoon par excellence. Later, he was depicted as the "natural" servant and slave, nonviolent and humble. There were variations on the theme of Sambo but in the main he emerged as the national jester.

The origins of the Sambo type are uncertain. Several significant characteristics, however, are related to the Negro's position of servitude. The status of the slave evoked strong expressions of disdain and intolerance. The psychology of the situation worked automatically against the servile man. As long as he remained at the lowest level of society, he could barely hope to improve his status; and unable to improve his status, he was powerless to change the white image of him as less than human. Thus the traits ascribed to Sambo are found in other cultures where slavery existed. "The white slaves of antiquity and the Middle Ages," states David B. Davis, "were often described in terms that fit the later stereotype of the Negro. Throughout history it has been said that slaves, though occasionally as loyal and faithful as good dogs, were for the most part lazy, irresponsible, cunning, rebellious, untrustworthy, and sexually promiscuous."[3] There existed, then, an historical precedent for anticipating the character of the black slave in America.

II

The child-Sambo apparently made his debut into the popular culture in the dramatic theater in the latter half of the eighteenth century. English plays often featured a white actor who wore blackface and who performed the role of a Negro. For example, in *The Padlock,* a play by Issac Bickerstaff performed in 1769, the character of Mungo, a Negro servant, suffered the insults of his master. In the English plays by George Colman, *Inkle and*

---

[2] Robert Penn Warren, *Who Speaks for the Negro?* (New York, 1965), p. 52.
[3] David B. Davis, *The Problem of Slavery in Western Culture,* pp. 59–60.

Yarico (1791) and *The Africans; or, War, Love and Duty* (1808), comic black figures spoke in dialect and sang nonsensical choruses.

The American contribution to the blackface tradition appeared immediately following the termination of hostilities with England in 1815. The Negro song and singer, as illustrated by a burnt-cork sailor who sang "The Siege of Plattsburg" or "Back Side Albany," was apparently the first staged Sambo type. The songs were written by Micab Hawkins, an American composer. Blackfaced performers also were seen in circuses where they sang and danced before delighted audiences.

By the 1820s, the characteristics of the Sambo form were clearly delineated in act and song. In 1822, a broadside "Sold by the Flying Booksellers" was circulating in Boston on the same day that the Negro population was parading through the city to celebrate the anniversary of the abolition of the slave trade. The statement was a parody of the event and was a ludicrous imitation of the black's dialect. The sheet contained instructions detailing the toasts to be made at a banquet, with the added ridicule: "40 cheer—4 grin all round de mout," "3 guess—5 sober look," "2 wink—7 sly look," and so forth. An example of the political barbs foreshadowed the type of statement which would be found in the minstrel act:

> De day is one of dose great nashumnal hepox which will call fort de sensumbility and de herhaw of good feelum of ebery son and daughter of Africa in dis world, and good many udder place beside, which you no find tell of in de jography, cause I spose Massa Morse what make um, dont know wedder deir any such place or not. De committee of derangement hab gib me full power to make de debiltry marshal mind what I say—else dey stand chance to get shin kick cause he no take de hint and act just like raw soger, who know nothing bout milintary dissumpleen.[4]

At the close of the decade, two songs heralded the development of a new American comic form. In "Coal Black Rose" and "My Long-Tail Blue," performed by comedian George Washington Dixon, two types of black men were impersonated. The two figures—the plantation hand and the city dandy—would become an integral part of the minstrel theater.

Just as the blackfaced figure became basic to the minstrel theater, the American minstrel theater developed as the most popular theatrical form of the nineteenth century. Today, however, minstrelsy in its old and true meaning, is a nostalgic segment of the American memory. The generation born after World War II knows little of the minstrel show, or of its impact upon the history of race relations in the United States. For it was the

[4] In Hans Nathan, *Dan Emmett and the Rise of Early Negro Minstrelsy* (Norman, Okla., 1962), p. 49.

minstrel show and its tradition, as it was adapted to other mass media, which fostered the national consciousness of the Sambo figure.

Minstrelsy, with its elaborate formulas for precise execution, with its blackfaced dandies whose conundrums kept pace with gaily beating bones, and whose carols of "way down south" wrung tears from city and farm folk, left an indelible mark upon drama and the popular stage. Its descendant lingered in blackfaced acts on the vaudeville stage, in the movies of Al Jolson and Eddie Cantor, in the stage productions of high schools and colleges, and in other events such as the annual Philadelphia Mummers Parade on New Year's Day.

It was with the advent of Thomas D. Rice's "Jim Crow" that minstrelsy was initiated into the theater. Every study of the minstrel show acknowledges the importance of the song and dance of "Jim Crow"—a name which would become synonymous with segregation in later years—as one of the most important contributors to the tradition. Rice was a well-known performer acting with a theatrical company which was booked at the Columbia Street Theater in New York in 1828–1829 when he observed the antics of Jim, a stable hand who worked in a livery stable owned by a man named Crow. The slave, lame and aging, entertained himself by dancing a funny little jig to an original tune which he sang,

> Wheel about, turn about,
>   Do jis so,
> An' ebery time I wheel about
>   I jump Jim Crow.

Verse was added to verse, the ending always the same. Rice one day conceived the idea of using the old slave's jig and song for an act of his own. He appeared wearing an outlandish costume which was wrinkled, ill-fitting, and "bumish." Singing new verses to new tunes, Rice basked in instantaneous success. From the moment of the first audience response, Rice became one of the foremost exponents of the minstrel character.

In 1836, Rice took his Jim Crow to England. By this time he had more fully developed the stage "dandy," the figure who was to be the convention of the future minstrel show. In the earlier minstrel form, the black was a burlesque of "plantation darkies"; Rice's black "dandy," however, was a parody of the white dandy of Main Street or Broadway. The plantation black had been joined by an urban counterpart. He was not as uncouth or as ignorant but he was ludicrous nevertheless.

In the next decade, a chance incident caused the formation of the first company of minstrels. Four well-known performers, Dan Emmett, Frank Brower, Bill Whitlock, and Dick Pelham, met in a New York hotel and contrived to browbeat one of the proprietors of the Bowery Circus into an engagement by making noise on a violin, tambourine, banjo, and bones. To their surprise, the proprietor asked them to perform as an act. The Virginia Minstrels were thus born.

At the outset, the troupe's act was highly fluid. They improvised their dialogue, sang, played, and danced to the "Essence of Old Virginia" and "Lucy Long Walk Around." It was Emmett who composed most of the tunes for the group. Among the famous numbers they performed were "Old Dan Tucker," "Boatman's Dance," "Walk Along John," and "Early in the Morning." Late in the 1850s, when Emmett was associated with the Bryant Minstrels, he composed a walk-around called "Dixie," which he introduced just before the opening of hostilities between the North and South.

Shortly after the Virginia Minstrels took the stage, other quartets began to imitate them and within several years an entire evening of theater entertainment was offered by a minstrel troupe. The format of the show became so highly ritualized that departure from the format was considered sacrilegious. The program was divided into three parts. The first consisted of an overture introduced by a stout gentleman of dark complexion who exclaimed "Gentlemen, be seated. We will commence with the overture." This was followed by catch-questions, passed between the end men and the master of ceremonies. On came the comic songs of Bones and Tambo, followed by sentimental ballads and a final walk-around.

The second part of the show was the olio which featured a series of incidental numbers, clog dances, a stump speech, and a comic number such as Rice's Jim Crow. This was usually followed by a burlesque play, which constituted the third part of the program. The burlesque might be a satire of a popular drama, or it might be any farce performed in Negro dialect. All the actors used burnt cork and wigs; the majority of the songs, however, were written by white men who had only the slightest contact with either the plantation slave or the free Negro in the North. Yet they spoke in dialect, moved rhythmically in an attempt to imitate the movement of the Negro, and wrote the stump speeches and other burlesques in what they considered to be black patois. Later, when Negro actors organized minstrel shows, they were forced to don blackface and speak in the same exaggerated manner. A writer contemporary with minstrel times was highly critical of the origin of the songs. Examining the songs of the minstrel performers, he concluded that there were not "more than ten which bear any trace of the cotton-field afflatus, and these ten, with only one exception, have been so patched and dressed up for drawingroom inspection, that they look like a bumpkin who has suddenly come into possession of fortune. . . ."[5]

Such criticisms went unnoticed, however. The songs, skits, and black-faced performances were accepted as an accurate representation of the

[5] "Negro Minstrelsy—Ancient and Modern," *Putnam's Magazine.* 5 (1855), p. 74.

Negro. In the summer of 1840, a New York editor, after attending a minstrel show, wrote ecstatically of his impressions:

> Entering the theater, we found it crammed from pit to dome, and the best representative of our American Negro that we ever saw was stretching every mouth in the house to its utmost tension. Such a natural gait!— such a laugh!— and such a twitching-up of the arm and shoulder! It was *the* Negro, par excellence. Long live James Crow, Esquire.[6]

Indeed, many whites established highly popular minstrel troupes which lasted for years. One of the best-known groups—its name would be used by a folksong group in the 1960s—was the Christy Minstrels. Much of the material used by the minstrel troupe was written by Byron Christy. One of his stump speeches reveals the degree to which the Negro image was twisted in the nineteenth century. The occasion was the Civil War:

Burlesque Political

STUMP SPEECH; OR, "ANY OTHER MAN"

Written and Delivered by Byron Christy throughout the United States

FELLER CITIZENS:—Correspondin' to your unanimous call I shall now hab de pleasure ob ondressin ebery one of you; an I'm gwine to stick to de pints and de confluence where by I am myself annihiliated.

When in de course ob human events it becomes necessary fur de colored portion ob dis pop'lation to look into and enquire into dis inexpressible conflict. It is—it is—it is— to return to our subject.

Dis is a day to be lookin' up, like a bob-tailed pullet on a ricketty henroost, or—or any other man!

Somethin' has bust—whar is we? You is dar—and I am here, and I'm a gwine to stay here till I take root, if you'll only shout out aloud for Clam Johnson, or—or—or any other man.

What do de folks mean talkin' 'bout de Norf and de Souf? Do dey want to separate us from our brederin in de sunshiney Souf? Do dey? Eh? umph? Do dese people (whats roamin' round like hungry lions seekin' whom dey may devour) want more? Eh? umph? It dey do let 'em hab New Jersey, Hardscrable, or—or—or any other man.

Do dese people want to tear up dat magnificent and magniglorious American flag what's ravelin' out in de breezes ob de atmosphere on de top ob de St. Nicholas Hotel? Eh? umph? Do dey want to strip it up and gib de stars to de Souf, and de stripes to de Norf? I answer you in clarion tones dat I hope may be heard from de risin' place ob de sun to de cheer in which he sets down. Dey can't do it, nor—nor any other man.

[6] "Jambo and Bones," in George C. D. Odell, *Annals of the New York Stage* (15 vols.; New York, 1927–1945), IV, p. 372.

Our patriotic canal-boat has indeed unshipped her rudder; our wigwams is tored to pieces and scattered to de winds like a delapidated shirt on a brush fence. Be we gwine to allow dese things to be did? Eh? umph?

Whar is our progressiveness—ness—ness is not our—is not our—our—our—to return to our subject.

I ask you in de name ob de shaggy-headed eagle, what's flyin' ober de cloud-capped summits ob de rockganey mountains; be gwine to be so extremporaneously bigoted in dis yer fashion? Eh? Answer me, as Shakspere says:

"Do not let me blush in ignorance," nor—nor—any other man.

What does our glorious constitution say on referrin' to dis lamentable subject? Does not our glorious constitution—shun—shun—Tution! Don't it? Eh? umph? I'll bet two dollars and a half it does.

Now, den, feller citizens, I've got a question to ask you all; I don't want you to go one side ob it nor on de toder side of it, but I want you all to keep huddled up togedder as you be. If de Democrats, de Aristocrats, de Autocrats, or any other rats, will elect me to be dere president, I'll tell you what I'll do for you; I shall hab de Japanese Embassy and de Prince ob Whales here once a week fur to look at you, and Johnny Heenan, de Magnesia Boy, shall hab de champion belt, or—or—or any other man.

Why, see here—look a'here—de members ob congress—gress—gress, don't dey take de advantage ob de Frankin' privilege? Eh? umph? Don't dey hab dere shirts washed 'way out home, and hab 'em sent back to 'em froo de postoffice widout payin' nary red cent postage on 'em.

My dear feller citizens, dat one act is against de glorious laws ob dis unimpeachable Onion.

What did my friend General Cass say when he signed de Decliclumption ob Dependence. I was dar—I seed him sign it. He said to me, (as he laid his right hand on my head), "Clem, my boy, who knows but what you might wake up some fine mornin' and find yourself de President ob dis glorious Unicorn; you might, or—or—any other man."[7]

The heyday of the minstrel lasted for more than fifty years, from the 1830s to the 1880s. It was one of the most popular forms of theater, reaching into all sections and into the most remote corners of America. By the early twentieth century, almost every community boasted of a minstrel group. Books, pamphlets, and scores provided minstrel compendiums from which schools, civic groups, church organizations, and others could chose materials to produce a show. *The Newsboys and Bootblacks Minstrel Show Book,* published in 1919, contained a complete show for "Unchanging Voices for Boys and Girls of the Upper Grammar Grades and Junior High Schools." Among the various characters in the show were Rastus, Rufus, and Mose. Typical of the hundreds of published shows was "The Masonic Lodge." The picture on the front cover depicts a young Negro woman wearing a funny cap, flanked by cabins with a watermelon patch

[7] Byron Christy, *Christy's New Songster and Black Joker* . . . (New York, 1863), pp. 9–11.

on the left side and cotton bales and a steamboat on the other side. The words of the characters, Obediah, Spoffit, and Jabez Fishpole, are grossly exaggerated as illustrated by "cum erlong," "inishiated," "arribe," and "serlissister." Common folk expressions were transposed into dialect as in "Punctiosity c'n be tief o' time."

The minstrel as a neighborhood production continued to the 1940s and reached millions of persons who rarely had first-hand knowledge of the black man. Indeed almost the only contact the immigrant groups who settled in the northern urban areas and midwestern towns had with the Negro was that acquired through the mass media. The minstrel show, in emphasizing the peculiarities of Negro dialect and in creating the vehicle for foolishness, buffoonery, and dance, transformed regional differences of language into signs of racial inferiority. As sociologist Arnold Rose stated regarding the speech pattern of the black man:

> To the Northern white man, although seldom to the Southern white man, the speech of the Negro seems unusual. In fact, the "Negro dialect" is an important cause of the Northern white's unconscious assumption that Negroes are of a different biological type from them.[8]

The stage Sambo also was reflected in the printed media. Its literary appearance occurred early in the ante-bellum period and coincided with the figures in the theatrical productions. Northern writing, no less than southern in the nineteenth century, contained many characters cast in the Sambo form. In James Fenimore Cooper's *The Spy* (1821), the minor though prominent figure of "Caesar" is used for comic relief. Caesar is faithful, extremely superstitious, and easily delighted with gaudy colors. "Spooks" unnerve him: "Best nebber tempt a Satan," he exclaimed as the whites of his rolling eyes revealed the glare of the fire. The Negro figure in Edgar Allan Poe's "The Gold Bug" (1843) is gregarious but ignorant. In his initial appearance, "Jupiter, grinning from ear to ear, bustled about to prepare some marsh hens for supper." Similar to Cooper's character, Jupiter is excessively superstitious; his entire intellect is absorbed by "de bug."

The plantation Sambo type was described by novelist John Pendleton Kennedy in *Swallow Barn* (1832), a work which endowed Virginia squires in the Old Dominion with "an overflowing hospitality which knows no ebb." *Swallow Barn* contributed generously to the concept of the slave as a proverbial child. "I am quite sure [Negroes] never could become a happier people than I find them here . . . he has the helplessness of a child . . . he is extravagantly imitative . . . In short, I think them the most good-natured, careless, light-hearted, and happily-constructed human beings I have ever seen."[9]

---

[8] Arnold Rose, *The Negro in America* (New York, 1944) pp. 300–301.

[9] John Pendleton Kennedy, *Swallow Barn* (New York, 1853), pp. 452–455.

Although the slave as a Sambo was accepted as a valid portrayal by people in the South, the figure was less comforting to them than to northerners. The fear of reprisals and revolts caused the southern white also to conceive of the slave as a Brute or as a Satan bent on destruction. Nevertheless, their writing went far to convince northerners and westerners that the traits describing the "agreeable" Negro personality represented an essential feature of his being.

The plantation Negro was given further definition in the stories of Joel Chandler Harris, one of the first writers to use the folktale as a literary medium. Harris' Uncle Remus stories were popular with children and adults for decades, and were adapted to the mass media in the twentieth century. On one level, the Uncle Remus tales, articles, and short stories stimulated interest in folklore. On another level, however, the animal stories of Brer Rabbit, the bear, fox, and wolf only served to satisfy the multitude that the fiction of the plantation had substance in reality. Despite the quality of shrewdness which enables Brer Rabbit to survive among bigger and fiercer foes, the traditional aspects of Sambo were present throughout his stories. The "darkies" singing and spinning yarns into the night, the kindly and gentle "Marse," the wide-eyed children listening to the gentle, white-haired old man who displayed no rancor or animosity, the watermelon-and-chicken aroma of the plantation, and the softness of the old plantation days were all pleasantly entertaining.

Harris' writings inspired similar but less effective stories. A typical work was *Mammy's Reminiscences and Other Sketches* (1898) by Martha S. Gielow of Alabama. Her sketches were gleaned from "actual happenings related to me by my own black Mammy" whose "immortality is due to her devotion and her loyalty, under circumstances which never before tried human hearts. . . ." The slaves, Gielow maintained, possessed "quaint humor" which reflected "their happy, simple natures." *Mammy's Reminiscences* consists of scenes in the cabin of the Old Plantation: "How Brer' Simon Got 'Erligion'," "De Painner Juett," "Seein' Sperrits," and similar tales, all delivered in heavy dialect.

Prestigious journals and magazines contributed to the stereotype. From the 1870s to the 1930s—a period of intensifying segregation in all areas of American society—popular publications such as *Harpers, Atlantic Monthly, Scribner's Monthly,* and responsible newspapers such as *The New York Times,* cast the black man as Brute or Sambo in their articles and stories. Identified as the "darkey," "African," "Aunt," "Uncle," or "negro," the black man was pictured as being addicted to alcohol, gambling, lying, stealing, superstitions, watermelons, 'taters and possum, and violence. Over a fifty year period, *Harper's* printed in each issue no less than two humorous incidents regarding the antics of the Negro; the number of anecdotes within each issue increased during the first two decades of the twentieth century. The contents of *Atlantic Monthly* were similar in tone and substance to the other periodicals. Former slaves were quoted in their recollection of the virtues of plantation life, the benevolence of their masters, and the joys of life before the great war that divided the nation. Fiction articles portrayed the Negro as lazy, dishonest, illiterate, and docile. *Scribner's Monthly* published the writings of southern authors, such as Thomas Nelson Page, Joel Chandler Harris, Harry Stillwell Edwards, George Washington Cable, and John E. Cooke. Their stories canonized the plantation whose masters were blustering but beneficent and whose slaves were, as usual, ignorant, fearful, possum loving, watermelon devouring, and loyal.

An outpouring of humor books, comic pamphlets, cartoons, burlesque essays, anthologies, and visual prints beginning in the latter third of the nineteenth century and continuing through the first third of the twentieth, furthered the Sambo image in the popular mind. Technological improvements in the printing industry and the visual media enabled publishers to reach a burgeoning reading and viewing public.

The central theme of these variegated materials was the "funny nigger," an image which was repeated with monotonous regularity. The Afro-American was invariably portrayed with wide, thick lips; a wide, grinning mouth; a big, black head; a round cheruby face; saucerlike eyes; lengthy arms; and a dull look. His speech was atrociously ridden with malapropisms and mispronounciations. Predictably, the majority of the humor books ridiculed the Negro's attempt to educate himself. A number of the books contained a message. Southern authors used the media to extol the region's advantages for the Negro. In a series of dialect stories by Samuel A. Beadle, significantly entitled *Adam Shuffler*—including one in which the main character is named Sambo—the Negro is exhorted to remain in the South and seek white approval. "I tells yer," says Adam in the main story, "dat de best place for de cullud brudder am in Mississippi, an' de best thing fur him ter do . . . is ter git on de white side uv public opinion."[10]

Joke books and single cartoons pictured the black American in identical fashion. Long before the development of the newspaper funnies Negroes were caricatured in cartoons and prints. Among the most popular prints in the nineteenth century were those published by Currier and Ives. Their graphic descriptions of American life could be found hanging on the walls of hotels, barbershops, firehouses, barrooms, schools, and homes. With few exceptions, the Negro in their prints was happy, dancing, jolly, and well fed. Whether he worked on the docks loading cotton, danced in a barn to a banjo, or assisted in landing fish for his employer, the Negro appeared contented and satisfied. The most prolific artist of black life was Thomas Worth. Born and raised in Greenwich Village, Worth's pictures comprise the largest single group among the stock prints. They are divided into the

[10] Samuel A. Beadle, *Adam Shuffler* (Jackson, Miss., 1901).

"Darktowns" and the "White Comics." The former are burlesques of Negro life which appeared in the 1880s and detailed Negro activities, both real and imaginary. Among others they included "The Darktown Fire Brigade," "Lawn Tennis at Darktown," and "The Darktown Hunt." The Negro was spoofed as a potential member of the middle and upper classes. In other prints the Negro could be seen in comic horse-racing scenes, oyster-eating contests, dice games, and watermelon-eating contests.

The single cartoon and the comic strip carried the stereotype into the twentieth century though with lessening exaggeration. Nevertheless, Negroes were pictured almost exclusively as Pullman porters, servants, comical jockeys, African natives, chauffeurs, cooks, "Mammies," and in other similar roles. Primitiveness, linguistic pretentiousness, and laziness were three themes pursued by white artists. There was a general tendency to present Africans as cannibals and American blacks as descendants of the cannibals.

The techniques of comic art were extended into an area of communication which had a profound impact upon the extension of the stereotype—the children's book. Among the early books reflecting the Sambo image was the Nicodemus series, written and illustrated by Inez Hogan. The author of more than thirty-five children's books, Hogan created in Nicodemus one of his most popular and enduring characters. Eleven books comprise the series, including *Nicodemus and the Houn' Dog, Nicodemus and the Little Black Pig, Nicodemus and his New Shoes,* and *Nicodemus and his Gran'pappy.* Nicodemus, coal-black, apelike, with thick red lips and extended arms, is given to foolish antics and fragmented dialogue. Books in the Nicodemus style became standard fare in libraries, schools, and reading groups. One popular work was *Epaminondas and His Auntie,* written by Sara Cone Bryant and illustrated by Inez Hogan. Published originally in 1907, it was reprinted at least three times, with the 1968 version completely restructured to conform to new tastes and values. The earlier editions depicted black creatures similar to Nicodemus dressed in vivid reds and yellows. As the story opens, the reader is taken down a yellow path leading to a black sharecropper's shack in the South. Epaminondas, a dull-witted boy with thick red lips, is given a task by his Auntie: he is asked to bring home a big piece of rich yellow cake. Epaminondas carried the cake "in his fist and held it all scrunched up tight and came along home. By the time he got home there wasn't anything left but a fistful of crumbs." His Mother, a round-figured woman with a bandanna swaddling her head, inquires, "What you got there, Epaminondas?" "Cake, Mammy," responds Epaminondas. "Cake! Epaminondas, you ain't got the sense you was born with! That's no way to carry cake. The way to carry cake is to wrap it all up nice in some leaves and put it in your hat, and put your hat on your head, and come along home. You hear me, Epaminondas?"

The next day, Epaminondas traveled to his Auntie who gave him a pound of fine, fresh, sweet butter. Following the instructions of the previous day, he wrapped up the butter in some leaves, placed it in his hat, put the hat on his head and went home. A hot sun melted the butter which ran down Epaminondas' face. His Mother scolded him. "Epaminondas, you ain't got the sense you was born with! . . . The way to carry butter is to wrap it all up in some leaves and take it down to the brook and cool it in the water, cool it in the water, cool it in the water and then take it in your hands, careful, and bring it along home." Soon afterward, Epaminondas receives a puppy dog from his Aunt which he cooled in the brook three times, nearly ending its life. In a continuing series of episodes Epaminondas plays the foolish unteachable black boy. His final act is carefully to step directly in the middle of six newly baked mince pies after his "Mammy" had instructed him to "be careful how you step on those pies."

III

The electronics industry in the twentieth century made heavy use of stereotypes developed in the previous century. Animated cartoons, stereoscopic slides, moving pictures, photographic stills, radio, and television are, by their very nature, intended to synthesize thoughts and attitudes into a visual pattern. Without doubt, the visual and oral media have been able to create a collective consciousness regarding people, ideas, and events. They have demonstrated their power to create, perpetuate, or destroy stereotypes and thus to influence reality.

For the Negro, the medium has been the message which, until the 1950s, reproduced and reinforced the illusion of Sambo. From their earliest development in the first half of the nineteenth century, visual devices employed images of Sambo as an aspect of their entertainment. Before the innovation of the moving picture, receptive audiences peered into gadgets which contained scenes of churches, exotic peoples, historic buildings, geographic wonders, and humorous events. The stereoscope, a device which permitted the viewer to look at two drawings simultaneously by moving the holder back and forth along a stationary wooden track, was a popular device used to convey visual images. Among its educational and entertainment subjects was the comic black man. In the stereographics, blacks were shown working in the fields, harvesting cotton, and cavorting in pranks. The photographs used were both of black and white actors in blackface with wide eyes and prominent lips, which were consistent with the popular view. One scene staged by blackfaced actors involved a man and a woman in an overturning boat. The man is half way in the water; the woman is trying to prevent his complete immersion. "Golly," she exclaims, "I jest can't hole dat nigger." Other scenes involve subjects such as thievery, a comical wedding ceremony, and horseplay between "darkies."

Sambo moved from the stereoscope to the silent movie. From its earliest years, the film industry made movies in which the black man's fondness for watermelon, chicken, dice, razors, and funny antics seemed to define his nature. In the 1890s, Thomas Edison's company used Negroes in several of its early films, particularly in the "Black Maria" series and in comic shorts. The titles of the movies provide insight into their plots: "Negro Lovers," "Chicken Thieves," and "Colored Boy Eating Watermelons."

Several years later, Edwin S. Porter, who had completed the classic film "The Great Train Robbery" in 1903, made a short film based on Harriet Beecher Stowe's novel *Uncle Tom's Cabin*. The movie was a series of short vignettes followed by a cakewalk scene. As in the minstrel theater, the characters were mainly white actors performing in blackface. Regardless of the script, the Afro-American in the silent film era was depicted in a manner virtually identical with his counterpart in the printed media. A series of short slapstick films, highly popular prior to World War I, were the "Rastus" shorts. In "Rastus in Zululand" and "How Rastus Got His Turkey," the main character was a buffoon of low intelligence. A black clown named "Sambo" represented the same caricature in a number of similar shorts. "Sambo" was also the title of a series of all-Negro comedies produced in Philadelphia which included "Coon Town Suffragettes," a movie which burlesqued the organizing antics of a group of southern "Mammys" bent on keeping their irresponsible husbands out of saloons.

In the "silents and sounds" of the 1920s and 1930s, the minstrel tradition was continued by such performers as Al Jolson and Eddie Cantor. Chorus lines and singing groups in the extravaganza movies of the 1930s also wore blackface. When Negroes were hired for parts, they were usually seen singing spirituals and dancing happily in movies whose plots centered on the Old South. They bubbled with gaiety in kitchens while serving food in dining cars, smiled broadly as they red-capped bags at railroad stations, and tap-danced snappily in a variety of scenes.

Several dimensions of the stereotype were particularly mimed in the movies. The superstitious black, whose fear related to the concept of the black man as a child, received featured billing in detective stories such as the Charlie Chan film series. Fear of natural and supernatural phenomena such as earthquakes and ghosts were accentuated and carried to comical heights by such actors as Mantan Moreland and Willie Best. Moreland, who played Charlie Chan's chauffeur, was adroit in the role. Upon encountering a ghost, his eyes bulged, his body swayed, his feet began to move quickly, and off he went exclaiming: "Tain't no disgrace to run when you git skeered." Hollywood displayed its ingenuity in inventing techniques to highlight the Negro's alleged fear of ghosts; hair stood on end, speech became incoherent, the face turned white and then black again. In one movie, a frightened black man outran people and animals, shouting to them as he passed, "Git out de way an' let a man run whut can *run*."

The epitomization of the stereotype in the movies was achieved by Lincoln Monroe Perry whose stage name, "Stepin Fetchit," became synonymous with Sambo. Perry performed in more than a dozen films as a stammering, foot-shuffling, lackadaisical, slack-jawed comic. His motto, according to a Fox studio release, was "take your time—time ain't gonna take you."

Not all movies, however, pictured the Negro in Sambo form. There were exceptions to the traditional role. A few films treated the servant with dignity and approached the problem of race seriously. In an occasional movie the Negro appeared as a middle-class professional. During World War II, the film industry departed from convention by making nearly a dozen important movies in which Negroes were more realistically portrayed. Nonetheless, these films were the exceptions. The more sympathetic portrayal of the black was far outweighed by the popularity of the Sambo stereotype.

With the development of the cinemagraphic cartoon in the 1930s the appeal of the Sambo figure became further evident. Several representative examples of cartoons of the 1940s and 1950s demonstrated the tenacity of the visual stereotype. Among the many short subjects released by Metro-Goldwyn-Mayer between 1947 and 1951 were "Uncle Tom's Cabana," "Old Rockin' Chair Tom," "His Mouse Friday," "Mouse Cleaning," and "Half-Pint Pygmy."

Of the five films, three featured the popular Hanna Barbera figures of the playful Tom and Jerry. In two of these cartoons, the ubiquitous Negro maid, who appeared in many Tom and Jerry stories, clearly carried the Sambo image. The maid was generally drawn so that only the lower part of her body was seen; her "character" graphically communicated a heavy-set, slippered "Mammy" who cleans, mops, shops, and chatters in dialect. In "Mouse Cleaning," the action opens as the maid, terrified at the sight of a mouse, calls for Tom in ungrammatical dialect. Following a chase, Tom is swept through a door by an avalanche of coal which transforms him into an Uncle Remus. Chattering in dialect, he saunters down the street in Stepin Fetchit style. In "Old Rockin' Chair Tom," Stephen Foster's "Old Black Joe" is used as theme music. In this cartoon the maid screams at Tom as he chases Jerry, who, as usual, eludes capture. The maid, losing her faith in Tom—"Thomas, if you is a mouse catcher, I is Lana Turner, which I ain't"—summons a supercat who resembles Satan. Tom is unceremoniously bounced out of the house. In the process he is suddenly transformed into an Uncle Tom complete with white sideburns and whiskers. Strains of "Old Black Joe" are heard in the background and watermelons are shown on the side of the road.

In comparison with the film media, radio programs in the same decades did not feature the variety of roles for the Negro, but its representatives were conspicuous by their type. When musical programs were popular, as they were in the early 1930s, Negro singers and orchestras were featured regularly. "But with drama replacing music as the radio staple," wrote a leading historian of radio, "the Negro found himself edged out. The drama was almost lily-white. Negroes who applied for auditions found only occasional servant roles given to those who sounded sufficiently 'Negro'."[11] Consequently, black performers had to affect a thick dialect in order to obtain a role associated with Negro life.

One of the most widely known Negro figures of the 1930s and 1940s was Rochester, née Eddie Anderson, who performed as Jack Benny's servant. Although Rochester spoke with less of a thick dialect and enjoyed outsmarting his "Boss," the standard relationship between a black man-servant and his white superior was obvious. That Benny's valet and chauffeur possessed only a single name was particularly insulting. Gilbert Osofsky incisively assesses the psychological effects of withholding a second name during slavery:

> When Muslims . . . relinquish their "given" names and search for others or replace them with an X, they touch upon one of the most debasing consequences of slavery — the denial of human identity. The right to have or choose one's own name is the right to *be*; the power to control a man's name is authority to subjugate the man himself. Most slaves seem to have been given Christian names of a Biblical nature, but some were ridiculed or burlesqued from birth with such labels as Bashful, Virtue, Frolic, Gamesome, Lady, Madame, Duchess, Cowslip, Spring, Summer, Caesar, Pompey, Strumpet, and so on. Nothing better reveals the derisive nature of slavery than the act of naming.[12]

Rochester was sassy and bested Benny on many occasions but he was also given to dice-throwing, drinking, playing around with women, and threatening with a razor.

Two other performers who possessed only first names were among the leading acts on radio in the period: Amos 'n Andy. The "Amos 'n Andy Show," begun in 1928, became one of radio's longest running serial programs. A year after its initial airing the program received 30,000 Christmas cards, indicating a popularity which would continue throughout most of its history.

In keeping with the minstrel tradition, Amos and Andy were white men, Freeman F. Gosden and Charles J. Correll, the former a song-and-dance-man from Virginia, the latter an amateur stage player from Illinois, who utilized the blackfaced style. For almost thirteen years, from 1929 to 1942, Americans listened to the urban travails of Amos 'n Andy for fifteen minutes, Monday through Saturday.

The show presumably depicted black life in Harlem. Andy, who was played by Correll, and Amos, performed by Gosden, were allegedly from the rural South. Having migrated to Harlem, the urban center of black American

[11] Erik Barnouw, *A History of Broadcasting in the United States* (3 vols.; New York, 1966–1968), II, p. 110.

[12] Gilbert Osofsky, *The Burden of Race: A Documentary History of Negro-White Relations in America* (New York, 1967), p. 32.

life, they were caught in the throes of an impersonal environment during the great Depression. In those years, the basic format of the show rarely varied. Amos 'n Andy became entangled in comical albiet reality-based situations. In the "soap-opera" serial style popular to radio at that time, no situation was ever quite resolved within one broadcast. The story line was developed and played out over a series of fifteen-minute program slots. The serial allegedly drew from the life of the urban black—as the white writers knew of it. Amos 'n Andy and their cohorts—single-named burlesqued characters such as the Kingfish, Lightnin', Sapphire, and the doubled-named Madame Queen—caricatured for more than thirty years the struggle for economic solvency and harmonious man-woman relationships. The various schemes pursued by the members of the program to achieve status and dignity were understandable to millions of unemployed and struggling wage earners. By their quest for success and their rejection of work relief, Amos 'n Andy were made commendable models of the urban Negro.

But for all its sophistication, the show was in reality an updated minstrel show adapted to the mass media audience. Correll and Gosden retained the accepted Negro idiom and the familiar characteristics of the minstrel stage. Thick dialect, intellectual presumptuousness, simple-mindedness, laziness, and buffoonery were integral aspects of the situations. In their attempt to become entrepreneurs, Amos 'n Andy organized "The Fresh Air Taxicab Company, Incorpulated." Andy immediately appointed himself president and made Amos "de chief mechanic's mate, fixer of de automobile, head driver of the company, an' chief buziness gitter." The taxicab venture was one of their few successful undertakings. Successively the pair owned and operated less profitable businesses such as "The Reducingest Reducing Company," "Okeh Hotel," and "The Fresh Air Garage." Despite their many failures, Amos 'n Andy, in keeping with the alleged statements of black slaves, effused optimistically about their stock in life:

> Andy: Yo' know Amos, times like dese is bad.
> Amos: Yeh, but on de other hand, times like dese does a lot o' good 'cause when dis is over, which is bound to be, an' good times come back again, people's like us dat is living today is goin' know what a rainy day means. People is done used de respression, "I is savin' up fo' a rainy day," but dey didn't even know what dey was talkin' 'bout. Now, when good times come back again people is gonna remember all dis an' what a rainy day is—so maybe after all, dis was a good thing to bring people back to dey're senses an' sort-a remind ev'ybody dat de sky AINT de limit.
> Andy: Yeh, yo' git some good out o' ev'thing, don't yo?[13]

[13] *Amos 'n Andy Radio Scripts,* #1210 (Feb. 6, 1932), p. 4. Manuscript Collection, University of Southern California.

The television version of the program, except for the replacement of Correll and Gosden by black actors, basically followed the same format. The longevity of the show attested to the power of the stereotype of the black man in American culture. White could imitate black despite the ignorance of black culture and habits; but the reverse was unacceptable. As a black author wrote in the 1920s, "There is an unwritten law in America that though white may imitate black, black, even when superlatively capable, may never imitate white. In other words, grease-paint may be used to darken but never to lighten."[14]

Such was the grip of Sambo that the inner voices of the black communities rarely were heard. For the most part, the Negro, as Ralph Ellison has powerfully written, was "invisible." With the exception of the beat of the jazz groups and dixieland bands, the sorrows of the blues singers, and the steps of the dancers, the everyday activities of the black man and woman were virtually unknown. Caucasian conceptions and sensitivities were well protected. Indeed, such was the irony of the separation of the races that while the white man was laughing at his Sambo, the black man was often laughing at his detractor. Within the concentric circles of humor, which overlapped infrequently, the tragedy of race relations in the country could be seen. Caucasian deafness was an integral part of the denial of the Negro as an equal.

IV

The life of Sambo was dependent upon the willingness of the black man to contain his anger and his own laughter from the white and upon the ability of the white to disavow the dual feelings of the oppressed blacks. While blackfaced comedians were strutting in front of the stage lights and across the film, and white actors were mispronouncing so-called Negroid words, blacks were organizing for the end of such demeaning activities. Opposition to the Sambo figure had always existed; its strident voice was heard far back into the eighteenth and nineteenth centuries. Conditions conducive to the elimination of Sambo, however, became considerably more favorable during and after World War II. The stark contrast between the combatants, a fascist nation which derived much of its sense of being from racist ideas and a democracy whose sense of identity derived from egalitarian ideas, proved to be a catalyst for many black individuals and organizations. The Supreme Court decision in *Brown* v. *the Board of Education of Topeka,* nine years after the conclusion of the war, threw the national spotlight on the practice of segregation.

[14] Jessie Fauset, "The Gift of Laughter," in Alain L. Locke, ed., *The New Negro* (New York, 1925), p. 164.

In 1955, the curtain rose on the act which would bury the stereotype. In that year, Mrs. Rosa Parks, a weary seamstress in Montgomery, Alabama, refused to relinquish her seat to a white man in a crowded bus. The driver ordered Mrs. Parks to move to the back of the vehicle. When she refused, the driver called a policeman who arrested her. The following day, after a night of meetings, the black community of Montgomery decided to boycott the buses until the restrictive regulation was removed. Led by Dr. Martin Luther King, Jr., the action was one of the first successful *communal* acts on the part of the black. It contributed significantly to the revolt of the late 1950s and 1960s.

The activities of black Americans during the civil rights and black power movements—the thousands of meetings, sit-ins, motel-ins, wade-ins, jailings, and beatings—profoundly altered the Negro's conception of himself. A powerful sense of group identity arose, pride in accomplishments grew, and a communal direction only rarely achieved in the past appeared. The new sense of self- and group-identity created an aggressiveness and a determination to bring about social change. In innumerable ways, blacks protested the white's conception of the past. Students at Hyde Park High School in Chicago in 1964 protested the use of the traditional triumphal march from "Aida" at graduation exercises because the central figure of the opera was a Negro slave. When the white principal of the school gave the students a choice of "Aida" or nothing, they chose to march in silence.

Similar episodes were repeated many times in the 1960s. More than a hundred Negro high school students in Bridgeport, Connecticut, turned in their social studies textbooks to protest the books' treatment of the Negro in American history. The young blacks in the 1960s manifested their fierce pride in race in the wearing of natural hairdos, the cult of "soul," the African dress, the slogan "black is beautiful," and the clasp of "brothers'" handshake.

The mass actions of the period created an ethos in which Sambo was attacked and subsequently demolished. There is little doubt that the cry of black power meant the termination of Sambo. The Shriners' traditional blackface Mummers Parade held annually on January 1 was challenged for its perpetuation of Sambo. After considerable protest from the National Association for the Advancement of Colored People and other local groups in Philadelphia, the Mummers replaced black with gold in 1965. A more amusing episode occurred in Rocky Mountain, North Carolina, in 1966 when Negro employees of a laundry firm refused to clean Ku Klux Klan robes. So adamant were the workers that the owner was forced to subcontract the dirty laundry.

Civil rights workers, black power ideologists, community leaders, comedians, performers of various types, and many others made ringing denunciations of the Sambo tradition. Comedian Godfrey Cambridge, twitted the stereotype in his act. Rushing onstage, Cambridge would pantingly tell his audience: "I hope you noticed how I rushed up here. No more shuffle after the revolution. We gotta be agile."

The efforts of blacks, coupled with the changing climate of opinion in the late 1950s and early 1960s, effected changes in the mass media as well. The use of the stereotype in the radio, movies, television, and short subjects was gradually phased out. Bowing to pressure from the NAACP, and other civil rights groups, stereotypic symbols of Uncle Rastus were eliminated. In 1963, M-G-M announced that the "Tom and Jerry" cartoons would no longer feature the Negro maid. With some exceptions, Africans depicted as cannibals disappeared from animated and other forms of short subjects. The "Stepin Fetchits" as a movie type were not reintroduced after the war.

Mounting pressure from blacks also forced the mass media to modify or eliminate specific programs, the most prominent being the "Amos 'n Andy" television show. Though audience interest had waned considerably, *Ebony* magazine clearly signaled the demise of both the radio and television programs in an article in 1961. "Perhaps the progress of the American Negro in the last 10 years," wrote Edward T. Clayton,

> can be measured in the disapproval and final demise of the radio show of A & A. For it is certain that in this age of youthful protestation, of sit-ins and freedom rides, Negro America is no longer amused by the buffoonery of the Mystic Knights of the Sea or the bungling machinations of such as the King-fish. [15]

Consequently, the trappings of the minstrel, such as the use of the black-face and dialect, as well as the minstrel show itself, became a relic of past attitudes.

By the mid-1960s, attractive and light-skinned Afro-Americans were slowly beginning to make their way into various levels of the mass media. The first major use of blacks on a television network commercial occurred in 1963 on Art Linkletter's "House Party" show. On this inauspicious occasion, three Negroes were planted in the audience and one of them was drawn into the commercial for an instant. Billboards and magazines began to feature blacks in large ads; television news shows hired blacks as sports announcers and later as interviewers; black models made their appearance in all the media and in model shows. Importantly, major television shows utilized blacks in leading roles, the first being comedian Bill Cosby, who co-starred in the "I Spy" series. Interview and talk shows, such as the popular "Tonight" program, were hosted by well-known black entertainers and more blacks became members of panel shows. Black specials were produced by singer-actor Harry Belafonte which dealt with Harlem in the 1920s and

[15] Edward T. Clayton, "The Tragedy of Amos 'n Andy," *Ebony,* 16 (Oct. 21, 1961), p. 73.

black humor. By the end of the decade, more black actors were included in the network series shows.

The increasing emphasis on documentary coverage of black-white problems, which introduced the white audience to the highly articulate black leaders, made the Sambo image an irreconcilable contradiction. Similarly, films portrayed the blacks in a more realistic manner. More importantly, however, many black actors and writers such as Ossie Davis, author of the satirical play, *Purlie Victorious* began to produce their own films in a move to interpret their own past and present. Sensitive whites joined them in the reinterpretation of American attitudes and behavior as well. The increasing use of darker-skinned performers indicated a greater willingness among white Americans to deal with their own attitudes toward color.

The rise to national prominence of black comedians and humorists in the late 1950s and 1960s further reflected the changing concept and image of the Negro on the part of both blacks and whites. Before the 1960s, few whites had heard of talented black comics such as "Moms" Mabley, Redd Foxx, Dusty Fletcher, and Pigmeat Markham, who had been limited to all-black audiences, having been denied access to the popular stage. Within a few years, however, white Americans became aware of the bitterness and sweetness of Negro humor as it related both to themselves and to the black community. Beginning with Dick Gregory, who, like many Negro comics, began his career in a small night club but quickly gained fame on television, a series of talented men—Bill Cosby, Godfrey Cambridge, Nipsey Russell, Bill Pryor, Stu Gillam, and others—were piquing and regaling national audiences. Their materials were far removed from blackface or Sambo gyrations.

Thus the black revolt of the post-World War II period and the pressure of the drive toward egalitarianism brought an end to the Sambo image in popular culture. His demise was mourned only by those who had become enmeshed in its psychological labyrinths and who had utilized it as an instrument of racial denigration. A surge of events made the Sambo stereotype a ludicrous caricature of its own creators; only in the smallest way did it correspond with the reality of black life in America. Whatever the outcome of the conflict between blacks and whites in the twentieth century, it was thus no longer possible for the Sambo image to obfuscate the more complex social, economic, and racial problems.

9

The Pyschology
of Racism*

PETER LOEWENBERG

As the preceding essays have illustrated, racism in America has deep historical roots. A variety of factors—social, economic, political, and religious—have interacted over a period of almost 400 years to implant racial ideologies in the American culture and to imbed racism in our institutions.

But American racial prejudice cannot be understood simply in economic, political, and intellectual terms. Racism is also personal and social in origin. It must also be seen as a psychological function of the personality related to character structure, patterns of society, and adaptation to personal and social change. This essay explores the unconscious[1] as well as the

[1] The term *unconscious* means the type of symbolic preverbal thought that is the heritage of us all. It is how the mind of the infant works. It is where the language of dreams and the pure instinctual life prevail. The distinguishing features of the unconscious are that it fulfills wishes for pleasure; it is timeless—condensing the past, present, and future; and it knows no logic—the law of contradiction does not hold. Opposites are not mutually exclusive and may even coincide. The unconscious will hallucinate facts or objects if necessary to obtain gratification without delay.

*For many insights I have gained into the psychology of oppression and race conflict I am indebted to the brave youth of the Grenada County, Mississippi, Freedom Movement; The Bruin Grenada Project; and the Southern Christian Leadership Conference; also to Professor David O. Sears of University of California, Los Angeles, and Dr. Bernard Brickman of Beverly Hills.

conscious elements in individual race prejudice and suggests how racism functions in American society as a whole.

I

In order to understand the acquisition and tenacity of racial attitudes among both whites and blacks in America, it is necessary to consider the development of the personality as it grows from birth to maturity. The principles of mental functioning regarding the psychology of racism discussed in terms of white and black in this essay also apply to other racial and ethnic minorities, such as Mexican-Americans, Orientals and Jews. It is striking how universal these patterns of racist thought are. Be it in Europe, Africa, Asia, or America, one finds the same mental mechanisms in evidence. Each culture creates a special set of circumstances or situations to which the individual, with his needs and instincts, must adjust. On the issue of race, American society offers a prescribed set of responses which are clearly communicated—consciously and unconsciously—to all who reach adulthood in that society.

Prejudice is learned behavior. It is the natural result of participation in social patterns of prejudice. A child learns social behavior by watching and emulating the attitudes and conduct of the significant people around him—his parents, family, and friends. This is called identification. This is one of the processes by which racial attitudes are passed from generation to generation.

The typical American community, North as well as South, implies Negro inferiority in its pattern of living. The Negroes with whom the child comes into contact are likely to function as domestics, menials, or in some other subordinate role. The child early learns that Negroes live in one section of town. Patterns of socializing in church, home, and recreation centers are not shared with Negroes. The child assimilates these patterns of stratification and separation naturally, with no conscious effort.

A white child coming of age in this setting acquires prejudice as a matter of course by living in his environment and internalizing its values. It is not necessary to teach him any explicit ideology of racism. He has only to observe and participate in his world. He conducts himself in accord with the prevailing patterns of his home and community and comes to accept Negroes as social inferiors. By the time a white child hears for the first time that "Negroes are not inferior," it is usually too late. Even if he is intellectually convinced of their equality, it is difficult for him to escape the emotional consequences of his upbringing.

Ideas and behavior dramatically interact and influence each other. This has sometimes been called the device of the "self-fulfilling prophecy." Its workings often are seen in interpersonal relations. If one person has a fixed or stereotyped idea about another—for example that he is unreliable or aggressive—anticipatory behavior by the first man toward the second may actually elicit the expected irresponsible or hostile response. Then the induced behavior serves to confirm and reinforce the original stereotype. Thus, prejudiced behavior is in a real sense contagious and continuous, constantly reproducing itself. The social stereotype of the Negro as lazy, amoral, dirty, and dangerous, bears an inertia that is doubly hard to break, for his low status is sustained by the majority white image, which in turn keeps the Negro in a depressed social and economic position and induces impulse-gratifying and aggressive behavior.

Negro children, too, come to learn and internalize the values of the dominant white community. One of the most significant aspects of the school desegregation decision of 1954 is that Chief Justice Earl Warren, speaking for a unanimous United States Supreme Court, insisted on recognizing the damaging effects of segregation on the personality of the victim of race prejudice. Citing the research of psychologists and sociologists, the Court pointed to the harm done to the psyches of black children who are reminded by society each day that they are considered less worthy than white children. The court spoke explicitly of these Negro children's "feeling of inferiority as to their status in the community that may affect their hearts and minds in a way unlikely ever to be undone."

It is this feeling of being a second-class citizen that young Claude Brown expressed to his father as they returned to Harlem from a courtroom where they had not received due respect and consideration: "I guess we ain't nothin' or nobody, huh, Dad?"[2] The process of acquiring low self-esteem, self-directed hostility, and an injured self-image takes place early in life. The Negro child's recognition that dark skin color is less desirable and is to be associated with low value has been demonstrated in studies of preschool children. In one nursery school when Negro children were given a choice of a white and a brown doll to play with, they chose the white doll almost without exception.

When belonging to a minority group impedes the reaching of desired goals, the group affiliation assumes a negative connotation. Identifying with the group is a source of frustration because it limits freedom of action. The group member may gain status by moving away from or leaving the group. If this is not possible, he will accept the values and group stereotypes of the majority and give majority values a positive connotation. The verdict of the majority is accepted and aggression is turned in on one's group and on oneself. The phenomenon of self-hate is an aspect of psychological identification. It answers the basic question of the ego ideal: "Whom do I want to be like?" The primary objects of identification are almost always the parents. The child learns from them what it means to be a man or a woman.

---

[2] Claude Brown, *Manchild in the Promised Land* (New York, 1965), p. 98.

But for the Negro, the parent is a member of a disadvantaged and humiliated group. Their ethnic ideal bears with it the stigma of social handicap and internal inferiority feelings. No one can unambivalently embrace such an ideal.

The premium placed by many Negroes on a light shade of skin, straight hair, and Caucasian features, are all indicative of severely injured self-esteem and of the inferiority assumed in things Negro. James Baldwin's childhood memories may not be atypical:

> One's hair was always being attacked with hard brushes and combs and Vaseline: it was shameful to have nappy hair. One's legs and arms and face were always being greased, so that one would not look ashy in the wintertime. One was always being mercilessly scrubbed and polished, as though in the hope that a stain could thus be washed away. . . . The women were forever straightening and curling their hair, and using bleaching creams. And yet it was clear that none of this effort would release one from the stigma and danger of being a Negro; this effort merely increased the shame and rage.[3]

More recently Eldridge Cleaver has described "The Ogre"—his image of a white woman, clawing with dreadful power at the core of his being while he was in prison; and the "Black Eunuch," who would "jump over ten nigger bitches just to get to one white woman." The Black Eunuch felt that: "Ain't no such thing as an ugly white woman. A white woman is beautiful even if she's baldheaded and only has one tooth."[4] Such a profound self-hatred can only be the product of a social system that from infancy has crushed self-esteem and destroyed healthy self-images with which the growing Negro child can identify. An important study by two psychiatrists points out that "accepting the white ideal is a recipe for perpetual self-hatred, frustration, and for tying one's life to unattainable goals. It is a formula for living life on the delusional basis of 'as if.' The acceptance of the white ideal has acted on the Negro as a slow but cumulative and fatal psychological poison."[5] The poison is the disparity between the Negro's white ego ideal and the reality he experiences. The ideal is by its nature unachievable. A Negro child can never become a white adult. The most he can do is to strive for surrogate white attributes such as straight hair or a light-colored mate.

The true price that is paid in terms of human misery and damaged lives can only be perceived by looking at qualitative studies of the lasting trauma of race hate on the daily lives of American Negroes. An itinerant preacher who at age twelve had watched a shackled playmate in a cage waiting to be taken away and lynched never lost his feeling of panic. In the midst of a

---

[3] James Baldwin, *Nobody Knows My Name* (New York, 1961), p. 73.

[4] Eldridge Cleaver, *Soul on Ice* (New York, 1968), pp. 6, 159.

[5] Abram Kardiner and Lionel Ovesey, *The Mark of Oppression: A Psychosocial Study of the American Negro* (New York, 1951), p. 310.

sermon he would cry out: "How could they do that to a boy?"[6] One Negro woman had the frantic wish to have a white child. She dreamed of being in a hospital and giving birth to a white baby. In her rebirth fantasy she would shed her blackness and be reborn white. Whiteness would be the cure for all her troubles. Erik H. Erikson describes the case of a Negro child faced with the impossibility of making a satisfactory identification with the heroes of the mass media:

> I know a colored boy who, like our boys, listens every night to Red Rider. Then he sits up in bed, imagining that he is Red Rider. But the moment comes when he sees himself galloping after some masked offenders and suddenly notices that in his fancy Red Rider is a colored man. He stops his fantasy. While a small child, this boy was extremely expressive, both in his pleasures and in his sorrows. Today he is calm and always smiles; his language is soft and blurred; nobody can hurry or worry him—or please him. White people like him.[7]

In this vignette, we see how social discrimination produces low self-esteem. The reaction to this will be aggression, which may be unconscious. Aggressive acting out of impulses, which might be socially disastrous and are therefore feared, may then be defended against by ingratiating, passive behavior. But the Negro who denies his rage must pay a heavy price for this denial. He becomes removed, hesitant, and mistrustful. There is a general dulling of response which comes from the need to keep rage under control. Thus the self-abnegating, polite, cautious, and apologetic Negro is often holding down suppressed rage and sustained hatred. It should be no surprise that many superficially easygoing southern Negroes have a high incidence of hypertension and maintain consistently high blood pressure due to perpetual rage at their environment, which they feel powerless to change.

An encounter group of Negro students in the back rooms of a small Baptist church in the Deep South learned how these defenses against aggression operate. After some days of resistance to feelings of hostility against whites and protestations of "love" for the local red necks who had beat them during the difficult transition to integrated schools, the group leader suggested that roles be reversed and that the only white man in the group, a civil rights worker, be seen as Negro and that the Negroes act out the role of whites. The single white man was abused and heaped with contempt and ridicule as if he were black. They shouted at him: "You stink Nigger; look at his kinky hair; look at them old shoes, I bet he paid a dollar for them; why don't you go back to your own school; you're oily and smelly." The group had a chance to "identify with the aggressor," which is itself a

[6] William H. Grier and Price M. Cobbs, *Black Rage* (New York, 1968), p. 27.
[7] Erik H. Erikson, *Childhood and Society,* 2d edition (New York, 1963), p. 241.

defense against rage and impotence. It was a red-letter day for the group because the first layer of defense against feeling hate was cracked. Now they were able to begin confronting and working with the hatred and murderous wishes which all people who have been degraded harbor for their persecutors, and which they must either defend against by denial or deal with directly.

Negro and other minority psychiatric patients invariably discover in themselves varying degrees of self-hatred which they project on their whole race. One middle-class patient expressed it this way:

> It's when you see someone very black, uncouth, dressed like a bum in a bus. It's times like that I wish I weren't a Negro. It's when you see them acting a fool in the subway, bus, or street. I just want to commit manslaughter at times like that.[8]

Another lady felt she could not be proud of her little boy's kinky hair. She bathed him daily in hydrogen peroxide to lighten his skin. When this failed she tried washing him in Clorox for two months. This kind of degradation can only produce in the child the conviction that he is unlovable, the diminution of the capacity to feel, and vast amounts of hostility. American culture, in the words of Kardiner and Ovesey, gives the Negro "no possible basis for a healthy self-esteem and every incentive for self-hatred."[9]

The violent quality of the black militant movement arises from the discovery of power among those who have always seen themselves as powerless. What we are seeing is the dramatic consciousness of a reversal of roles: those who have been the victims of violence enjoy the prospect of exercising violence on their oppressors. The often bloody language of black power advocates is, among other things, a way of testing the surrounding white ambiance: How much can whites be frightened or hurt? Will whites respond, or perhaps overrespond, to threats and intimidation?

II

When we turn to how prejudice actually works in the mind, we find that all men, white and black, harbor desires that are inadmissable to consciousness because these wishes are not socially sanctioned and therefore arouse guilt. These desires—voluptuous, murderous, and incestuous—are kept hidden in the unconscious. One means of defense against unconscious wishes is projection. Projection is perceiving in others that which one wishes to deny in oneself. It is the process of saying: "the evil impulses are out there, not here in me." What is outside can be repudiated and destroyed.

---

[8] Kardiner and Ovesey, *The Mark of Oppression*, p. 228.
[9] Kardiner and Ovesey, *The Mark of Oppression*, p. 297.

One of the classic themes in modern literature and drama concerns persons whose guilt about their own erotic feelings is assuaged by condemning them in others. The minister in Somerset Maugham's *Rain* is a poignant example of this. He castigates the prostitute for her promiscuity when the true, unrecognized seat of sexual craving is in himself. In Robert Anderson's *Tea and Sympathy,* and Arthur Miller's *View from the Bridge,* the heroes perceive homoerotic feelings in others in order to defend against admitting such feelings in themselves.

When forbidden desires emerge in a white man, he can facilitate their repression by projecting them onto blacks or members of other racial minorities. In the unconscious of the bigot the black represents his own repressed instincts which he fears and hates and which are forbidden by his conscience as it struggles to conform to the values professed by society. This is why the black man becomes the personification of sexuality, lewdness, laziness, dirtiness, and unbridled hostility. He is the symbol of voluptuousness and the immediate gratification of pleasure. In the deepest recesses of the minds of white Americans, Negroes are associated with lowly and debased objects or with sexuality and violence. In our society children are taught at an early age that their excrement is disgusting, smelly, and dirty, and that sexual and hostile feelings are bad and dangerous. These feelings are easily associated with low status or tabooed groups such as Negroes. Blacks are pictured in the unconscious imagery of the white majority as dark and odorous, aggressive, libidinal, and threatening.

Internal ambivalence—the experiencing of contradictory feelings at the same time—frequently is resolved by projection. All elements of the population in the United States are in conflict over the emotionally loaded issue of race. The official ideal of equality teaches that each man has inalienable rights to be protected by the democratic political system. Yet in reality, American society condones the ghetto and other discriminatory situational and institutional practices. White people who practice discrimination must repress in themselves their own equalitarian impulses and project them onto white liberal "nigger lovers" who are then seen as the sole source of integrationist sentiment. On the other hand, white advocates of civil rights must repress in themselves racist stereotypes and view such ideas as emanating exclusively from bigoted segregationists. The difference between the white liberal and the white bigot is chiefly a difference in ideals. The liberal feels shame and guilt for his prejudiced ideas and therefore tries to make his conduct conform to the demands of his democratic ideals and his conscience; the bigot does not.

The process of projection becomes dangerous to the bigot when he perceives that he is hated as the exploiter and oppressor and that he must fear the revenge of the blacks. It has become apparent in recent years that centuries of denigration and humiliation have been unsuccessful in keeping the Negro "in his place." Blacks, sometimes with the initial aid of whites, have persisted in rising on all fronts: educationally, socially, legally, and politically. These efforts have often been interpreted in the white mind as preludes to hostile vengefulness by blacks. This, again, is largely a projection. Bigoted whites cannot imagine blacks who are not vengeful because they identify projectively with the targets of their prejudice and they know how revengeful they themselves would be in similar circumstances. White ambivalence vitiates the capacity of the majority to understand black militancy. Many whites overreact to black militancy and violence by conjuring up fantasies of revenge: that the oppressed will now conquer and rule their oppressors. This is pure fantasy since no black group or leader has advocated ruling over the whites. Most whites interpret black threats as final intentions of annihilation rather than tests of reality by those who have until now been powerless. Such overanxious whites reason, on a primitive archaic level, that an injury can be undone or must be punished by a similar deed inflicted on themselves. Whites accordingly are preoccupied with protecting themselves from black violence, which blacks in turn misapprehend as a preparation for accelerated white oppression and even genocide.

The mechanism of projection frequently coincides with and is complemented by displacement. This is when the anxiety, frustration, or cause of misery, whether social or instinctual, is attributed to a person or object which is less threatening and more accessible than the real source. The classic example is the man who is mistreated or misunderstood by his boss at work, and then comes home to yell at his wife and beat his children. It is safe to express his anger against them. His hostility is displaced from its true source, which is too remote or powerful to be attacked, to a closer defenseless object. Small children often express their rage against their parents by abusing their pets. It is far too dangerous to risk the loss of mother's love, so the anger is displaced onto a kitten or puppy which is easily available and without means of retaliation.

Displacement is seen dramatically in a famous study correlating lynchings of Negroes in the South to the price of cotton during the years from 1882 to 1930. Whenever the income from cotton declined and economic hardship ensued, the number of lynchings rose, suggesting that material frustration caused anger that could not effectively or immediately be directed at an abstract social and economic system, and that this hostility was instead discharged by being displaced onto blacks.

Another important dimension of the psychology of racism concerns interracial sex relations. People with the most guilt about their own sexual desires also have the greatest prejudice involving sexual fears. A study of prison inmates showed that men with high sexual anxiety are more hostile toward racial minorities and tend to commit more sexual offenses than men who are sexually more secure.

A southern author, Wilbur J. Cash has brilliantly portrayed the sexual patterns of southern men who have historically exploited black women. In *The Mind of the South,* Cash stresses the mental mechanism of guilt which has impelled these men to make white women into desexualized objects of worship. This is the peculiar southern variant of a common tendency in the mind of the Western world to divide women into mutually exclusive categories. The first, which corresponds to what Denis De Rougemont has called courtly romantic love, views woman as a spiritualized pure image to be worshiped from a distance. The other regards her as a debased, voluptuous, and sensual creature to be used for sexual pleasure. These images coexist in the mind and are split, or ascribed to different women. In a society with a highly differentiated class or racial structure, the erotic and sensual qualities tend to be ascribed to the women of a minority race or a lower social class, while the women of the dominant or upper-class group are depicted as pure, virginal, desexualized, domestic—and therefore more incestually taboo. This is why in the South white womanhood was glorified in courtly chivalric terms while sexual gratification was obtained from the black women of the slave quarters and shanty towns.

Though Cash does not explore the linkage between the guilt induced by this emotional splitting and white attitudes toward black men, the connection is apparent. If he desires and sexually uses black women, the white man fantasizes and fears that black men will claim the same right and desire. Thus the white man who uses black women sexually perceives the black man as a menace to him and his women. By projection, the black man is seen as the one who lusts after white womanhood. This projection— "it is he, not I, who is lascivious"—is both guilt-evading and self-assuring because the evil doer who violates social morality is the other man, not oneself. Thus the "badness" is externalized.

However, Negroes are not only equated with dirt and uncontrolled violence in the mind of white America. The emotions of race are much more conflicted and ambivalent than that. In the same white minds Negroes are also the symbols of warmth, fecundity, and wild voluptuousness. Two such apparently contradictory feelings may coexist with equanimity because elements of mystery and forbiddenness heighten attraction in a society which places, as does our own, many inhibitions on the enjoyment of the body and the senses. What is attractive must therefore also be degraded and forbidden.

A number of outstanding works of American literature vividly present the theme of the erotic attraction of the white imagination to the tabooed people of dark skin. To cite from three classics: James Fenimore Cooper's Natty Bumppo and Chingachgook, Herman Melville's Ishmael and Queequeg, and Mark Twain's Huck and Jim give to each other the love, trust, tenderness, and comradeship which they could not find in the world of women. In each case two men, one dark hued, the other light skinned, shared what the critic Leslie A. Fiedler has called the "archetypal relationship" which "haunts the American psyche."[10] It is highly suggestive that the

---

[10] Leslie A. Fiedler, *Love and Death in the American Novel* (Cleveland and New York, 1960), p. 187.

favorite epithet of bigots for the white liberal is "Niggerlover." The very word itself suggests that those who use it are enmeshed in their own projected feelings of attraction.

Gordon W. Allport illustrates this phenomenon by citing the response of an urban housewife when questioned as to whether she would object to Negroes moving on to her street:

> I wouldn't want to live with Negroes. They smell too much. They're of a different race. That's what creates racial hatreds. When I sleep with a Negro in the same bed, I'll live with them. But you know we can't.[11]

We are startled to see how a woman's unconscious sexual fantasies have intruded themselves into an unrelated problem, namely residence on on the same street. After all, the fact of living on the same block is not the criterion by which most people select their sexual partners. We note that her mind first goes to the supposed distinctive unpleasant odor of Negroes, an assumption for which there is no scientific evidence. The woman's mental associations then move from images of body products that are intimate and disgusting to the theme of forbidden sexuality. We may see here how unconscious aggressive, sexual, and other repressed feelings emerge into consciousness in association with Negroes and are defended against by projection and displacement onto Negroes. This is one reason that repression of Negroes is maintained with such vehemence and that reaction to efforts at social or residential racial mixing is so irrational and intense. The deepest emotions concerning body products and repressed desires threaten to burst out of control. Inner panic must be avoided by new defenses against unconscious wishes; hence outer social segregation must be re-enforced.

The social effect of sexual projection and the inequality of the administration of justice in the United States are dramatically displayed in the pattern of criminal convictions for interracial sex offenders. The conviction of black males for sex offenses with white women has been disproportionately heavy, although the majority of interracial sex offenses are committed by white men. In thirteen southern states where blacks made up 24 percent of the population 15 whites and 187 Negroes were executed for rape between 1938 and 1948.

III

We are often led to ask: why are some people more susceptible than others to racial hatred? In recent years social scientists have conducted extensive research on the personalities of prejudiced people in search of an answer to this question. Their work demonstrates a correlation between personality, ideas, and racial prejudice. Feelings of personal insecurity,

[11] Gordon W. Allport, *The Nature of Prejudice* (Cambridge, Mass., 1954), p. 373.

deprivation, anxiety, and hostility are all linked to prejudice. N. W. Acker-man and Marie Jahoda have described anti-Semitism as a culturally pro-vided projective test, "the Jewish inkblot," onto which people project all the negative feelings of which they disapprove.

A famous study, by T. W. Adorno and his associates, *The Authoritarian Personality,* found that the primary feature of the racially prejudiced personality is authoritarianism—a preoccupation with issues of power such as who is strong and who is weak. The study used questionnaires, in-depth interviews, and projective tests. The central finding is that prejudiced at-titudes express inner needs. The authoritarian individual is a weak and de-pendent person who lacks the capacity for genuine experience of himself or others. Behind his façade of strength lurks a shaky sense of order and safety. His world is one of rigidly stereotyped categories of power, success, and punitive moralism. He seeks to align himself with the conventional, and with what is regarded by others as good and strong. But these are not his own values. He has underlying feelings of weakness and self-contempt which he suppresses and projects onto ethnic minorities and other out-groups. The authoritarian thinks in rigid categories of dominance and sub-mission, those who command and those who obey, masters and slaves. For him weakness is contemptuous. It is associated with guilt. His identi-fication with those in power is a reaction to deep feelings of inadequacy and weakness. He acts the role of the "tough guy," trying to appear hypermascu-line, while in reality he has strong feminine dependent tendencies that he denies. His conceptions of masculinity and femininity are exaggerated and rigid. Therefore he fears and rejects all that appears as soft, feminine, or weak.

Authoritarian personalities tend to describe their fathers as distant, stern, and bad tempered. The relationship between father and child is cold and remote. The son tends to see his father as an oppressor, but his uncon-scious hostility is concealed from himself and others by an attitude of sub-mission and admiration. This submission to the father, a relation of love for the powerful man, determines the later projection of the dominance-submission dimension on all relationships. It also creates a compelling fear of weakness which is defended against by a façade of toughness. There follows a projection of all sinful, aggressive, and sexual impulses on out-groups and condemnation of these groups because of this projection. The authors of *The Authoritarian Personality* concluded:

> Thus a basically hierarchical, authoritarian, exploitative parent-child re-lationship is apt to carry over into a power-oriented . . . political philosophy and social outlook which has no room for anything but a desperate clinging to what appears to be strong and a disdainful rejection of whatever is relegated to the bottom.[12]

[12] T. W. Adorno, Else Frenkel-Brunswick, Daniel J. Levinson, R. Nevitt Sanford, and collaborators, *The Authoritarian Personality* (New York, 1950), p. 971.

Thus, a close relationship exists between sexual anxiety and intense prejudice. Men who hate racial minorities show "masculine" protest against sexual passivity, semi-impotence, or homosexual trends. They defend against these passive and feminine feelings by exaggerated toughness, pseudomasculinity, hostility, and racial prejudice.

Something vital is missing, however, from the extensive scholarship on prejudice carried out after World War II. The thrust of this scholarship was to suggest that prejudiced people were emotionally sick and that emotionally healthy people were ethnically tolerant. A direct relationship was posited between neurosis and prejudice. What this formulation disregards is the covering over and apparently strengthening qualities that may be conferred by racial prejudice. The greater the underlying anxiety of a person, the more prejudiced he is, because the pressure of his anxiety weakens his personal controls. Thus weakened, he seeks relief through prejudice, which serves to reduce anxiety because prejudice facilitates the discharge of hostility. If hostility is discharged, regardless of whether it is toward the "realistic" object of hate or not, anxiety is reduced. Prejudice suggests to the person that he is better than others, hence he does not need to feel so anxious. Thus prejudice can help a person protect his individuality and maintain the emotional balance of a distorted personality.

One of the striking changes in the views of several prominent social scientists, such as Bettelheim and Janowitz, in recent years is the discovery that prejudice may indeed be an integrating psychological force. The prejudiced person needs his hate to maintain his feeling of selfhood. The chief psychiatrist for the Netherlands army in World War II described the ego-strengthening effect of the release of hatred on some of his patients:

> Hatred gives man new social status among all those who share his feelings, and a feeling of magic power. The hater lives in a constant inner ecstasy. Even a pathological idiot assumes a pseudo-personality when he preaches hate and destruction. Several egoless patients of mine became (in their own estimation) new personalities when the Nazis, who occupied their homeland, gave them the opportunity to feel real hatred. The reality hatred cured them of their obsessive defenses against their inner hostility. [13]

Thus we can see how prejudice may permit the bigot to function better in society. A discharge of tension through racial hostility (projection and displacement onto minorities) permits the re-establishment of control over the rest of his instinctual forces. Prejudice may meet the need for emotional strength and personal control. For those who fail to achieve an effective personal identity, prejudice may become a permanent part of their identity. This reaction is involved whenever a person is threatened by self-doubt, feelings of confusion about who he is, a fear that he may be a "nobody." When a person has strong doubts about his ethnic, sexual, vocational,

[13] Joost A. M. Meerloo, *That Difficult Peace* (Great Neck, N.Y., 1961), p. 69.

social, national, or personal identity, he may unconsciously adopt prejudice against others to compensate for a lack of certainty about who or what he is.

An intellectual or emotional attack on prejudice may threaten a weak identity. Efforts to break down segregation are interpreted as an attack on the inner sense of identity of the prejudiced. Criticism increases their guilt feelings, which are often not even conscious. This may also work in reverse. Some white "liberals" derive their identity from their stance for social justice. By fighting the evils of racism in this society they can ally themselves with the forces of ethical purity and morality and thus assuage consciences that are guilty for reasons that may have no relation to racism. When these "liberals" engage the bigot, it is a confrontation between two types of people whose identities are committed to winning at the expense of their opponent's identity. Neither is willing to sacrifice the basis on which his identity rests—for the white liberal his identity as a fighter for the good, and for the bigot his feeling of superiority to other groups. In a sense, each says to the other: "Give up that which grants you a feeling of well being as a whole person, so that I can enhance my own security and fight my own feelings of inner aimlessness and emptiness." Each feels the self-seeking nature of this pressure. The underlying motive of this variety of white liberal is sensed by the prejudiced person, who also feels entitled to the benefits to the self which can be achieved by clinging to his prejudice. Blacks also sense the self-serving nature of some white liberals. In recent years, white Americans who have worked for racial justice have been discomfited to hear black spokesmen claim that avowed white racists are often more open, honest, and "straight" than white liberals.

This disillusionment with white liberalism is one reason for the collapse of the civil rights movement in the 1960s. This failure occurred when blacks realized that the legal promises of the civil rights legislation would not bring them either social integration or a middle-class standard of living. To be brought within sight of the goal and then to realize that one is barred from reaching it has caused depression, militancy, and violence. Bitterness and rage have grown among blacks as they have made gains that heighten their expectations of equality while the ultimate promise remains unfulfilled. Many minority leaders have asked why freedom and equality guaranteed by the Constitution are regarded as privileges to be obtained gradually. Others question whether equality will ever be gained by nonviolent or evolutionary means.

A recent analysis of the collapse of the civil rights movement points out the psychological difficulties of interracial relationships, even when the best motives underlie social action. Charles J. Levy has found that white field workers in southern communities and instructors in southern Negro colleges have experienced severe personal crises in attempting to work for integration as a social and political program.[14]

[14] Charles J. Levy, *Voluntary Servitude: Whites in the Negro Movement* (New York, 1968), *passim.*

Levy focuses on the element of trust in interracial programs. Do both black and white view their relationship in the same way? Is it a consistent relationship? Trust cannot be maintained in one area and broken in another. Both parties must feel that they are better off in the relationship than by acting alone. Both parties must understand and subscribe to each other's motives. Each must have the conviction that the other has nothing to gain by acting contrary to his stated purpose. Each must be convinced that the other will not change for the worse once trust has been conferred. The rewards to blacks cannot appear to be greater than the rewards to whites. The white must have stronger ties to the blacks in the movement than to other whites. They must form a collectivity. The operational test for trust is this: Will black and white act the same in each other's absence as they will in each other's presence?

Unfortunately, trust has not prevailed in the interracial civil rights movement. The dynamics of white involvement have been the dynamics of unrequited love. The white worker mentally seeks to identify with blacks. He psychologically tries to become black. But trust is withheld by blacks because whites in the civil rights movement are in fact exempt from the penalties of being black. Whiteness itself created the objective circumstances of a special relation to blacks and their movement. White engagement is for a limited time only and can always be terminated by withdrawal. The assumed "blackness" of a pseudoconversion can be shed at will. The white worker is viewed as having nothing to lose, while the local Negroes have everything to lose. They are vulnerable to economic and physical reprisals. Should violence occur, the white workers, it is felt, are treated better than the blacks. Bail money is generally more available to them and they are protected by attention from the national news media.

Of course there are also substantial and unique disadvantages to being a white civil rights worker in the South. The presence of a new white worker is instantly noticed in the Deep South. There is no community of friendly whites where the civil rights worker can go for comfort or protection. The white worker is alone, accepted by neither the Negro nor the southern white community. His presence is a declaration of war on southern traditions and he is an unmistakable target for hostility. In the end, the white civil rights worker discovers that there is a point beyond which he can never go in identifying with blacks.

IV

In spite of the failures of the civil rights movement, some basis exists for believing that racial attitudes are changing. Among the most promising findings of social scientists is that federal policy and government action have conditioned and influenced public opinion on desegregation. Since 1942, the first year intensive surveys on this subject were taken, there has been a long-term trend toward the acceptance of racial integration, regardless of dramatic racial crises such as the Little Rock conflict of 1957 and the sit-ins of the early 1960s. In 1942, fewer than a third of all whites in America, including both North and South, favored school integration. By 1956, two years after the Supreme Court school desegregation decision, approximately half of the white Americans approved of integrated schools. In 1963, a solid majority of the white community endorsed school integration.

Perhaps the best testing ground for changes in attitudes is white opinion in the South. Statistics for this region reveal even more dramatic changes. In 1942, only one person out of fifty favored public school integration in the sixteen southern and border states. Twelve years later the number was one in seven. Recent figures show that the trend has accelerated in the South. As of 1963, 30 percent of white southerners endorsed school integration. These findings have led two eminent social scientists to conclude that "in those parts of the South where some measure of school integration has taken place official action has *preceded* public sentiment, and public sentiment has then attempted to accommodate itself to the new situation."[15]

Acceptance by white Americans of residential integration and interracial marriage has been much slower than acceptance of the integration of schools and public transportation. The support of white Americans for residential integration rose nationally from 35 percent in 1942 to 64 percent in 1963. During the same period approval of integrated public transportation rose from 44 to 78 percent among whites. But in December 1963, 80 percent of white southerners and 53 percent of white northerners favored laws prohibiting interracial marriages.

The chief factors conducive to support for integration among whites are exposure to integration, higher levels of education, and younger age. What has been termed the "revolutionary change" undergone by southern opinion during the first eighteen months of school integration in that region is striking proof that exposure to integration does promote favorable attitudes toward desegregation. This "revolutionary change" is a turn from 30 percent of white southerners who favored integration in December 1963 to an absolute majority, 55 percent, in June 1965. In the same period the proportion of white southerners who had no objection to residential desegregation rose from 51 percent to 66 percent. When school districts are broken down by level of segregation, 74 percent of the southern white parents whose children were in desegregated schools favored integration, whereas only 48 percent of parents of children who still were segregated favored a change.[16] The evidence is clear: where integration is an accomplished fact, even in the South, white citizens will support it after a short period.

[15] Herbert H. Hyman and Paul B. Sheatsley, "Attitudes Toward Desegregation," *Scientific American,* 211 (July 1964), p. 20.

[16] Hyman and Sheatsley, "Attitudes Toward Desegregation," p. 20.

When we turn to educational level, which correlates with occupation and earning power, the findings show that the higher an individual's socio-economic status, as measured by education, vocation, and income, the greater the likelihood that he will support integration. Throughout America the older age groups are more segregationist than the younger ones. People aged sixty-five and over are more segregationist than those between forty-five and sixty-four, and these in turn are less tolerant than persons aged twenty-four to forty-four. This suggests a genuine and important shift in the attitudinal structure of the American people. Our nation's greatest challenge is to convert this into a movement for the institutional reforms necessary for the achievement of racial equality.

Further Reading

The student who wishes to extend his study of race and racism in America will find a long list of books on the subject—one indication of the prominent place which the subject has occupied in the American mind over the past three centuries. These books, as a rule, do not focus on white racial attitudes but offer valuable information on the context in which these attitudes developed and flourished. The following books are only a partial list of relevant and available materials. The interested student can glean further references from the footnotes and bibliographies of each of these works.

Colonial and Early National Period, 1607–1820

Every person concerned with the roots of racism in England and America will want to read Winthrop D. Jordan, *White Over Black: American Attitudes Toward the Negro, 1550–1812* (Chapel Hill, N.C., 1968). Jordan's analysis of the formation and transmission of racial attitudes in the colonial and early national periods is useful for understanding racism in our more recent history as well. Roy Harvey Pearce's *The Savages of America: A Study of the Indian and the Idea of Civilization* (Baltimore, 1953) is the best attempt to deal with American attitudes toward the Indian in the colonial period, though much remains to be done on this important topic.

Also of significance are Alden T. Vaughan, *New England Frontier: Puritans and Indians, 1620–1675* (Boston, 1965); Chapman J. Milling, *Red Carolinians* (Chapel Hill, N.C., 1940); and Almon W. Lauber, *Indian Slavery in Colonial Times within the Present Limits of the United States* (New York, 1913). For the antislavery impulse and racial attitudes imbedded in the ideology of abolitionism in the eighteenth century, David Brion Davis' *The Problem of Slavery in Western Culture* (Ithaca, N.Y., 1966) is invaluable. Arthur Zilversmit, *The First Emancipation: The Abolition of Slavery in the North* (Chicago, 1967) carries the subject further. Of the many studies of slavery in the colonial period, the most useful in analyzing racial attitudes are Lorenzo J. Greene, *The Negro in Colonial New England, 1620–1776* (New York, 1942); Thad W. Tate, Jr., *The Negro in Eighteenth-Century Williamsburg* (Charlottesville, Va., 1966); Thomas E. Drake, *Quakers and Slavery in America* (New Haven, Conn., 1950); Frank Tannenbaum, *Slave and Citizen: The Negro in the Americas* (New York, 1947); and Stanley M. Elkins, *Slavery: A Problem in American Institutional and Intellectual Life* (Chicago, 1959).

National Expansion and Industrial Growth, 1820–1890

One of the most perceptive analyses of racial attitudes in nineteenth-century America is also one of the oldest: Alexis de Tocqueville, *Democracy in America,* published in many editions since its first translation into English in 1835. Racial ideology is treated in Thomas F. Gossett, *Race: The History of an Idea in America* (Dallas, 1963), and with great insight in William Stanton's *The Leopard's Spots: Scientific Attitudes Toward Race in America, 1815–1859* (Chicago, 1960). Wilbur J. Cash, *The Mind of the South* (New York, 1941) is of signal importance, as is Leon F. Litwack, *North of Slavery: The Negro in the Free States, 1790–1860* (Chicago, 1961). For the effect of slavery at its apogee on racial thinking in the antebellum period, one should turn to Kenneth M. Stampp, *The Peculiar Institution: Slavery in the Ante-Bellum South* (New York, 1956). William S. Jenkin's *Pro-Slavery Thought in the Old South* (Chapel Hill, N.C., 1935) examines the racial ideology of the defenders of slavery.

For the period of Civil War and Reconstruction much can be learned from James M. McPherson, *The Struggle for Equality: Abolitionists and the Negro in the Civil War and Reconstruction* (Princeton, N.J., 1964) and from the essays collected in Martin B. Duberman, ed., *The Antislavery Vanguard; New Essays on the Abolitionists* (Princeton, N.J., 1965). Those who did not befriend the Negro are portrayed in Forrest G. Wood, *Black Scare: The Racist Response to Emancipation and Reconstruction* (Berkeley and Los Angeles, 1968). Studies at the state level are too numerous to mention but two regional studies are worthy of note: Jacques V.

Voegeli, *Free but Not Equal: The Midwest and the Negro during the Civil War* (Chicago, 1967) and Eugene H. Berwanger, *The Frontier Against Slavery: Western Anti-Negro Prejudice and the Slavery Extension Controversy* (Urbana, Ill., 1967).

The Indian, whose plight worsened almost to the point of extinction in the era of continental expansion, also figured importantly in white racial ideology. Two good introductions to the attitudes of westward-moving Americans are Albert K. Weinberg, *Manifest Destiny* (Baltimore, 1935) and William T. Hagan, *American Indians* (Chicago, 1961). Lewis O. Saum, *The Fur Trader and the Indian* (Seattle, 1965) should be read in conjunction with Hoxie N. Fairchild, *The Noble Savage: A Study in Romantic Naturalism* (New York, 1928) so as to compare the image of the Indian as it was refracted in the minds of land-hungry frontiersmen and literary easterners and Englishmen. The attitudes of still another social group are examined in Robert F. Berkhofer, *Salvation and the Savage: American Protestant Missions and American Indian Response, 1787–1862* (Lexington, Ky., 1965). Also of value is Henry E. Fritz, *The Movement for Indian Assimilation, 1800–1890* (Philadelphia, 1963).

The ideology of racism, profoundly affected in the post-Civil War period by the rise of the social sciences, is treated with penetration by George W. Stocking, Jr., *Race, Culture, and Evolution* (New York, 1968). More general, but still helpful, are Richard Hofstadter, *Social Darwinism in American Thought* (New York, 1959); and Oscar Handlin, *Race and Nationality in American Life* (Boston, 1957).

Racist patterns of thought conditioned the response of Americans to the flood of immigrants that entered the United States in the nineteenth and twentieth centuries. Informative, in this connection, is John Higham's *Strangers in the Land: Patterns of American Nativism, 1860–1925* (New Brunswick, N.J., 1955). More specialized treatments of nativism, as it applied to various ethnic groups, are Gunther Barth, *Bitter Strength: A History of the Chinese in the United States, 1850–1870* (Cambridge, Mass., 1964); Stuart C. Miller *The Unwelcome Immigrant: The American Image of the Chinese, 1785–1882* (Berkeley and Los Angeles, 1969); Roger Daniels, *The Politics of Prejudice: The Anti-Japanese Movement in California and the Struggle for Japanese Exclusion* (Berkeley and Los Angeles, 1962); Leonard Pitt, *The Decline of the Californios: A Social History of the Spanish-Speaking Californians, 1846–1890* (Berkeley and Los Angeles, 1966); and Barbara M. Solomon, *Ancestors and Immigrants; A Changing New England Tradition* (Cambridge, Mass., 1956).

Modern America, 1890–1960

A deluge of books have been written in an attempt to understand the problem of race relations in twentieth-century America. One of the most important is C. Vann Woodward, *The Strange Career of Jim Crow* (New York, 1955), which traces the hardening of attitudes in the South at the end of the nineteenth century. The story is carried into the twentieth century in Ray Stannard Baker, *Following the Color Line; An Account of Negro Citizenship in the American Democracy* (New York, 1908), and in I. A. Newby, *Jim Crow's Defense: Anti-Negro Thought in America, 1900– 1930* (Baton Rouge, La., 1965). Outside the South, racial hostilities also intensified as evidenced by the rise of the Ku Klux Klan. New appraisals of the Klan are offered in Kenneth T. Jackson, *The Ku Klux Klan in the City, 1915–1930* (New York, 1967) and Charles C. Alexander, *The Ku Klux Klan in the Southwest* (Lexington, Ky., 1965). In Elliott M. Rudwick's *Race Riot at East St. Louis* (Carbondale, Ill. 1964) the student will find a case study of the racial confrontation experienced in northern cities during and immediately after World War I. The relationship between white attitudes and the growth of northern black ghettos is considered in Gilbert Osofsky, *Harlem: The Making of a Ghetto; Negro New York, 1890–1930* (New York, 1966); and Allen H. Spear, *Black Chicago; The Making of a Negro Ghetto, 1890–1920* (Chicago, 1967). Also valuable is Ray Marshall, *The Negro and Organized Labor* (New York, 1965), and Julius Jacobson, ed., *The Negro and the American Labor Movement* (Garden City, N.Y., 1968). A modern classic on race relations and racial attitudes, completed during World War II, is Gunnar Myrdal, *An American Dilemma; The Negro Problem and Modern Democracy* (New York, 1944). The problem in the setting of a small town is examined in John Dollard, *Caste and Class in a Southern Town* (New Haven, Conn., 1937). A moving personal memoir which can still be read with profit is Lillian Smith's *Killers of the Dream* (New York, 1949).

The efforts of white leaders to achieve racial justice during World War II and thereafter can be followed in Dennis D. Nelson, *The Integration of the Negro into the United States Navy* (New York, 1951); Lee Nichols, *Breakthrough on the Color Front* (New York, 1954); and Arthur I. Waskow, *From Race Riot to Sit In* (Garden City, N.Y., 1966). For opposition to these struggles see I. A. Newby, *Challenge to the Court; Social Scientists and the Defense of Segregation, 1954–1966* (Baton Rouge, La., 1967). The most significant books on the racial trauma of the 1960s are Stokely Carmichael and Charles V. Hamilton, *Black Power; The Politics of Liberation in America* (New York, 1967); Robert Conot, *Rivers of Blood, Years of Darkness* (New York, 1967); Harold Cruse, *Rebellion or Revolution* (New York, 1968); John Hersey, *The Algiers Motel Incident* (New York, 1968); Louis E. Lomax, *The Negro Revolt* (New York, 1962); and Charles E. Silberman, *Crisis in Black and White* (New York, 1964).

Of special significance for other racial minorities in the twentieth century are Carey McWilliams, *North from Mexico: The Spanish-Speaking People of the United States* (Philadelphia, 1949); Julian Samora, ed., *La*

Raza: Forgotten Americans (South Bend, Ind., 1967); Stan Steiner, *La Raza: The Mexican Americans* (New York, 1970); and Jacobus ten Broek, Edward N. Barnhart, and Floyd W. Matson, *Prejudice, War and the Constitution* (Berkeley and Los Angeles, 1954), the latter a study of the internment of the Japanese-Americans, both citizens and resident aliens, during World War II.

As racial attitudes became imbedded in the thought and institutions of American society, they were mirrored in literature and the arts. A number of noteworthy books have attempted to trace this diffusion of ideas. Among them are Peter Noble, *The Negro in Films* (London, 1948); Charles Keil, *Urban Blues* (Chicago, 1966); Lindsey Patterson, ed., *The Negro in Music and Art* (New York, 1967); Sterling A. Brown, *The Negro in American Fiction* (Washington, D.C., 1937); Robert A. Bone, *The Negro Novel in America* (New Haven, Conn., 1958); Joseph Boskin, *The Life and Death of Sambo* (New York, 1970); Cecil Robinson, *With the Ears of Strangers: The Mexican in American Literature* (Albuquerque, New M., 1963), Albert Keiser, *The Indian in American Literature* (New York, 1933); and Leslie A. Fiedler, *The Return of the Vanishing America* (New York, 1968).

Only recently has it been widely recognized that the victims of racism often understand the phenomenon better than its practitioners. This is because oppressed minorities have learned that their security—and sometimes their survival—depends upon patterning their behavior so as to minimize the effects of racism. Thus, some of the most penetrating and provocative critiques of racial ideology and behavior have come from the pens of minority novelists, poets, and social critics. No student of racial attitudes in America should overlook Richard Wright's *Black Boy* (New York, 1947) and *Native Son* (New York, 1940); Ralph Ellison's *Invisible Man* (New York, 1947); James Baldwin's *Another Country* (New York, 1960), *Nobody Knows My Name* (New York, 1961), *Notes of a Native Son* (New York 1964); and Claude Brown's *Manchild in the Promised Land* (New York, 1965). Some of the most important reflections on white racism to emerge in recent decades are Harold Cruse, *The Crisis of the Negro Intellectual* (New York, 1967); *The Autobiography of Malcolm X* (New York, 1964); Eldridge Cleaver, *Soul on Ice* (New York, 1968); and Julius Lester, *In Search of the Land* (New York, 1969). Similarly, Vine Deloria's *Custer Died for Your Sins* (New York, 1969) offers insights into white attitudes toward the Indian which have heretofore escaped white scholars.

Studies of the social and psychological dynamics of racism have proliferated in recent years. Many of them stem from earlier studies of anti-Semitism and must be read with that in mind. Among the best are T. W. Adorno, Else Frenkel-Brunswick, D. J. Levinson, and R. N. Sanford, *The Authoritarian Personality* (New York, 1950); Gordon W. Allport, *The Nature of Prejudice* (Cambridge, Mass., 1954); Bruno Bettelheim and

Morris Janowitz, *Social Change and Prejudice Including Dynamics of Prejudice* (New York, 1964); Kenneth B. Clark, *Dark Ghetto, Dilemmas of Social Power* (New York, 1965); William H. Grier and Price Cobbs, *Black Rage* (New York, 1968); Abram Kardiner and Lionel Ovesey, *The Mark of Oppression: A Psychosocial Study of the American Negro* (New York, 1951); and John P. Kirscht and Ronald C. Dillehay, *Dimensions of Authoritarianism: A Review of Research and Theory* (Lexington, Ky., 1967).

Index

Abercrombie, Thomas, 154
Abolitionism, 24–25, 29, 31, 34
Ackerman, N. W., 196
Adam Shuffler (Beadle), 175
Adams, Charles Francis, Jr., 56
Adams, John, 21, 92
Adams, John Quincy, 82
Adams, Sam, 112
Adorno, T. W., 196
AFL-CIO, 120
African Blood Brotherhood, 163–164
Africans, American Revolution and,
    21–26
  attitudes toward (*see* Attitudes, racial)
  characteristics of, 11–13, 32–33, 35,
    36, 167, 174, 175
  emancipated, 24–26
  image of, 27–44, 165–185
  introduction to America, 10
  See also Blacks
Africans, The (Colman), 167–168
Alien and Sedition Acts, 122
Alien Land Law, 150
Allport, Gordon W., 195
American Anthropological Society, 94
American Antiquarian Society, 92
American Breeders Association, 136
American Dilemma (Myrdal), 118
American Ethnological Society, 93
American Eugenics Society, 137
American Federation of Labor (AFL),
    104–107, 114–120
  anti-Orientalism, 114–115
American Federationist, 115
American Legion, 150
American Philosophical Society, 92
American Protective League, 129
American Revolution, slavery and the,
    21–26, 29

Amos 'n Andy, 180–182, 184
Anderson, Eddie, 180
Anderson, Robert, 192
Anglo-Saxon, the cult of the, 122,
    129–131
Anti-Catholicism, 122, 129, 130
Anti-Orientalism, 107–117
Antislavery crusade, 29, 34
Asiatic Exclusion League, 114, 149
Atlantic Monthly, 174
Attitudes, racial, change in, 199–201
  Civil War and, 45–58
  colonies and, 1–26
  English, 1–26
  Iberian, 13
  industrialization and, 121–143
  labor movement and, 98–120
  prior to Civil War, 27–44
  Reconstruction era, 58–70
  after World War I, 144–146
Authoritarian Personality, The (Adorno
    and associates), 196

Baldwin, James, 189
Baltimore and Ohio Railroad, 126
Bancroft, Hubert Howe, 93
Bandolier, Adolph, 93
Beadle, Samuel A., 175
Belafonte, Harry, 184
Benny, Jack, 180
Best, Willie, 178
Bettelheim, Bruno, 197
Beveridge, A., Senator (Indiana), 131
Beverley, Robert, 9, 20
Bickerstaff, Issac, 167
Bird, Robert Montgomery, 75–76, 94
"Birth of a Nation, The," 156, 166
*Black Diamonds Gathered in the Darkey
    Homes of the South* (Pollard), 36

209